DESIGNING MEANING-BASED INTERVENTIONS FOR STRUGGLING READERS

DESIGNING MEANING-BASED INTERVENTIONS for Struggling Readers

ANDREW P. JOHNSON

THE GUILFORD PRESS
New York London

A Division of Guilford Publications, Inc.
370 Seventh Avenue, Suite 1200, New York, NY 10001

www.guilford.com

Printed in the United States of America

This book is printed on acid-free paper.

Last digit is print number: 9 8 7 6 5 4 3 2 1

Library of Congress Cataloging-in-Publication Data

Names: Johnson, Andrew P. (Andrew Paul), author.
Title: Designing meaning-based interventions for struggling readers / Andrew P. Johnson.
Description: New York : The Guilford Press, [2021] | Includes bibliographical references and index.
Identifiers: LCCN 2020053568 | ISBN 9781462545773 (paperback) | ISBN 9781462545780 (hardcover)
Subjects: LCSH: Reading—Remedial teaching. | Reading disability. | Response to intervention (Learning disabled children)
Classification: LCC LB1050.5 .J5832 2020 | DDC 372.43—dc23
LC record available at *https://lccn.loc.gov/2020053568*

To all the graduate students I have worked with in the Department of Special Education at Minnesota State University, Mankato, over the last 20 years. Many of you changed careers to become special education teachers. You decided to make the world a better place through your teaching. I felt your passion to make a difference.

I am humbled and honored that you shared a small part of your teaching journey with me. I want you to know that I learned from you. I am inspired by you. And it has been a joy and a privilege to be your professor.

Teaching is hard work. I thank you and all other teachers for your service. You are changing the world one kid at a time.

About the Author

Andrew P. Johnson, PhD, is Professor of Literacy Instruction and Distinguished Faculty Scholar at Minnesota State University, Mankato. He specializes in literacy instruction for students with intellectual and learning disabilities, response to intervention (RTI) for reading and writing, strategies for the inclusive classroom, and advanced pedagogy. Prior to his university career, he taught in elementary, middle, and high school classrooms for 9 years. Dr. Johnson is the author of 13 books and numerous book chapters and academic articles related to literacy, learning, and the human condition. He hosts a podcast, *The Reading Instruction Show,* at *https://rss.com/podcasts/drandy*.

Preface

Erik was one of my students when I first started teaching. I was a second-grade teacher back in 1982. I still remember him. He was a happy little guy when school started in the fall. He was also a happy little guy when I saw him outside at recess playing with his friends. But as the year went along, he became less happy. He began to slump in his desk. He seemed to draw into himself. Thirty-eight years later I still remember Erik. As teachers, we tend to remember our failures. Erik struggled with his reading, and I failed to give him the kind of reading instruction and support that he needed. I did not have the knowledge or skills to help him back then. Erik's test scores were below the 10th percentile, and he could barely write or spell.

At the spring conference with his mother, I described Erik in terms of numbers on a continuum and told his mother all the things he could not do. All Erik learned from me was that he could not read or write and that he was a failure.

Of course, Erik was not the failure. I was.

At that spring conference with Erik's mother, I am ashamed to admit that I recommended that Erik repeat second grade. That is the only intervention strategy I had back then. Run him through the second-grade conveyor belt one more time; add the same parts, in the same way and at the same places. I remember his mother crying when I told her this. She said that her family was moving to Texas because of a job opportunity—and that she would not be following my recommendation (thankfully). Several years later, I would read research showing that while retention may result in slight short-term gains, there is little to no long-term effect on students' academic performance (McCoy & Reynolds, 1999). At the same time, it can have a devastating social and emotional impact on students.

Erik would be in his early 40s now. I often wonder what became of him. How did I affect his self-esteem and self-efficacy? Did he eventually experience success in school? Did he graduate from high school? Did he ever become a proficient reader? Is he realizing his full potential?

I had a wholly inadequate knowledge base related to literacy and learning in 1982. I wish I had a do-over. But I do not. The best I can do today is to provide knowledge related to struggling readers, reading instruction, and reading interventions so that you will not have to look back 38 years from now, wishing for a do-over.

ACKNOWLEDGMENTS

I would like to acknowledge the influence of my wife, Dr. Nancy Fitzsimons, in helping me understand some of the issues and problems in and around the special education system. Her descriptions of the systemic problems in schools and other institutions that limit the potential of people with disabilities have influenced my thinking greatly. Her work as an ally and advocate for people with disabilities has shown me the power of one: One person, living her values, committed to making a difference, can make a difference. Thank you, Dr. Fitzsimons.

Finally, this book was written in the ugly shadow of the murder of George Floyd in Minneapolis. Change needs to occur. Let us be agents of change. If we all do little things, big things will happen.

Contents

PART II. ELEMENTS OF A MEANING-BASED INTERVENTION FOR READING

PART V. DESIGNING READING INTERVENTIONS

PART VI. ISSUES IN SPECIAL EDUCATION

Introduction

THIS IS NOT ANOTHER RTI BOOK

This is not another book about implementing a response-to-intervention (RTI) model for reading. Instead, it is a book about designing meaning-based reading interventions. It just so happens that the strategies described here can be used within an RTI context. They can also be used as part of reading interventions or instruction separate from an RTI model.

The basic RTI model described in this chapter is used for reading, writing, or math. Understanding the basics of this model will provide context for the specific strategies and other information that follow. Chapter 20 contains ideas for designing an RTI program specifically for reading. After reading this book, you will be able to design effective reading interventions within or apart from an RTI context.

A GENERAL OVERVIEW OF RTI FOR READING, WRITING, AND MATH

RTI is an integrated assessment (identification) and intervention program designed to provide immediate instructional help for students who struggle in reading, writing, and math without having to be formally identified for special education programs.

- **Identification.** RTI, as originally described in the Individuals with Disabilities Education Act (IDEA) of 2004, was to be used as a mechanism for identifying students with learning disabilities. Here students with learning disabilities are defined and identified by how they respond to scientifically

based interventions in each of the three content areas (reading, writing, and math). This is different from the discrepancy model, where a learning disability is defined as a difference between potential (usually defined by an IQ score) and achievement (usually defined by a score on an academic achievement test).
- **Intervention.** RTI is also seen as an intervention model for students who struggle with reading, writing, and math. It is a way to provide early and immediate specialized instruction so that special education services can be avoided (Averill, Baker, & Rinaldi, 2014; International Reading Association [IRA], 2010; Wixson & Valencia, 2011). Here the benchmarks are used, not to identify, but as formative assessment to determine the effectiveness of the intervention and to see what change, if any, needs to be made.

RTI then proposes that three tiers of intervention be used for students who are struggling: (1) Tier 1, which includes high-quality classroom instruction, screening, and group interventions; (2) Tier 2, which includes targeted instruction; and (3) Tier 3, which includes intensive interventions and comprehensive evaluation. Each tier is described next.

TIER 1

Tier 1 interventions take place within the general education classroom. They include high-quality classroom instruction, screening, and group interventions.

High-Quality Classroom Instruction

High-quality instruction refers to the curriculum, the approach and pedagogical strategies used, and the specifics of lesson delivery for each of the three content areas: reading, writing, and math. High-quality instruction cannot occur in the absence of high-quality teachers. These are teachers with expertise in the content area being taught as well as pedagogical strategies related to that content area. High-quality teachers also have knowledge and a broad understanding of learning, learning theories, research, and assessment in the content area being taught (Johnson, 2017).

Screening

Screening in Tier 1 is used to see if all students are responding appropriately to the instruction found within the general education curriculum. Screening consists of (1) establishing a baseline, (2) setting goals or benchmarks, and (3) monitoring progress.

1. **Establishing a baseline.** The baseline is a measure of students' current level of academic performance. Any type of measure used here must be simple and pragmatic. This means it needs to be administered in a large group. It also needs to be a valid indicator of students' ability in the area being measured, whether reading, writing, or math.
2. **Setting goals.** The RTI goals identify where you think students should be at various times during the year. These are sometimes called benchmark goals or simply benchmarks. Identifying benchmark goals and showing how they will be measured must be carefully considered as these decisions greatly impact and define the type of interventions students receive. Benchmark goals should be set at three (and sometimes four) points during the year.
3. **Monitoring progress.** If screening shows that students are not making adequate progress toward established benchmark goals, a Tier 1 intervention is used. This is where a progress monitoring system is implemented to check students' progress at shorter intervals.

Group Interventions: In-Class Supplemental Instruction

Tier 1 interventions involve supplemental instruction that occurs in the general education classroom. Small-group, in-class supplemental instruction is usually used here. And because classroom teachers are still responsible for teaching the general education curriculum, Tier 1 must be simple, pragmatic, and effective.

Finally, interventions at all tiers should be coordinated with classroom instruction (Averill et al., 2014; IRA, 2010). That is, they should reflect the types of research-based instruction and activities used with the general education curriculum. In this way, students' learning experiences do not become splintered or fragmented. Instead, the intervention builds upon and reinforces good classroom instruction. RTI at all tiers is not meant to replace good classroom instruction; rather, it is meant to enhance it.

TIER 2

Students not meeting Tier 1 benchmark goals are identified for a Tier 2 intervention. Tier 2 interventions (most often done in small groups) involve targeted instruction and usually occur outside the general education classroom. These groups can be cross-graded. Instruction should build upon the Tier 1 intervention to the greatest extent possible.

Data-Based Decision Making

RTI calls for data-based decision making to be used throughout (Averill et al., 2014). This means that data need to be collected at various points during the intervention and used to inform instruction. Data-based decision making also means that the specific intervention for each student should be based on solid, diagnostic data. Thus, some type of measure needs to be used to diagnose the cause of the reading, writing, or math difficulty before a student moves into a Tier 2 intervention.

Targeted Instruction

Tier 2 instruction should be targeted. Targeted instruction means that the intervention targets the specific deficit area. It does not mean simply implementing a program, curriculum, or method. There is no single evidence-based program, research-based curriculum, or scientifically based teaching method in any curriculum area that works best for all students (Allington, 2012). There are, however, a variety of strategies that research has shown to be effective with certain students, for certain tasks or skills, and in certain situations. Thus, teachers implementing any type of intervention must have a variety of pedagogical tools (strategies) in their teaching toolbox. They must also be empowered to make the decisions necessary to best meet the needs of their students.

TIER 3

Tier 3 involves intensive interventions and comprehensive evaluation. If students are not making adequate progress in Tier 2, they are targeted for a Tier 3 intervention. Tier 3 should build upon Tier 2 instruction to the greatest degree possible. The main difference between Tier 2 and Tier 3 is that Tier 3 interventions should be increased in both frequency and intensity (Swanson & Vaughn, 2011). Students not making the desired level progress in response to the Tier 3 intervention should then be referred for a comprehensive evaluation to see if they are eligible for special education services under IDEA 2004 (National Center for Learning Disabilities, 2014).

Tier 3 is often synonymous with special education; however, RTI was specifically designed to avoid special education labels and services. IDEA calls for Tier 3 interventions to be delivered primarily in a general education setting by a general education teacher and additional staff. If special educators do become involved at this level, it should be under the guidance of the classroom teacher or a specialist in that area (reading, writing, or math). There must also be careful planning and continued communication with all parties in all phases.

IMPLEMENTING RTI FLEXIBLY

One of RTI's strengths is its flexibility (IRA, 2010). It is expected that there will be wide variation in how these regulations are interpreted and implemented. However, to be successful, any RTI plan must be economical, practical, and effective. Also, RTI requires that evidence-based pedagogy be used in each tier (Averill et al., 2014). This is quite different from a specific program or method. As will be stated throughout this book, there is no single evidence-based program, research-based curriculum, or scientifically based teaching method that works best for all students (Allington, 2012). Thus, RTI plans for any area should comprise research-based strategies that enable teachers to apply them flexibly in ways that best meet the needs of their students.

ORGANIZATION OF THIS BOOK

When I set out to write this book, I had a very good idea of where I wanted to go. My initial outline contained 15 tidy little chapters all written in an objective, third-person voice. However, something happened along the way. It soon became clear that this book had its own, very different, idea of where it wanted to go. I have found that things that need saying will not go away until you say them. Thus, this became a book that says what needs saying about reading interventions for struggling readers.

Part I. Background Information

The first section of this book lays the foundation for the chapters that follow. Chapter 1 describes exactly what is meant by a reading intervention. Chapter 2 describes two common theoretical models of reading used to design reading research as well as reading instruction and interventions. Chapter 3 describes how our brains create meaning with print. And Chapter 4 defines commonly misunderstood terms and concepts related to reading instruction and interventions.

Part II. Elements of a Meaning-Based Intervention for Reading

The second section of this book contains 10 chapters that describe a variety of strategies that can be used to address each of the three reading deficit areas: word identification, fluency, and comprehension. Included here are all the pedagogical elements necessary to design effective reading interventions. However, since struggling readers are not a homogeneous group, you will need to select only those strategies that work best for you and your teaching situation. Adopt and adapt them based on the specific needs of the students with whom you work.

Part III. Diagnosing, Assessing, and Monitoring Progress

The third section of this book focuses on quantifying students' ability to create meaning with print. Chapter 15 examines standardized tests, their role in identifying students with reading difficulties, and their limitations when used as a diagnostic tool for reading. Chapter 16 describes more valid methods that can be used to diagnose problems related to each of the three reading-deficit areas. These more valid methods include a student attitude survey or questionnaire, a diagnostic reading assessment (or informal reading inventory), a miscue analysis, words-per-minute for fluency, and maze and retelling strategies for comprehension. Chapter 17 describes a variety of simple progress-monitoring strategies that can be used to assess students' responsiveness to the types of strategies used in a reading intervention as well as to document their progress.

Part IV. Individualized Education Programs

The fourth section of this book focuses on individualized education programs (IEPs). Chapter 18 unpacks federal guidelines to enable you to design IEPs for reading that are simple, clear, pragmatic, and effective in enhancing students' ability to create meaning with print. Since federal guidelines require special education services to be based on "peer-reviewed research to the extent practical," Chapter 19 is devoted solely to understanding the peer review process, its strengths, and its limitations.

Part V. Designing Reading Interventions

The fifth section of this book focuses on designing effective reading interventions. Chapter 20 describes how the elements contained in this book fit into an RTI context. When RTI is used as an assessment mechanism, students are identified for special education services based on how they respond to interventions that are supported by scientifically based research. Thus, Chapter 21 provides an explanation of scientifically based research. In so doing, the limitations of the U.S. Department of Education's simplistic view of this construct becomes evident. Chapter 22 provides an example and analysis of a severely flawed research study that meets all the standards imposed by the U.S. Department of Education. This analysis, along with Chapter 23, is designed to help you become a more critical consumer of educational research. Finally, Chapter 24 examines the construct known as dyslexia and describes specific interventions and supports.

Part VI. Issues in Special Education

Students with reading difficulties often intersect with special education services in some form. Chapter 25 describes the special education world as a broken system and identifies how systematic reform might begin so that this system may be restored.

NEW IDEAS

In the chapters that follow, you may encounter some ideas that are at odds with your previous ways of thinking. In fact, some of these ideas may directly conflict with what you believe to be true regarding how children learn to read and how you should teach them to read. This is as is should be. Dissonance and disequilibrium are important parts of learning. I urge you to neither accept nor reject these new ideas. Instead, touch them. Carry them with you for a bit. Let them settle. See what sticks. Sort it out. This is how we grow, how we change, how we continue to evolve. But in considering these new ideas, keep your focus on the larger goal—to help children create meaning with print.

PART I
BACKGROUND INFORMATION

CHAPTER 1

Instruction and Interventions

DEFINING OUR TERMS

This book describes how to design and implement meaning-based interventions for struggling readers (mild, moderate, and severe). So, let us first define two important terms: (1) a *reading intervention* and (2) a *meaning-based reading intervention.*

A Reading Intervention

A reading intervention is a focused instructional plan that supplements existing reading instruction (Allington, 2012; Wharton-McDonald, 2011). Like any type of intervention, reading interventions are designed to be used for short durations. In other words, an effective reading intervention should enhance students' current reading levels such that the reading intervention is no longer needed. That is the goal. For some students, the duration of the reading intervention could be a matter of weeks. Other students (students with severe reading difficulties) may need a bit longer.

Again, a reading intervention should supplement effective research-based reading instruction taking place in a general education setting. In other words, it should not be substantially different. When an intervention or remedial program is different from classroom instruction, it creates a splintered curriculum. Here struggling readers are presented with different types of instruction and learn different sorts of skills in different places throughout the day. This makes it harder for them to develop their reading skills, not easier.

Imagine if you were a struggling tennis player and you were sent first to one instructor who did a set of drills and asked you to swing the racquet a certain way in the morning, and then to a different instructor who did different sets of drills and asked you to swing the racquet a different way in the afternoon. This would make it difficult to develop your tennis skills. Yet, this is what occurs with struggling readers when interventions and remediation provided outside the classroom look substantially different from good classroom instruction. Struggling readers need consistency in order to reinforce developing skills.

A Meaning-Based Reading Intervention

A meaning-based intervention is a reading intervention that seeks to keep the language used in literacy learning whole, complete, and meaningful. That is, it seeks to minimize those instances where students are asked to focus on individual words or letter parts in isolation. Instead, phonics and other reading subskills are taught within the context of meaningful sentences or whole connected text to the greatest extent possible. So instead of asking students to master a series of reading subskills (like sounding out words), a meaning-based intervention asks students to create meaning with print. The specific elements of what you might include in a meaning-based intervention will become clear as you read the chapters that follow.

DAILY READING INSTRUCTION

As mentioned above, an effective reading intervention is based on effective reading instruction. There are seven basic elements necessary for effective daily reading instruction. Although not every element need be included every day, most elements should be included most days. The frequency and duration of each would be determined by the age and ability of the students with whom you work. Good teaching is not an algorithm or a recipe to follow. Rather, good teaching is watching your students and responding to their needs.

Daily Reading Practice

All students at all levels need practice reading books that they have selected. Like any skill, one needs to practice in order to improve. Would you expect to learn to play the piano if you never practiced? Could you learn to play the piano if you did not have good music to play? Could you learn to play the piano if all the music given to you was too hard? So it is with reading.

Reading widely is one of the best methods that will enhance students' comprehension, word identification, and fluency skills as well as vocabulary and conceptual knowledge (Allington, 2012; Krashen, 2004). Also, reading practice enables students to practice newly learned skills in authentic reading contexts. Nancy Atwell (1998) recommends that 70–80% of each reading class be used for self-selected reading practice and 20–30% for skills work. In most classrooms, these percentages are just the opposite. Students are asked to find a book to read only when they finish their "work." Instead, finding a good book to read should be the main work occurring in reading class.

Thus, instead of reading *class,* it might be more constructive to think of it as reading *practice*. Here students would be provided a variety of good books to read at their independent level or below, as well as lots of time to practice and enjoy reading. In such an approach to reading instruction (known as reading workshop), small bits of targeted skills instruction would be provided based on students' individual needs and set within a meaningful context to the greatest extent possible.

Social Interaction and Conversation around Good Books

Social interaction enhances high-level thinking and literacy learning. It may involve a variety of activities, including book talks, literature circles, book clubs, book evaluations and critiques, top 10 lists, journal entries and responses, and planned discussions. These experiences need not be long, but they should be planned and purposeful.

Authentic Writing Experiences

An authentic writing experience is one in which students are asked to use writing to describe, express, and share their ideas and experiences. Like social interaction, these writing activities do not need to be long. As you will see in this book, they can also be designed to be used as pre- or postreading activities or to reinforce target letter patterns.

Activities and Instruction to Develop Cueing Systems

As described fully in Chapter 3, the brain uses three cueing systems to recognize words during the act of reading: phonological, semantic, and syntax. The phonological cueing system uses letter sounds and letter patterns to recognize words; the semantic cueing system uses meaning or context to recognize words; and the syntactic cueing system uses grammar and word order to recognize words. Effective reading instruction includes activities to develop all three systems. Formal instruction and activities are generally discontinued when students are reading comfortably at the third-grade level.

Activities and Instruction for Word Identification Strategies

Students use certain strategies to identify words that are in their lexicon but not immediately recognized. There are four basic word identification strategies:

(1) analogy (word families), (2) morphemic awareness (prefix, suffix, affix, root), (3) context clues (semantics), and (4) phonics. All four of these strategies should be included in a reading curriculum. Formal instruction related to word identification is generally discontinued as a word identification strategy when students are reading comfortably at the third-grade level. However, they should be continued as part of vocabulary development.

Comprehension Instruction

Comprehension instruction refers to the specific strategies and skills used to create meaning with narrative and expository text. This is one of the most underinstructed elements in most reading programs (Allington, 2012; Pearson & Cervetti, 2017). Here, study skills are taught for use with expository text. Direct instruction is also used to teach the cognitive operations effective readers use with narrative and expository text.

Activities to Develop Word Knowledge (Vocabulary)

Wide reading is the most efficient and effective way to develop students' vocabulary. However, a variety of pedagogical strategies should also be used to expand the depth and breadth of students' word knowledge (Johnson, 2016b).

EFFECTIVE READING INTERVENTIONS

Interventions for struggling readers should build on the elements described above and include more intense versions of classroom reading instruction, a balanced approach to reading instruction, and expert reading teachers.

More Intense Versions of Classroom Reading Instruction

There is a misconception that struggling readers need some sort of super-secret specialized teaching strategies that only specially certified teachers can use. In reality, struggling readers do not need dramatically different kinds of instruction than other readers do (Wharton-McDonald, 2011). What they need is more intense versions of the kinds of research-based instruction they receive in a general education setting (see above). Intensity here refers to (1) more time, (2) more time on task, (3) more time engaged in authentic literacy activities (reading and writing), and (4) smaller instructional groups (three to seven students) (Allington, 2012). Intense, supplemental instruction (or an intervention) can occur within or outside of a general education classroom setting. This is not to say that there are no differences in instruction between students with and without reading difficulties; however, these differences are in emphasis and intensity, not in kind.

A Balanced Approach to Reading Instruction

What struggling readers often receive in intervention programs is a steady diet of phonics and low-level reading skills (Allington, 2012). While research has shown that phonics-based instruction can lead to increased scores on phonics-based measures (Fautsch-Patridge, McMaster, & Hupp, 2011; Hill, 2016), too often there is little transfer of these skills to authentic reading conditions (ILA, 2016a; Weaver, 2009). As well, there is little evidence to demonstrate that this kind of instruction has any long-term effect on students' ability to create meaning with print (Allington, 2012; Strauss, 2011b).

This is not to say that phonics instruction is not necessary. Phonics instruction in some form is an important part of an intervention given to many students who are struggling readers; however, it should occur within a meaningful context to the greatest extent possible (Fawcett & Nicolson, 2007; Johnson, 2016b). And it should be part of a balanced literacy program that includes practice reading real books, a focus on higher-order reading skills, and word work that develops all three cueing systems (phonological, semantic, and syntactic).

Expert Reading Teachers

Successful reading intervention is dependent on having teachers who are experts in reading instruction (IRA, 2010; Wixson, Lipson, & Valencia, 2014). Expert reading teachers have knowledge and a broad understanding of the following areas: (1) human learning, (2) the processes used by the brain to create meaning with print, (3) literacy teaching and learning, (4) literacy research, (5) literacy assessment and diagnosis, and (6) literacy pedagogy.

THEY ALREADY KNOW HOW TO READ

I know how to play the piano. I know that the little dots on the page represent individual notes, the places on the piano where I am supposed to plink my fingers, and the duration of each finger plink. The problem is, I am not very good at it. I need some basic instruction and lots of practice.

In the same way, with any type of reading instruction or intervention, you will not be teaching students how to read. (I know this last sentence will be freaking out some of you. Take a deep breath.) Most students already know how to do this. That is, they understand the process. They know that letters stand for sounds, that you put the letter symbols together to create words, and that these words go together to create ideas. They know that this is what you do when you read. The problem is, they are not very good at it. So, what do you do when you are not very good at something? You practice. Reading practice is necessary for readers to develop the higher-level cognitive processes involved in creating meaning with print (Portes & Salas, 2009). Instruction is necessary but not sufficient for struggling readers. Any reading intervention should also include a goodly amount of reading practice.

THREE BIG IDEAS

The chapters that follow describe specific strategies that might be included in reading interventions for struggling readers. There are three big ideas to take from this chapter:

1. A reading intervention should supplement research-based reading instruction already taking place in a general education setting.
2. Instruction and activities in a reading intervention should occur within a meaningful context to the greatest extent possible.
3. Daily reading instruction should include (a) daily reading practice, (b) social interaction and conversation around books, (c) authentic writing experiences, (d) activities and instruction to develop all three cueing systems, (e) activities and instruction for word identification strategies, (f) comprehension instruction, and (g) activities to develop word knowledge.

CHAPTER 2

Educational Research and Theoretical Models

THEORETICAL MODELS

Educational research is used to create the theories through which we design educational policies and practices. Theories help to organize relevant empirical facts (i.e., to observe or measure them) in order to create a context for understanding phenomena. Put another way, a theory is a way to explain a set of facts. If reality were a dot-to-dot picture, a theory would be a way to connect a set of data dots (see Figure 2.1).

Theories are built, not on a single research study, but on a collection of data gleaned from a variety of different research studies. Good theories are well substantiated, connecting a wide variety of data dots, all of which have been confirmed through experiment and observation.

Theoretical models of reading are used to understand the reading process as well as to design and evaluate instructional practices. As such, the theoretical model

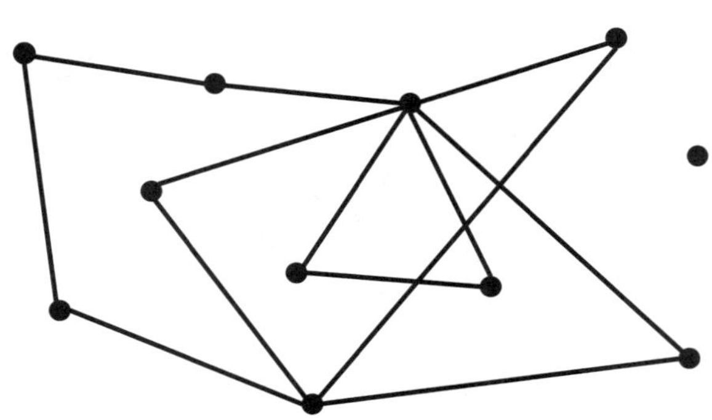

FIGURE 2.1. Theories connect a set of data dots.

of reading one adheres to has tremendous impact on the type of reading instruction and interventions that are used. Described below are two common theoretical models of reading, phonological processing and the neurocognitive models, each providing vastly different views of the reading process and struggling readers.

The Phonological Processing Model

The phonological processing model is based on the premise that reading is simply the act of sounding out words (Ehri, 2005; Fawcett & Nicolson, 2007; Kershner, 2016; Roberts, Torgesen, Boardman, & Scammacca, 2008; Shaywitz, & Shaywitz, 2008; Snowling, 2008; Torgesen et al., 2001). This is known as the phonological processing model. James Hoffman (2017) calls it a simple view of reading. In this model, the reading process is thought to involve four subprocesses: (1) perceiving the words and letters on the page, (2) giving sounds to all the letters in each word, (3) putting the individual sounds together to identify words, and (4) putting the words together to create ideas. This process is thought to create a form of speech-in-the-head that the reader listens to during reading. According to this model, a proficient reader is one who can sound out words automatically and fluently so that the speech-in-the-head is uninterrupted. From this perspective, a struggling reader would be one who has a sounding-out-words deficit (see Figure 2.2).

According to this model, what struggling readers need is more sounding-out-words instruction (phonics) along with lots of drill and practice (Adams, 1990; Chall, 1989; Gaskins, 2011; Shaywitz, Morris, & Shaywitz, 2008; Sweet, 2016). The goal of this type of instruction is to develop students' ability to sound out words. The thinking is that if students were proficient with this skill, their reading problems

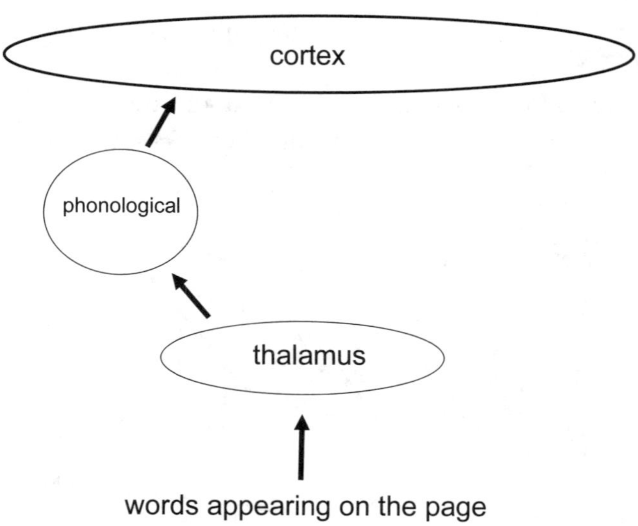

FIGURE 2.2. The phonological processing model.

would vanish. But this is not the case. As described in Chapter 1, students may get marginally better at sounding out isolated words in the short term, but usually there is little transfer of these skills to authentic reading situations (Weaver, 2009). And in the long term, there is no noticeable improvement in students' ability to create meaning with print in authentic reading situations (Lipson & Wixson, 2009).

The phonological processing model is limited because it does not account for a wide array of data, including the following four facts:

First, proficient readers do not look fully at one-third of the words on the page (Paulson, 2005; Weaver, 2009). This indicates that readers are using more than the words and letters on the page to create meaning. They are using semantic and syntactic information along with background knowledge to fill in the blanks as they read.

Second, proficient readers often insert words that are semantically or syntactically correct (Paulson, 2005). Again, this points to the fact that information besides what is on the page is being used to construct meaning.

Third, the ratio of corticothalamic nerve fibers to the thalamocortical fibers is 10 to 1 (Alitto, & Usrey, 2003; Hawkins, 2004; Sherman, & Guillery, 2002; Sillito & Jones, 2002; Strauss, 2014). In other words, during the act of reading, almost 10 times more information is flowing from the cortex down to the thalamus than is flowing up from the page to the thalamus and then up to the cortex. This shows that what is in the head is being used along with text clues to create meaning.

And finally, information from the cortex is used to direct the eyes during that act of reading (Rayner, Liversedge, White, & Vergilino-Perez, 2003). In other words, higher-level processes drive or mediate lower-level processes (Paulson & Freeman, 2003; Straus 2011).

The Neurocognitive Model

The neurocognitive model (sometimes referred to as the psycholinguistic model) accounts for these four facts. Here, reading is defined as the process of creating meaning with print. During this meaning-making process, the brain uses the three cueing systems discussed in Chapter 1 to recognize words on the page: phonological, semantic, and syntactic (Anderson, 2013; Hruby & Goswami, 2013; Paulson & Goodman, 2008; Ruddel & Unrau, 2013; Strauss, 2011a; Weaver, 2009). Readers use what is in their head (schemata) to make sense of what is on the page (Strauss, 2011b) (see Figure 2.3).

Also, during the process of reading, our eyes fixate on approximately 60% of the words on the page (Paulson & Freeman, 2003). Of these fixated words, our eyes usually stop on only one or two letters. Since we can perceive only those things our eyes fixate on, it is clear that our brain fills in the blanks to create meaning during the reading process (Strauss, Goodman, & Paulson, 2009). It is clear as well that the eyes are directed by information in the cortex much more so than information on the page during the act of reading (Paulson, 2005; Rayner et al., 2003; Weaver,

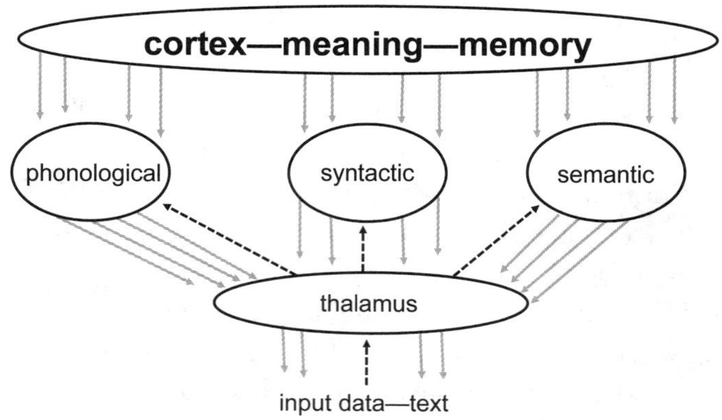

FIGURE 2.3. The neurocognitive model.

2009). Syntactic cues, semantic cues, and minimal letter cues are used along with information in our cortex to confirm or revise words as the brain seeks to create meaning with print (Paulson & Freeman, 2003).

According to this model, a proficient reader is one who can orchestrate a variety of strategies to construct meaning during the process of reading (Weaver, 1994). These strategies include using knowledge and contextual clues to predict and infer, monitoring comprehension, and employing fix-up strategies when comprehension breaks down. From this perspective, a struggling reader is one who is ineffective in the use or coordination of these strategies (Strauss, 2011a). What struggling readers need then (according to this model) is direct instruction related to meaning-making strategies, direct instruction related to the four word identification strategies (morphemic analysis, analogy, context clues, and phonics), and activities to develop all three cueing systems. These should all occur within a meaningful context to the greatest extent possible (Goodman & Goodman, 2009).

RESEARCH AND THEORETICAL MODELS

Theoretical models are the lens through which reality is viewed and interpreted. However, clinging too tightly to a particular theoretical model can constrain the type of research undertaken, limit the research questions asked, and constrict the type of data collected (Unrau, Alvermann, & Sailors, 2019). And with the thickening of the lens, the theory becomes increasingly data-resistant, to the point that only data that support the theory are considered valid. New data that fall outside the theoretical model are either ignored or forced into a preformed, reductively inflexible box. In this way, the continued growth and evolution of the field is stymied (Kuhn, 1996). This appears to be what has happened in fields such as special education where the phonological processing model dominates.

Sounder-Outer Researchers

Despite a wealth of research data from a wide variety of areas supporting a neurocognitive model of reading, there are still many researchers who choose to understand the reading process only in terms of the phonological processing model. I call them *sounder-outers*. Sounder-outers design research studies to examine the effectiveness of sounding-out-word instruction. Their research invariably finds that sounding-out-word instruction is effective in helping students to sound out words.

Typical sounder-outer research goes something like this: A treatment group is given intensive instruction in sounding out words. A control group does not receive intensive instruction in sounding out words. On posttreatment measures assessing students' ability to sound out words, the treatment group scores significantly higher than the control group. Or else, students are pulled out of their normal classroom and given intensive one-on-one sounding-out-word instruction by specially trained research assistants. After several weeks of intensive sounding-out-word instruction, it is found that these students have made statistically significant gains in their ability to sound out words as determined by sounding-out-word measures.

Scientifically Based Research

Since the research studies discussed in this chapter meet all of the U.S. Department of Education's requirements for scientifically based research (see Chapter 21), sounding-out-word instruction is deemed to be scientifically based reading instruction. Commercial sounding-out-word programs are then designed based on this sounding-out-word research. They stamp "Research-Based" on the side of the box. Schools buy these expensive programs and require teachers to use them with "fidelity." This means that teachers are told they must follow the directions exactly as written in the instructions regardless of whether or not it meets their students' needs (see Introduction).

However, even if the tightly controlled sounding-out-word research is "scientifically based" and methodologically sound, it is based on a false premise: that reading is simply sounding out words. Any research based on a false premise will always give you misleading results. In addition, sounder-outers rarely (if ever) consider some of the following research questions: Does sounding-out-word instruction enhance or impede students' ability to create meaning with print? Is sounding-out-word instruction more effective than meaning-based instruction in helping students create meaning with print? When comparisons are made with comparable groups and comparable teaching, can you say with certainty that sounding-out-word instruction is the most effective form of instruction to use with regard to the long-term effectiveness on comprehension, word identification, fluency, vocabulary, and/or voluntary reading? Is sounding-out-word instruction the most effective form of reading instruction for all struggling readers?

CHAPTER 3

Understanding the Reading Process

HOW THE BRAIN CREATES MEANING WITH PRINT

Reading is a thinking process, not a responding process as depicted in the phonological processing model. This chapter describes how our brain functions during this thinking process known as reading.

Three Cueing Systems

In the act of reading, we use the knowledge stored in our cortex to constantly reach out and predict the words in the sentences we are reading (Johnson, 2016b). This enables our brain to work more efficiently. Our brain uses three cueing systems to make these predictions: (1) semantic, (2) syntactic, and (3) phonological (see Figure 3.1).

Semantic

The semantic cueing system is the most efficient of the three in terms of speed and space required in working memory. Semantics refers to meaning. As you read, you use context and background knowledge to identify words and figure out what the next word might be. (You are doing it right now.) This is the semantic cueing system.

For example, in the sentence below, there are several possible words that would make sense: a pail, a lake, the ocean, water, or the tank.

Fish swim in _ _ _ _ _.

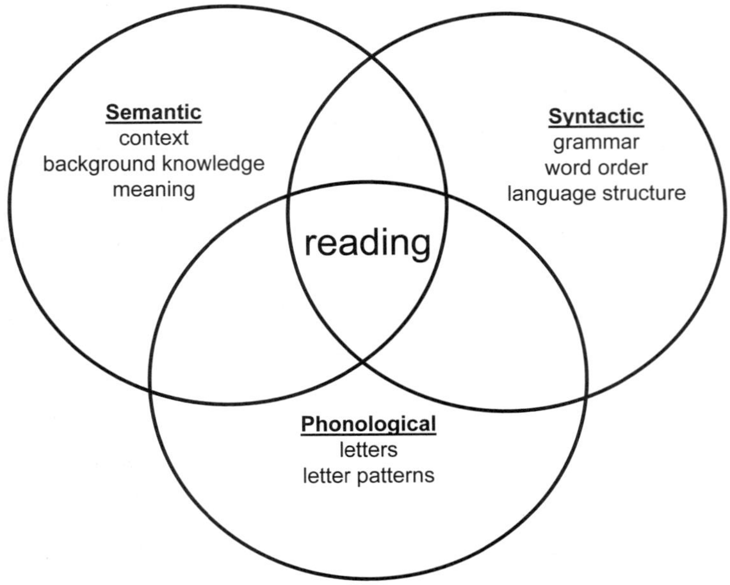

FIGURE 3.1. Three cueing systems.

In the next sentence, most readers would not need the four additional letters to recognize the word *water.* The beginning letter is a sufficient clue. It would be inefficient to attend to each letter.

Fish swim in w__ __ __ __.

Syntactic

Syntax has to do with the grammatical structure of the language. As your brain reads you also use your knowledge of grammar, sentence structure, word order, tense and plurality, prefixes and suffixes, nouns and verbs, and function words (prepositions, pronouns, etc.) to recognize words. This is the second most efficient cueing system.

Phonetic

The phonetic (or phonological) cueing system uses letter sounds to predict what the next word might be. Of the three cueing systems, this one is the least efficient (Strauss, 2005). Why? It focuses on individual letters and letter patterns instead of words and ideas. Working memory has very limited capacity. It can hold a few letters, a few words, or a few ideas. And since ideas contain far more information than individual letters, it is more efficient to focus on ideas (or meaning) than individual letters.

Proof of the Three Cueing Systems

There are some who still insist that reading is simply sounding out words, that the three cueing systems for identifying words during reading (semantic, syntactic, and phonological) are part of a myth foisted upon education by ivory-tower professors bent on ruining America. (I get a lot of responses like this online.) Let me demonstrate first by asking you to examine your own eye movement. Read the sentence in Figure 3.2. Now look at the word in Figure 3.3. Notice how the movement of your eyes differs when you see the same word (*stampede*) in the context of a sentence and when you see it in isolation. Reread these again.

Now read the paragraph in Figure 3.4. Since buffalos are often associated with stampedes, this word acts as a primer as you encounter the word *stampede*. In the context of the sentence your eyes probably just touched on just the beginning letter blend of this word. Now, if you go back to read the isolated word in Figure 3.3, you will notice that your eyes probably start at the beginning, move all the way through the letters in a choppy fashion, then zip back again. Even though you saw the word in the previous sentences, your eyes do this.

Why is this? Syntax and semantics.

Still don't believe me? The paragraph in Figure 3.4 contains 110 words. Read the paragraph as quickly as you can and time yourself. Figure 3.5 contains the same 110 words. Read them as quickly as you can and time yourself. Was your reading rate the same? What about fluency? Did you go smoothly from word to word? How about your eye movement?

The buffalos started to stampede toward Billy.

FIGURE 3.2. A word in a sentence.

stampede

FIGURE 3.3. A word in isolation.

Billy was traveling from Minnesota to California. As he was driving through South Dakota, he stopped at a rest stop to stretch his legs and buy a can of pop. When he got out of his car, he saw a herd of buffalo off in the distance. He was very interested. Billy started walking toward the buffalos so that he could take a picture to send to his friend, Molly. Suddenly, there was a loud bang! Somebody at the rest stop had thrown a large firecracker into the air. The buffalos started to stampede toward Billy. Billy ran as fast as he could, jumped into his car, and drove away.

FIGURE 3.4. A paragraph with 110 words.

> Away drove and car his in jumped could he as fast as ran Billy. Billy toward stampede to started buffalo the. Air the into firecracker large a thrown had stop rest the at somebody. Ban loud a was there suddenly. Molly friend his to send to picture a take could he that so buffalo the toward walking started Billy. Interested very was he. Distance the in off buffalo of herd a saw he car his of out got he when. Pop of can a buy and legs his stretch to stop rest a at stopped he Dakota South through driving was he as. California to Minnesota from traveling was Billy.

FIGURE 3.5. A paragraph with the same 110 words.

> **Passage #1**
>
> Billy was traveling from Minnesota to California. As he was driving through South Dakota, he stopped at a rest stop to stretch his legs and buy a can of pop.
>
> **Passage #2**
>
> Pop of can a buy and legs his stretch to stop rest a at stopped he Dakota South through driving was he as. California to Minnesota from traveling was Billy.

FIGURE 3.6. A two-sentence passage with 30 words.

Now try it with the two-sentence passage in Figure 3.6. The passage on top makes sense. The passage on the bottom contains the exact same words, but they are presented backward. If reading was simply sounding out words, and if the syntactic and semantic cueing systems were nonsense, your rate, accuracy, fluency, and eye movement would have been the same in both paragraphs and with both sentences. But they were not. You most likely read word by word in a very choppy, stilted manner—very much like a struggling reader who is trying to use only letter clues and not semantic or syntactic clues to create meaning.

Two-Way Flow of Information

So here is how it all works: As visual data is taken in from the eyes, it moves to the relay station in the brain called the thalamus. All three cueing systems are then used to recognize words and make sense of this data before it moves to the cortex. The cortex is the part of the brain responsible for higher thinking and memory.

As stated above, information does not flow just one way from the page up to the cortex (bottom up). Brain-imaging research shows that as we process data taken in by the various senses, information flows from the cortex down to the thalamus as well as from the thalamus up to the cortex (Engel, Fries, & Singer, 2001; Hawkins,

2004; Hruby, 2011; Johnson, 2016b; Koch, 2004). As stated in Chapter 2, there is almost 10 times more information flowing down from that cortex to the thalamus than up from the thalamus to the cortex.

We perceive and interpret all of reality (including reading) in terms of the information, images, and patterns stored in our cortex (Engel et al., 2001; Siegel, 2007). These various forms of data are used to reach out and make predictions about what we are about to experience or encounter (Hawkins, 2004). Sense data is then used to confirm, revise, or deconstruct these predictions and construct our current version of reality. The data used to make predictions is called a *schema* (plural is *schemata*). Schemata are the file folders in your head related to specific concepts and experiences. You use schemata to help you understand what you are reading or experiencing, as well as to predict what you are about to read or experience.

Eye Movement

As you noticed in the little experiment above, your eyes do not move evenly from left to right as you read. Instead, they move in small, jerky movements called *saccades*. Your eyes will skip some words, stop on some words, and even go back and stop on words previously read. It only appears as if your eyes move smoothly from left to right because your brain is filling in the blanks. The movement of your eyes across the page while reading is illustrated by Figure 3.7. The line represents the path your eyes take, and the dots are stopping points or *fixations*.

Your eyes fixate on approximately 60% of the words as you read (Paulson & Goodman, 2008). Of these fixated words, your eyes usually stop on only one or two letters. Since we can perceive only those things upon which our eyes fixate, it is clear that your brain is filling in the blanks as we read. During reading, minimal letter cues are used, along with syntactic cues, semantic cues, and the information in our cortex, to confirm or revise words as your brain creates meaning with print.

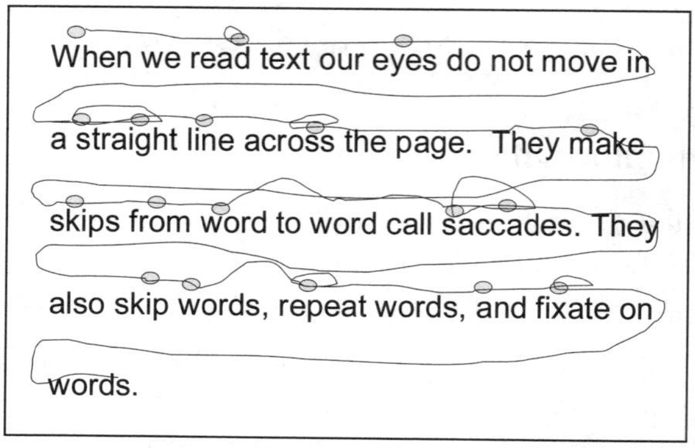

FIGURE 3.7. Eye movement.

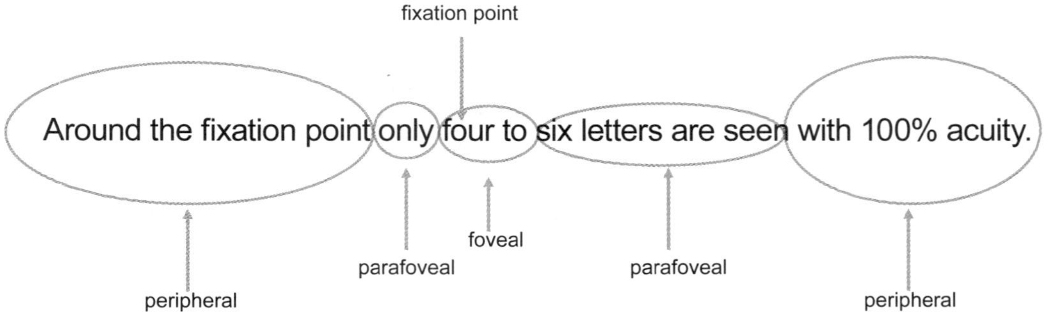

FIGURE 3.8. Foveal, parafoveal, and peripheral regions.

Your eye has three visual regions: foveal, parafoveal, and peripheral (see Figure 3.8). The *foveal* takes up only 1–2% of your total vision. This is the point of fixation where you are able to see clearly and process details. You can take in only about three to six letters here. The *parafoveal* is the region directly surrounding the foveal region. Here you are able to take in about 24 to 30 letters, but not very clearly. In this region you can identify gross shapes, but without some sort of context, the strings of letters are indistinguishable. The *peripheral* region is everything else. Here you are able to perceive only gross shapes.

So, with this very small in-focus viewing area, how is anybody able to read more than 10 words per minute? Efficient readers are able to read quickly because of the top-down flow of information as described in the last chapter. When we read, we use the information in our head along with the context of what we are reading (semantics) and the syntax of the sentences to make predictions about the upcoming text. These predictions enable us to make sense of the semi-blurred letters found in the parafoveal regions and to identify words. Efficient readers do not process every letter in a word or every word in a sentence (Kucer, 2014); rather, they recognize words using semantics, syntax, and minimal letter clues. Because we are creating meaning with print, our brain only tricks us into thinking we have looked at every letter in every word.

CHAPTER 4

Coming to a Common Understanding

Much of the great "debate" related to reading instruction and interventions is based on misunderstandings of some basic terms and concepts. The purpose of this chapter is to bring clarity to three areas: (1) essential literacy terms; (2) methods, strategies, and direct instruction; and (3) direct instruction in a meaning-based approach.

EIGHT ESSENTIAL LITERACY TERMS

Below are eight commonly misunderstood terms related to reading instruction.

1. **Reading.** As described in previous chapters, *reading* is *not* sounding out words. Reading is creating meaning with print. Misunderstanding this basic concept has led to the design of many ineffective reading interventions.

2. **Word recognition.** Word recognition and word identification are not synonymous terms. *Word recognition* refers to instant and automatic identification of a word. You see the word and you know what it is without having to use any word identification strategies. This is a desired end state of word work.

3. **Word identification.** *Word identification* refers to the conscious employment of a strategy (see below) to figure out words in print that are known (in a student's lexicon) but unrecognized. Strategies to identify words include (a) morphemic analysis, (b) context clues, (c) analogy, and (d) phonics. Of these four strategies, using phonics is the least efficient in terms of efficiency and the amount of space required in short-term memory.

4. **Decoding.** *Decoding* refers to using the code (letter or symbol code) to identify unrecognized words in print—in other words, using phonics to sound out letters and identify words.

5. **Strategy.** A *strategy* is a cognitive process that one consciously applies to a task. Students should be taught to consciously apply all four of the word identification strategies above as well as comprehension and study skill strategies (see Chapter 13).

6. **Skill.** A *skill* is a cognitive process that has become automated. That is, you do not have to think about it. In reading, we teach the strategy to develop the skill. This means that we teach a variety of word identification and comprehension strategies so that students use them automatically and effortlessly while reading.

7. **Systematic phonics instruction.** Almost all teachers and researchers believe that *systematic phonics instruction* is an important part of any reading curriculum or intervention. However, systematic phonics instruction does not mean that you start at one end of a scope-and-sequence chart and work your way through it in standardized fashion and in a prescribed sequence without consideration of your students' needs (Braunger & Lewis, 2006). This would be educational malpractice. Systematic phonics instruction also does not mean that phonics skills should be taught in isolation apart from meaningful contexts. Instead, systematic phonics instruction means that some system or arrangement is in place to make sure that essential skills are taught, to document when they are taught, and to document when students have learned them (see Chapter 17). Also, teacher knowledge and expertise should be utilized to make the instructional decisions about what is taught, in what order, and in what context.

8. **A balanced approach.** A *balanced approach* to classroom literacy instruction means that there are appropriate amounts of (a) essential skills instruction and word work, (b) reading practice using real texts, (c) writing for authentic purposes, and (d) social interaction around books and writing. What are the appropriate amounts? Since students are not standardized products, this varies depending on students' needs. However, as mentioned in an earlier chapter, no more than 20–30% of literacy instruction occurring in a general education setting should be used for skills instruction. If this seems like too little skills instruction, keep in mind that students learn literacy skills best in the context of authentic literacy activities (see below) and not in isolated drill and practice routines.

METHODS, STRATEGIES, AND DIRECT INSTRUCTION

The terms *method, strategy,* and *direct instruction* need a bit of clarification as well.

A Strategy Is Not a Method

A *method* in education usually refers to a defined process or specific set of techniques that are used exclusively in a prescribed fashion for instruction in a particular subject area (Johnson, 2017). Example: reading methods, math methods, or social studies methods. In contrast, a *pedagogical strategy* is a specific teaching technique that is used selectively in a variety of subject areas for a specific purpose. *Direct instruction* is one such pedagogical strategy and should not be considered a method. There are instances when direct instruction is the most effective strategy to use; there are other instances when it is the least efficient strategy to use. Like any pedagogical strategy, its effectiveness is dependent on how it is used and for what purpose.

Using direct instruction as a method of reading instruction is an example of educational malpractice. In such a case, it is the only strategy (or the main strategy) used to teach reading. Sadly, this is what often occurs with struggling readers and writers (Allington, 2012). They are given a steady diet of low-level skills instruction, with little or no chance to develop the high-level thinking skills associated with reading and writing. And those who need reading practice the most are given the least amount of time to engage in free, voluntary reading practice (Spear-Swerling, 2012). Thus, students who do little reading are exposed to significantly fewer words (see Figure 4.1) and have fewer opportunities to practice and develop meaning-making skills necessary for reading.

Direct instruction is effective for learning low-level facts and skills, but it is not very effective for higher-level learning (Eppley & Dudley-Marling, 2018). Direct instruction comes in a variety of forms, with titles such as programmed instruction, criterion-referenced instruction (CRI), conditions of learning, mastery learning, mastery teaching, strategic instruction, learning strategies, direct instruction, explicit direct instruction, or supported instruction. All of these can be useful tools in certain instances for specific purposes (like mastery of low-level reading skills). However, they all have limitations and should never be or become a method of instruction for anything. Direct instruction can be used to teach specific skills, but the goal of any type of instruction or reading intervention is to develop students' ability to create meaning with print rather than enable them to master a set of reading skills.

An analogy: I used to be a wrestling coach. My wrestlers needed direct instruction on specific wrestling skills (moves). We did small amounts of direct instruction during every practice. However, if all we did was drill and practice wrestling skills without any chance to actually use them to wrestle, my wrestlers would not be very successful. They might be able to demonstrate mastery of individual wrestling skills, but they would not have a good sense of how and when to use them. Thus, initially

Achievement percentile	Minutes a day reading	Words per year
90th	40.4	2,357,000
50th	12.9	601,000
10th	1.6	51,000

FIGURE 4.1. The amount of voluntary reading is highly correlated with achievement: Fifth-grade student data from Anderson, Wilson, and Fielding (1988).

I used direct instruction to teach wrestling skills, but most of wrestling practice was used to practice wrestling, that is, to actually engage in real-life wrestling.

DIRECT INSTRUCTION IN A MEANING-BASED APPROACH

In reading, some form of direct instruction should be used to teach things such as letter–sound associations, letter patterns, word identification skills, comprehension skills, and study skill strategies. Direct instruction should be a small part of any reading class or intervention. The specific form that direct instruction takes and the amount necessary vary; however, it usually includes variations of the following five elements (Johnson, 2019):

1. **Clearly defined purpose.** Direct instruction learning experience is designed to teach a specific skill, procedure, or concept. It is purposeful as opposed to experiential.

2. **Explicit input with demonstration or modeling.** The input is the specific information that students need to know. When teaching a skill or procedure, this would include a description of the skill or procedure, how to use it, the specific steps, and then examples or teacher modeling. Effective input for direct instruction lessons is well organized, with a logical structure to enhance students' assimilation and encoding of information. If you are teaching a specific skill, the input should not be of great duration.

3. **Guided practice.** Guided practice enables students to practice the skill under the guidance of the teacher. The goal here is for students to use or apply the new skill as the teacher monitors to assess learning (formative assessment). In using guided practice, the teacher provides a scaffold with a gradual release of responsibility that enables all students to be successful. Small-group activities can be effective here because they enable the teacher to see many students simultaneously and to hear their thought processes as they discuss ideas with others.

4. **Independent practice.** Independent practice is the application of what students already know or can do. It is learning practice used to reinforce the skill taught. This is not the place to challenge students; rather, this is the place for them to apply and practice what they have learned. Thus, students should be able to complete independent practice activities with 95–100% success.

5. **Provision of opportunities for review and practice.** Learning occurs over time. You cannot expect to teach any skill once and achieve student mastery. You must revisit, review, and reinforce skills many times, in different ways, at successively higher levels over time for real learning to occur (Johnson, 2016b). This is especially true with severely struggling readers who often have difficulties recognizing letter patterns. As skills are revisited in a variety of contexts and settings, learning becomes more complete.

The "How" and "How Much" of Direct Instruction

Almost all teachers, researchers, and scholars believe that direct and explicit instruction is one important part of reading instruction and interventions. It is not the *what* of direct instruction; it is the *how* and the *how much* of direct instruction in which there are often differing views. In this regard, here are three suggestions for enhancing the effectiveness of direction instruction:

1. **Use the least amount necessary.** The goal for any reading intervention is not for students to master a particular set of reading skills; rather, it is to enhance their ability to create meaning with print. So, how much direct instruction should be used in a reading intervention? The least amount necessary.

2. **The initial instruction must be whole-to-part.** Complex learning of any kind occurs best when it is whole-to-part (Donnelly & Davidoff, 1999; Helmut, 2005; Julia, 2006; Lim, Reiser, & Olina, 2009). We learn skills best if we are able to get a sense of the whole first and then we are taught individual skills. In literacy instruction, this means that students should be immersed in authentic reading and writing experiences first and then taught the skills necessary to decode, identify words, comprehend, or write. This approach enables learners to see the big picture as context for the subskills related to reading and writing. This means that any type of word work should occur, to the greatest extent possible, within the context of authentic texts or sentences.

3. **Instruction should be briskly paced.** Figure 4.2 shows the recommended duration for direct instruction (Jensen, 2005). Outside of this, learning is reduced significantly. This does not mean that the duration of the entire reading lesson or intervention should be this short; instead, small bits of direct instruction should be used that are briskly paced (2 to no more than 8 minutes for a single element) with a pause or reflective activity between (see Figure 4.2). The brain learns best when instruction is provided in small bits followed by a pause for students to process or do something with the new instructional input (Johnson, 2016b).

Grade level	Appropriate amount of direct instruction
K–2	5–8 minutes
3–5	8–12 minutes
6–8	12–15 minutes
9–12	12–15 minutes
Adults	15–18 minutes

FIGURE 4.2. Appropriate amount of direction instruction.

PART II

ELEMENTS OF A MEANING-BASED INTERVENTION FOR READING

CHAPTER 5

How a Meaning-Based Intervention for Reading Works

Here the rubber starts to meet the road. This chapter provides an overview of what might be included in a meaning-based intervention for struggling readers.

INTERVENTIONS AND EDUCATIONAL MALPRACTICE

As has been described in previous chapters, there is no single evidence-based program, research-based curriculum, or scientifically based teaching strategy that works best for all students who struggle with reading. There are; however, a variety of strategies that research has shown to be effective with certain students, for certain skills, in certain situations. The effectiveness or ineffectiveness of any strategy is dependent on how, when, where, for whom, and for what purpose it is used or applied. Based on this information, teachers implementing an intervention for reading must have a variety of tools (strategies) in their teaching toolbox. Teachers must also be empowered to make decisions regarding these tools so that they can best meet the needs of their students (Lyons et al., 2013). Thus, an effective approach to reading interventions should include a variety of research-based strategies; but teachers must be able to use only those strategies they deem to be appropriate for their teaching situation and to flexibly apply them in ways that best meet the needs of their students.

Fidelity or Educational Malpractice

Fidelity is a term often misused by the designers of commercially prepared reading interventions and by decision makers outside the classroom. Teachers are told they must implement an evidence-based program with "fidelity." This term has been misinterpreted in an educational setting to mean following the instructional recipe exactly as written. In other words, fidelity means that teachers are required to dismiss their own knowledge and experience and instead follow the directions and do exactly what the program designers tell them to do without question or variation when implementing a reading intervention.

Following this logic, a teacher working with struggling readers in a third-grade classroom in Blackwater, Arizona, would be required to give the same "treatment" in exactly the same way as a teacher working with struggling readers in a third-grade classroom in Edina, Minnesota. Program designers have already made this decision for them even though they know nothing about these schools, teachers, teaching situations, and the individual students.

While this concept of fidelity may be appropriate for experimental research where control and treatment groups need to follow strict parameters in order to isolate a variable; it is neither effective nor appropriate when educating real students in the uncontrolled confines of the real world (Bradley & Reinking, 2011). Our job as reading teachers operating in this real world is not to isolate variables; it is to help real human beings develop their ability to create meaning with print. Moreover, since real human beings are not standardized products, it would be a form of educational malpractice to insist that teachers follow any educational recipe with fidelity. This would, in fact, prevent them from being able to adequately meet the needs of their students.

Can you image an engineer being told to implement a particular bridge design with fidelity when he or she found that the particular terrain on which the bridge was being built had elements that were not considered up front? If you were undergoing a complex medical procedure, would you want your doctor to implement the procedure with fidelity without considering any of your particular medical variables? Would you want the lawyer representing you to simply follow some sort of lawyer algorithm with fidelity in court? How then is it appropriate for a teacher to implement any sort of reading instruction or intervention with fidelity with all the multitude of unaccounted for variables present in a classroom of actual human beings?

If you still insist on implementing something with fidelity, know that there are two understandings of the term. It can refer to the exactness with which something is copied or reproduced. However, it can also refer to one's faithfulness to a person, cause, or belief. Unless one is conducting experimental research in a controlled environment, the latter definition should be used when teaching real human beings in the real world. Thus, the appropriate understanding of fidelity regarding reading interventions (or any instructional program) would be to understand and accurately apply the research-based principles on which the intervention is based. This would enable teachers to adopt the strategies they deem to be most appropriate for their students and to flexibly apply them in ways that best meet their needs. In this way, teachers are able to use their knowledge, expertise, and experience to make the decisions that are best for their students.

INTERVENTION SESSIONS FOR READING

Depending on students' needs, intervention sessions for reading should include some or all of the following seven elements:

1. **Word work.** Students receive short bits of instruction and practice related to letters and letter patterns. This includes synthetic phonics, analytic phonics, and large unit phonics (see Chapter 7).
2. **Word identification.** Students receive short bits of instruction and practice related to one of the word identification strategies: (a) analogy, (b) morphemic analysis, (c) context clues, and (d) phonics (see Chapter 9).
3. **Maze and cloze work.** Students practice identifying words within sentences based on context clues. Cloze and maze sentences can also be used as pre- or postreading activities or to reinforce word work (see Chapter 10).
4. **Writing.** Students write using language experience activities (LEA), simple one- or two-sentence writing activities, structured writing activities, daily journal writing, and other short activities where students use writing to describe their ideas (see Chapter 11).
5. **Fluency work.** Students engage in repeated reading and other activities used to develop fluency (see Chapter 12).
6. **Comprehension.** Students receive short bits of instruction and practice related to the cognitive processes used in comprehension as well as study skills strategies for older students (see Chapter 13). Often, comprehension work is used with reading practice (see below).
7. **Reading practice.** Students read and respond to authentic texts that they have chosen. For emergent level readers, this could also include teacher read-alouds (Braunger & Lewis, 2006) and scaffolded oral reading (Johnson, 2016b; see Chapter 14).

Again, students are *not* standardized products. A single type of intervention will never meet all the needs of all struggling readers. However, by adopting and adapting the strategies and activities presented in this book, it is more likely that you will be able to help students to achieve their full literacy potential. Individual sessions generally consist of three to five of the activities above. It is not effective to focus on only one or two of these.

Schedule, Intensity, Pace, and Duration

To have an impact, intervention sessions for reading should occur a minimum of 3 days a week (this would be comparable to RTI Tier 2). More intense interventions should occur daily (this would be comparable to RTI Tier 3). Shorter bits of focused instruction and activities are always more effective than longer bits of instruction

Beginning level	Intermediate level
1. LEA	1. Journal writing
2. Word work	2. Word work
3. Cloze–maze	3. Cloze–maze
4. Fluency	4. Fluency
5. Reading practice—comprehension	5. Writing
	6. Reading practice—comprehension

FIGURE 5.1. Ideas for daily intervention sessions.

and activities in which students are not actively engaged. Thus, intervention sessions should be short and briskly paced (15 to no more than 40 minutes daily). These sessions should move quickly from one activity to the next, with each activity lasting 2–8 minutes. This brisk pace maintains students' focus while developing a full range of literacy skills. Keep in mind that you are not teaching students to read as much as you are developing their ability to create meaning with print. Also keep in mind that your reading interventions should build upon and enhance good classroom reading instruction.

Figure 5.1 contains examples of what intervention sessions might look like for two levels. Each session consists of five or six briskly paced activities. Always adopt and adapt to meet the needs of your students. This means that, depending on students' needs and level, you might add more or fewer activities, or you might use different kinds of activities for your daily intervention sessions. Also, the activities in Figure 5.1 can be used with individual or small groups of students.

FINAL WORD

This chapter provides suggested templates for individual intervention sessions as well as an example of what daily sessions might look like. Specific activities are described in the chapters that follow. Again, the selection of activities for a reading intervention should be based on diagnostic information that identifies strength and deficit areas related to reading.

CHAPTER 6

Language Experience Activities

AN EXPERIENCE WITH LANGUAGE

Language experience activities (LEA) are an effective strategy to use with beginning-level readers. Here students dictate an experience or story to the teacher. The teacher then records what students say. I strongly recommended that you use this activity with each intervention session for two reasons: First, on an interpersonal level, language experience activities enable you to make personal connections with your students. You can find out what is going on in their lives as well as what they find interesting or significant. It also creates conversation around these events. This enhances your ability to relate to your students. Relationships are important in any kind of teaching, but especially so when dealing with struggling readers, as their self-efficacy and motivation are often low.

Second, on an instructional level, LEA enable students to practice reading using words that are in their lexicon as well as their experiences and ideas. This makes learning to read easier. Analytic phonics (modeled below) can then be used to develop letter–sound relationships with these familiar words and experiences.

STEPS

LEA can be used with large groups, small groups, pairs, or individual students. Here are the specific steps.

Writing

Ask students to describe an experience. You might ask, "What do you want to say today?" Then write down what is said. For example, if the class took a field trip to the zoo, you might say, "We took a trip to the zoo yesterday. What should we say about that?" A student might say something like "We went on a bus and it was a long trip and it was really, really fun and we had lots of candy." Often, you need to paraphrase or break up their long sentences into two or three short sentences. This makes it easier to read and thus, more likely that students will be successful. Here you would write something like "We went on the bus. It was a long trip. We had lots of candy." You then can ask, "What else do you want to say?"

Figure 6.1 contains some prompts that can be used for LEA. Let students know that you will be asking for a minimum number of sentences. With severely struggling readers in the early grades, two to three sentences should be the goal. With other readers, use a four- or five-sentence minimum.

Language experience entries (sometimes called stories) should always be put in paragraph form (vs. lists of sentences). This reflects the type of reading students will encounter. Also, if students say something that is grammatically incorrect, include the correct version as you write. Use cognitive modeling to teach writing mechanics such as punctuation, indentations, and capitalization. These are very powerful ways to teach these skills directly and explicitly in the context in which they are used.

Reading

Use scaffolded oral reading (ScORe) to read the story with students. ScORe is a technique that enables students to successfully engage with text that is a little above their independent reading level. It is a variation of the neurological impress method (Flood, Lapp, & Fisher, 2005; Oladele, 2013). Here you and the student read the text together aloud. You act as a scaffold by reading just a millisecond ahead of the student in order to maintain a steady, comfortable pace. If the student pauses or stumbles, you keep reading. Do not stop to let the student sound out the

1. What did you do yesterday?
2. What did you do after school?
3. What are you going to do this weekend?
4. What is something interesting that happened?
5. Tell me about something you like to do?
6. What should we say about [*insert event here*]?
7. What happened at [*insert event*]?
8. What do you think is interesting about [*insert event*]?
9. What do you want to say today?
10. What should we write about today?

FIGURE 6.1. Prompts to use for LEA.

word. The student learns to rely on your voice to act as a scaffold to identify words during the process of reading.

During ScORe you should read using a quiet voice, providing just enough support to keep the pace moving. Point to the words as you are reading. If the student seems to be reading fluently, provide less scaffolding by sounding out just the beginning parts of some words or by dropping out completely in places. The goal is to act as a scaffold to enable students to read at a reasonable pace without frustrating them or having to stop to figure out any of the words. This also allows students to enjoy reading the book while lessening the cognitive demands on working memory used to identify words.

In a small group, this becomes a form of choral reading. Just like ScORe that is done individually, point to the words as they are being read and keep the pace moving. You will also find that ScORe is effective with many of the other activities in a meaning-based intervention for reading.

Developing Fluency

Have students reread the passage independently until fluency is achieved. This usually occurs after two or three readings.

Analytic Phonics

Use analytic phonics to teach and reinforce letter sounds and patterns. Here you would ask students to identify and read aloud words that contain target letter sounds or patterns—for example: "There's a word in the first line that ends in the /duh/ sound. What word is this?"; "Find the word in the second line that ends with the /ch/ sound"; "What is the same about /bat/ and /tub/?"

Date and Store

Date and save these stories (see Figure 6.2). You can use these for reading practice on subsequent days. As well, students enjoy looking back to see what they were thinking and experiencing at different times of the year.

Tuesday, November 30, 2019

I went to my grandma's house for Thanksgiving. My cousin was there. We had turkey, stuffing, and mashed potatoes. It was great.

FIGURE 6.2. Example of an LEA story.

TIPS

Students should be able to see the words forming as you are writing them. With groups, use a smartboard or projector. You can use poster, but it does not work as well. When doing language experience with individuals or pairs, use a computer monitor. Turn the monitor so that it is directly facing students. If needed, put the keyboard in your lap so that it does not interfere. Increase the font size to 24 points or larger, depending on the age and level of your students. Use 1.5 or 2.0 spacing so that words are easily seen.

Figure 6.3 contains an example of an LEA done with an individual student (Pat). A Word document was created and saved with the date of the entry posted on top. The teacher printed out entries and used them to create books. Pat was asked to draw a picture to go with each entry. These were used to practice reading. Also, a variety of meaning-based activities and mini-lessons were designed using Pat's own writing. This made the lessons much more impactful than it would be by breaking down words in isolation or on a worksheet.

If you are doing LEA with groups, you can also make books. Students can take turns drawing pictures to go with each entry. These can be bound, put in a classroom library, and used for reading practice in subsequent years. (I do not recommend putting students' individual books in a classroom library.) Students love reading what other students (especially older students) have written.

Friday, September 8, 2019

We went on a field trip. We went to a wildlife area. I saw lots of animals and birds. I saw a heron. It was great.

FIGURE 6.3. Pat's LEA entry with a space to draw a picture.

CHAPTER 7

Word Work

Word work activities are used to strengthen students' ability to perceive letter–sound relationships and recognize letter patterns. These types of activities emphasize the phonological cueing system and should be one part of the total intervention for students whose deficit area is word identification. Also included here should be activities to develop the semantic and syntactic cueing systems. These will be described in Chapters 9 and 10. To be most effective, word work activities should occur within a meaningful context to the greatest extent possible. And of course, students should be given ample opportunities to read authentic texts so that they can practice using the skills they have learned.

PHONICS

Meaning-based reading teachers are sometimes accused of ignoring phonics instruction. Of course, this is an absurd notion. Effective meaning-based reading teachers use very direct and explicit phonics instruction when appropriate. It is not the *what* of phonics instruction in which there are differing views; it is the *how* and the *how much* of phonics instruction. Whereas a skills-based approach sees phonics instruction as the main part of a reading intervention, a meaning-based approach sees phonics instruction as one of many parts of an effective reading intervention. As a result, skills-based reading teachers develop only one of the brain's cueing systems, while meaning-based reading teachers develop all three.

Three Types of Phonics Instruction

Three types of phonics instruction are synthetic phonics, analytic phonics, and large-unit phonics.

1. **Synthetic phonics.** Synthetic phonics instruction is the traditional skills-based approach that most people associate with phonics instruction. This is part-to-whole instruction in which students are asked to put letter sounds together to create words. Synthetic phonics usually occurs in isolation (outside a meaningful reading context), using workbooks, flashcards, and other nonreading materials. It usually involves some form of direct instruction. There is a place for this type of instruction. However, it should not be the only place, nor should it be the largest place.

2. **Analytic phonics.** Analytic phonics instruction asks students to analyze sounds with the words they encounter in print. This instruction occurs within in the context of authentic reading experiences. Chapter 6 describes how this was done with LEA. It can also be done with big books, books students are reading, or in small-group guided reading activities.

3. **Large-unit phonics.** Large-unit phonics is based on the brain's natural inclination to notice patterns and complete configurations based on partial data (Gazzaniga, Ivry, & Mangun, 2000; Revlin, 2013). When we look at words on the page, we tend to notice letter patterns much more than individual letters (Weaver, 2009). So instead of using individual letters to recognize or construct words, proficient readers tend to use internalized letter patterns from familiar words stored in long-term memory (Moustafa, 1998; Weaver, 2009). These patterns include the 30 most common phonograms, or word families, shown in Figure 7.1 (Fry, 1998) and common prefixes, suffixes, and root words presented in Figure 7.2. To utilize large-unit phonics as a word identification strategy, students are taught to look for familiar letter patterns (Allington, 2002; Cunningham & Cunningham, 2002). The word identification strategies related to this are called *analogy* and *morphological analysis* and are described in more detail in the next chapter. However, large-unit phonics can also be used to develop students' ability to recognize words. To do this, activities focus on word parts and letter patterns. Some of these are described below.

Activities Using Large-Unit Phonics

Shared Reading for Large-Unit Phonics

Margaret Moustafa describes shared reading for large-unit phonics in her book *Beyond Traditional Phonics* (1997). With modification, it can be used with students at any level in individual, small-group, or large-group settings. These are the steps:

- First, the teacher reads a book to students. Each student should have a copy of the text and follow along.
- Second, students read the text independently or with a partner using buddy reading. (Buddy reading is where students find a partner and take turns reading paragraphs or sections orally.)

ay	ag	ot	ain	op	ow
ill	ack	ing	eed	in	ew
ip	ank	ap	y	an	ore
at	ick	unk	out	est	ed
am	ell	all	ug	ink	ab

FIGURE 7.1. The 30 most common phonograms.

- Third, students identify interesting or important words from the selection. Depending on the level of students and the size of the group, the total number of words should be 8–15. The teacher records these words on a board, poster, or screen so that everyone can see the list. For younger students, the teacher writes the words on 3″ × 5″ cards. Older students can simply look at the list.
- Fourth, students are asked to create groups based on letter patterns.
- And finally, students create a word wall or poster that includes the title of the book or text, the groups, and the words within each group. Students should be able to see and reference these groups and words.

Any word-sorting activity like this is effective in helping students notice letter patterns (see below). The duration of this initial activity should be 10 to no more than 20 minutes. You can extend this by using one or more words as a writing prompt, to play bingo, or to play letter rummy (below). It may be appropriate to occasionally do a sorting activity like this using a list of words that the teacher

Prefixes	Suffixes
un	s, es
re	ed
in, im, ir, il	ing
dis	ly
en	er, or
non	ion, tion, ation, ition
in, im, in, into	able, ible
over	al, ial
mis	y
sub	ness

FIGURE 7.2. The 10 most common prefixes and suffixes.

creates in order to reinforce target letter patterns. However, encountering the words in a meaningful context first makes it a meaning-based activity. While not every word work activity can be meaning-based, you should strive to maximize meaningful encounters with letters and words.

Word Sorts

Word sorts are used to reinforce the target letter sound or pattern. You can include words from books you are reading (shared reading above), words that students encounter in their daily lives, words from other curriculum areas, or words used to reinforce target letter sound or patterns. This activity can be done individually but works best in pairs. Here, students are given 6–20 individual words cards. Students must look for and arrange the word cards into groups. A group is two or more things that are the same. Groups can be based on letter patterns (beginning, middle, or ending), on sounds, or on meaning.

Word-sort activities of any kind invite students to use inductive reasoning to notice letter patterns, including prefixes, suffixes, and roots. Inductive reasoning is a cognitive operation in which broad generalizations are made based on specific observations (Johnson, 2000). Whereas deductive reasoning proceeds step by step along a predetermined path to teach new concepts, inductive reasoning enables students to quickly perceive reoccurring patterns and construct a big conceptual picture. Learning based on this type of thinking tends to be more meaningful and often goes beyond what is presented in the lesson when compared to teacher-directed, deductive types of activities (Lefrancois, 2011).

Word Building

Word-building activities involve putting word parts together to create whole words. Three types of word-building activities are as follows.

1. **Word construction or onset–rime.** Here, students are shown a beginning letter or consonant cluster (onset) and a phonogram (rime) and are then asked to put them together to create a word. Figure 7.3 shows the two levels of word construction activities used to reinforce the /ad/ phonogram. Students are first shown the initial letter and the phonogram. They are asked to say each part and then to put them together—for example: "/b/ plus /ad/ is ______." Provide just enough

b — ad bad	p — add — ed padded

FIGURE 7.3. Word construction activities for the /ad/ phonogram.

scaffolding to enable students to identify the word. As students put the two parts together and begin to form the word, they should then be shown the complete word. If you are using PowerPoint for this activity, the complete word should appear beneath the construction.

Word construction activities can be used to develop students' ability to recognize letter patterns. As well, they can be used to reinforce letter sounds. For example, to reinforce the short-*a* vowel sound, phonograms containing the short *a* for word construction activities are used. Figure 7.4 contains common short-*a* phonograms. The point is that many activities can be designed to reinforce letter sounds and letter patterns.

2. **Letter with phonograms.** Here a beginning letter is presented with different phonograms (see Figure 7.5). Students are asked to connect the beginning letter with each phonogram to create words. The complete word is shown once it is assembled.

3. **Phonogram with letters.** Here a word family is presented with different letters (see Figure 7.6). Students are asked to connect different letters to the beginning of the same word family to create words. The complete word is shown once it is assembled.

ad	bad, mad, had
ap	cap, tap,
at	bat, rat, mat
am	ham, jam,
ack	back, tack, track
an	can, fan, ran
ag	bag, drag, tag
ab	cab, lab, nap
ash	bash, cask, dash

FIGURE 7.4. Common short-*a* phonograms.

m	**- ad**	mad
	- ap	map
	- at	mat

FIGURE 7.5. Letter with phonograms.

b	**- at**	bat
c		cat
h		hat
m		mat

FIGURE 7.6. Word family with letters.

Word-building activities can be designed using paper, dry erase boards, scrabble letters, simple letter cards, or PowerPoint. I prefer using PowerPoint or some other slide format in order to use color to highlight the target letter patterns and to be able to move quickly from one activity to another. Remember, you are not teaching anything here; you are strengthening neural pathways in order to enhance students' ability to notice letter patterns within words. This ability develops over time and is not mastered in a single session or in a single unit. Word-building activities should be briskly paced, lasting from 2 to no more than 10 minutes (usually less). You should use 8 to no more than 15 examples here.

Word Discrimination

Word discrimination activities are used to reinforce target letter patterns or sounds. Students are presented with a picture clue and three words, one of which is related to the picture (see Figure 7.7). They must analyze the three words and identify the correct one. You could also speak the word (without a picture clue) while presenting the three options. The series of words used here should reinforce a letter sound or letter pattern, for example, all short-*a* words. As students attend to these words, they inductively learn about phonemes and letter patterns within words. Learning by inductive analysis is a more powerful and immediate way of learning when compared to direct instruction (Bruner, 1977).

The three words used here should be similar enough to invite students to fully analyze each word. In Figure 7.7, notice how the first word is the same except for the last letter *t*. The second word is the same except for the middle letter *u*. The three words contain all the necessary letter sounds. This activity should be briskly paced, lasting 2 to no more than 8 minutes. Students should be asked to analyze 8–15 sets of words in a single setting.

Word Wall Riddle Review

Here students are given a simple riddle. The answer appears on a word wall with 6 to 10 choices, all of which contain the target letter pattern. They must select the correct answer from the word wall (see Figure 7.8). If you are in a classroom

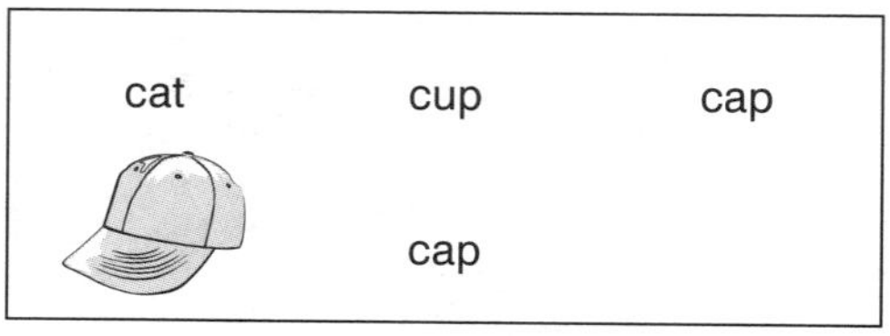

FIGURE 7.7. Word discrimination.

or a consistent teaching space, it is recommended that these words be posted on an actual wall or bulletin board. This enables you to review past letter sounds or patterns quickly. In addition, students can eventually think of and ask their own riddles. Words on a word wall can also be used for writing or speaking prompts, spelling work, and other activities.

Pattern Recognition

Students are shown a simple sentence or paragraph and asked to identify words with a particular letter pattern. For beginning level students, you may need to read the sentence or paragraph. Again, the goal with this type of activity is to develop students' ability to notice or recognize letter patterns.

Replay Analysis

This is a variation of retrospective miscue analysis (see below) described by Goodman, Martens, and Flurkey (2016). Here, students are presented three to six sentences on a piece of paper (see Figure 7.9). In order to reinforce target letter sounds or patterns, each sentence includes at least one word containing the target. Students read the sentences aloud as they are audio recorded. Next, they listen to the recording and underline any miscues or stumble words. After this, they review the "stumble" words, then reread, and again record the sentences. This process is repeated until fluency is achieved with no miscues or stumbles.

If six sentences are overwhelming for students, start with three. When teaching in small groups, students can work in pairs. One student serves as the recorder operator and helps the other identify stumble words, while the other is the reader. You can extend this by asking students to identify words containing the target letter sound or pattern in each sentence.

not happy	cap
	bad
	mat
sad	slam
	glad
	pan
	sad

FIGURE 7.8. Word wall riddle review.

Replay Analysis Sentences
1. I will clap my hands.
2. I have a small hat.
3. The car needs gas.
4. Fill the tank with gas.
5. You do not want to fall.
6. Use the pan to cook the ham.

FIGURE 7.9. Replay analysis to reinforce the short-*a* sound.

Retrospective Miscue Analysis

A more advanced version of replay analysis is retrospective miscue analysis (Goodman, Goodman, & Allen, 2017). This strategy can be used to enhance word recognition and identification for older students; however, it also serves to develop comprehension and helps students understand their own reading process. Here the student reads aloud a passage at his or her instructional level. This is recorded. The teacher conducts a miscue analysis of the passage, marking the text to identify meaningful miscues, meaning-disrupting miscues, and self-corrections (see Chapter 16). The next day, the teacher and student listen to the recording and go through the text together, noting the types of miscues and instances when meaning was disrupted and not disrupted. This invites further analysis of words and recognition of common miscues, but more importantly, students begin to understand their own strengths and weaknesses as readers, and they begin to move away from a view of reading as simply correctly identifying words. Over time, students can learn to do miscue analyses of their own readings and those of classmates.

Sentence Dictation

Here, the teacher (or partner) reads three simple sentences to students. Each sentence contains at least one word with the target letter sound or pattern (see Figure 7.10). Students write the sentence. After each sentence, they are asked to look for words that "do not look right" and underline them. Students are then shown the complete sentence with correct spelling. They cross out any misspelled words and write the correct spelling on top. (They cross out instead of erasing so that they can see the difference between the correct and incorrect spelling.) When the correct spellings are in place, students skip a line and go to the next sentence. When all three sentences are completed, they reread them until fluency is achieved.

Word Parsicle

This activity is designed to develop students' ability to perceive parts of words. To parse a word means to analyze it or break it into parts. In word parsicle, students are given parts of a word as clues and asked to identify the mystery word (see Figure 7.11). With each successive guess, students are given additional clues until the word

1. It is bad.
2. The cat ate the ham.
3. He sat on my hat.

FIGURE 7.10. Sentence dictation for short *a*.

is correctly identified. The mystery word should contain the target letter sound or patterns you are trying to reinforce. Like all activities in this chapter, this activity should be kept short and briskly paced. A whiteboard, poster, or paper can be used here; however, PowerPoint enables you to quickly move through this activity.

Activities for Analogy

After the word identification strategy has been taught, the activities below can be used to develop students' ability to perceive letter patterns. Activities like these should be approximately 2–8 minutes in duration. PowerPoint is preferred (but not required) because it allows you to move quickly from one set to another and use color to highlight target phonograms.

Word Wall

Word walls are words that are displayed on a wall or bulletin board for quick reference and review. You can post words with common word families or phonograms like those shown in Figure 7.12. Word wall riddle reviews can be used to reinforce target phonograms. Here students are asked a simple riddle based on a letter pattern—for example: "I am thinking of an /ay/ word. Cows eat it"; "I am thinking of an /in/ word. It is on a fish." The riddle review is a quick and easy way to review and reinforce. Eventually, you can encourage students to think of their own riddles.

Phonogram Categories

Which word doesn't belong? Students see three words. One of the words is not like the other. Categories here should be based solely on phonograms. Even though all the words in Figure 7.13 have the long-*a* sound, only two of them have the same /ay/ phonogram.

gr______
gr_bb___
gr_bb_ng
grabb_ng
grabbing

FIGURE 7.11. Word parsicle.

ay	in	ate
hay may day say lay pay stay play	tin bin kin fin chin pin win shin	hate late Kate date fate mate gate plate

FIGURE 7.12. Word walls based on phonograms.

say
late
play

FIGURE 7.13. Phonogram categories.

Phonograms

ay	ip	ill

FIGURE 7.14. Example of a data retrieval chart for phonograms.

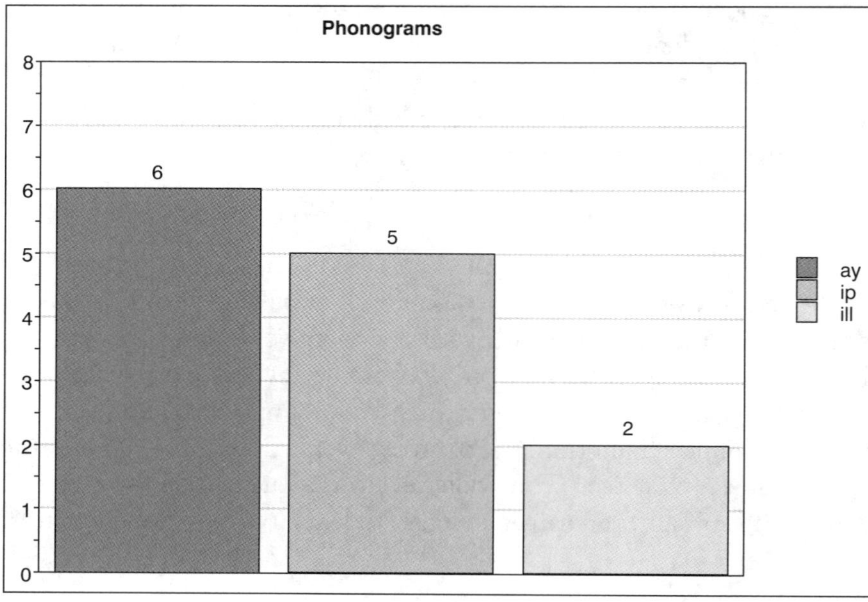

FIGURE 7.15. Phonogram bar graph.

Phonogram Inquiry

Similar to the sight inquiry described in Chapter 8, inquiry activities can also be used with phonograms. Using a book they have already read, students are given a data retrieval chart (Figure 7.14) and asked to look for words with specific phonograms. Tally marks are used to indicate instances of words with target phonograms. This activity can be extended by having students create bar graphs based on their data (see Figure 7.15).

HOW TO TEACH PHONICS

Direct Instruction

Direct instruction used as a pedagogical strategy is an integral part of any reading intervention. However, what often occurs in remedial programs and interventions for reading is that struggling readers get an unhealthy dose of direct phonics instruction used to teach letter–sound skills (Allington, 2012; Braunger & Lewis, 2006). However, you cannot direct-instruction your way into reading proficiency (Eppley & Dudley-Marling, 2018). Direct instruction used to teach letter–sound skills may result in small, temporary gains on word-level measures; however, there is little significant transference of these skills to authentic reading contexts or gains in comprehension (Eppley & Dudley-Marling, 2018). Direct instruction is effective for learning low-level skills, but not for high-level cognitive processes related to comprehension. Teaching only low-level skills is one way to ensure that low-level readers stay low-level.

Phonics Instruction in PreK

Students should enter first grade knowing their letter sounds and 25–40 sight words. In preschool, phonics instruction should be fun, short, highly incidental, and within the context of authentic literacy experiences to the greatest degree possible. For example, you might teach the /d/ sound by reading *Danny and the Dinosaur.* A short mini-lesson lasting 30 seconds to no more than 2 minutes would occur before reading. During reading, you would stop to identify words that begin with the /d/ sound. And after reading, you would review with /d/ words and maybe write them on a poster. Under no circumstances is it developmentally appropriate to have formalized phonics lessons using direct instruction and worksheets at the PreK level.

Review and Reinforce

Once students know their letter sounds and can recognize common letter patterns, instruction and interventions should consist largely of activities designed to review and reinforce this knowledge. Remember, the goal is to strengthen neural pathways and expand neural networks in order to enhance students' ability to recognize letter patterns during reading. As described in Chapter 1, you are not teaching reading. Instead, you are enhancing students' ability to create meaning with print. In so doing, you cannot totally eliminate isolated word study; however, these kinds of activities should take place within the context of sentences or authentic reading to the greatest extent possible. Most important, students should be able to apply phonics and other reading subskills by reading a variety of interesting and engaging texts at their independent level and below. Helping children fall in love with books is one of the best reading intervention strategies of all.

Temporary Spelling

Temporary spelling (sometimes called *invented spelling*) is an effective method to use to develop both phonemic awareness and letter–sound relationships. This method can be used starting in kindergarten and going through all levels. This means that when writing, students should be taught to use letters or approximate spellings to hold the idea. Capturing the idea is more important than the arrangement of individual letters. This does not mean that spelling is not important. However, just like real writers who are writing in the real world, editing occurs as the last step before publishing, and not during the drafting or revising stages.

GAMES

Ending a reading class or intervention session with some sort of game or activity gives students something to look forward to and creates a positive emotional tone. Below are some simple games that can be used to reinforce letter sounds and patterns. Adopt and adapt as necessary.

Word Rummy

The goal of this game is to be the first person to get rid of his or her cards. A deck is created on 3″ × 5″ cards using words from the share reading activity (above), or words that target one or more letter patterns. Cut the cards in half to create card decks. These smaller cards are easier to handle. Create four examples of the target letter sound or pattern. For example, if you work focusing on the /ack/ phonogram, you could use *black, sack, tack, back*. Each player is dealt five cards (you can vary this number), and they are asked to create groups. Players need at least three of a kind to create a group. Before their turn, each player draws a card. After every turn, a play discards a card. When a player gets a group, those cards are set down face up. If somebody has the fourth part of that group, that card can be laid down (just like real rummy). The player who gets rid of his or her hand first is the winner.

Letter Rummy

This game works best with two to four players at the emergent or beginning levels. Create letter cards with a single letter on them. You will need several examples of the most common letters. Then create 5–10 word cards that have words containing target letter sounds or patterns on them. Players draw a word card and put it in front of them face up. Players are dealt five (this may vary) letter cards. The goal of the game is to spell the word on the word card in front of them using the individual letter cards. Players take turns drawing and discarding. When players have a letter card in their hand that is in their word, they lay it down in front of them. The first person to spell the word on the word card is the winner. When you initially begin playing this game, leave the word cards face up so that students notice the cards of other players. This enables them to be strategic about which letters they discard. The goal here is for students to look at and notice letter patterns. Eventually, you may choose to deal the word cards face down. This creates an interesting variation.

Pairs

This game is played using the word cards created to reinforce target letter sounds or letter patterns. Cards are turned over and mixed up. There are two of every word card. Students take turns turning them over to look for pairs. As the card is turned, students must read and pronounce the word on the card. As students discover a pair, the cards are taken off the board. The person with the most pairs is the winner. Initially, a pair would be a card with the same word on it. You can extend or create variations by making the pairs words that have the same beginning letter, the same vowel sound, or the same ending letter.

Wild Monkey

This game is similar to Crazy Eights. The goal is to be the first person to get rid of all the cards in his or her hand. A simple deck is created that includes words with a similar letter sound or letter pattern and a symbol (see Figure 7.16). Two or three Wild Monkey cards should be included. These are wild cards. Players are dealt five (or seven cards). The remainder of the cards are placed face down. The top card is turned over. To place a card down, it must have a similar vowel sound or symbol. If a player cannot make a match, that person draws a card. If a player has the Wild Monkey card, that person can change the symbol. Play continues until one person has no more cards.

Old Monkey

The goal is to not be the person with the Old Monkey card at the end of the game. The deck in Figure 7.16 is used here with one monkey card included. All the cards are dealt. Any pairs are laid down. A pair is a card that has the same vowel sound and symbol. Players take turns drawing from the player on their right. When a player has no more cards, that player is safe. Play continues until one player is left holding the Old Monkey.

Guess the Secret Word

This is a word-guessing game that can be played individually, in teams, or with a friend. The purpose is to reinforce targeted vowel sounds and letter patterns. Similar to *Wheel of Fortune*, students are shown blank spaces representing letters in the secret word (see Figure 7.17). They must guess the letters until the secret word can

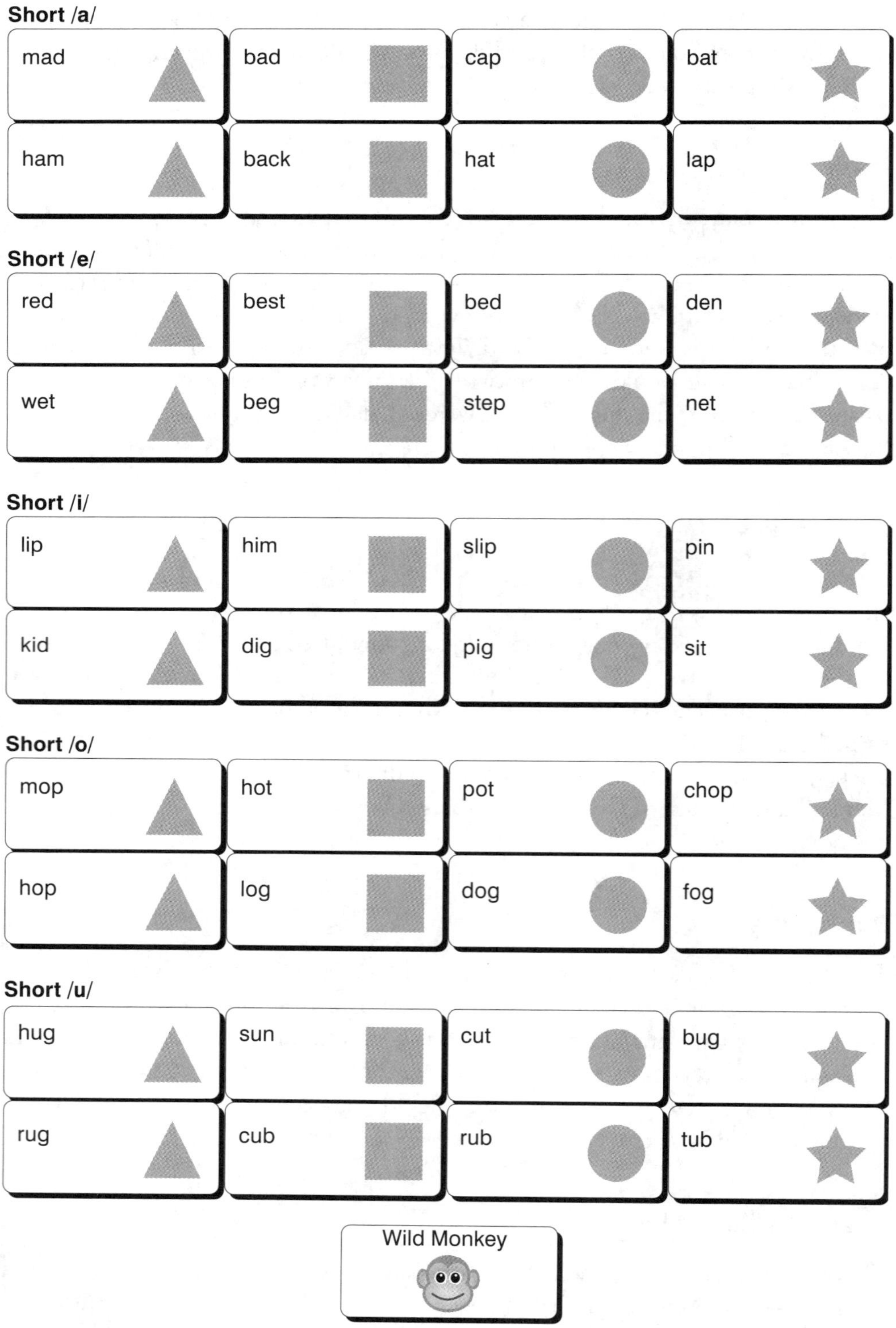

FIGURE 7.16. Deck for Wild Monkey.

— — — — — — — —
(clapped)
Word bank—short-*a* words: added, clapped, napping, backed, grabbed, calling, packing, flashed, dragging, unpack, thanks, thankful, planned, dragging, bashful, trash, crashed, smallest, grabbing

FIGURE 7.17. Guess the secret word: short *a*.

Letter Box s y a t m l p u t b e k
stay   — — —   mat   may   play   tub   yes   bake   ray   lake

FIGURE 7.18. Guess the secret word: long *a*.

be identified. To provide structure for younger students or struggling readers, you can include a letter box as well as a list of possible words (see Figure 7.18). Creating these games using PowerPoint enables you to do several of them quickly. You can also play this game in teams. The conversation that takes place is an important part of learning.

Wordo

This game is similar to Bingo. Students are given a blank Wordo card (see Figure 7.19). For younger students, use a Word card. Create 15–20 word cards to reinforce letter patterns or vowel sounds. As students are shown the cards being used for the game, they are to write the word anyplace on their Wordo card. (Words can be written more than once.) Students can place an "X" anyplace on their card as a wild spot. Use pennies or game chips as markers. The word cards are shuffled and drawn one at a time. As the word is shown and read, students find the word on their Wordo card. (Include two cards for every word.) The winner is the player who gets five (or four) in a row.

w	o	r	d	o

w	o	r	d

FIGURE 7.19. Wordo or word cards.

THE BEST APPROACH TO PHONICS INSTRUCTION

So which type of phonics instruction should you use: synthetic, analytic, or large-unit phonics instruction? You should include all of them. There is no research to support the effectiveness of any one of these approaches over the other; however, there is strong research to support the use of phonics instruction within the context of authentic literacy experiences versus in isolation (Braunger & Lewis, 2006). From a neurological perspective, using multiple types of phonics instruction creates more expansive neural networks than does a single approach to phonics instruction.

The optimal amount of phonics instruction is the minimal amount needed to become an independent reader. Good phonics instruction (and word work of any kind) also includes opportunities to practice reading words in authentic reading contexts. There is a place for examining words in isolation—but most words should be encountered in context. In the real world, we never encounter a single word in isolation. Even signs and labels are found in contexts that make sense.

Word work activities come in a variety of forms. All activities described in this chapter should be briskly paced, lasting 2–8 minutes. As suggested in an earlier chapter, word work should be one part of a daily lesson for reading interventions if word identification is a deficit area. It should not be the reading intervention.

CHAPTER 8

Sight Words and Scope and Sequence Charts

This chapter describes strategies for attending to sight words in a meaning-based approach to reading. It ends with an examination of scope and sequence charts.

SIGHT WORDS

Sight words are the words that students recognize instantly (on sight) without having to use letter cues, word parts, or context clues. These words can be found on lists of most common words, which include the 100–200 words that students will encounter most often in print. These words are composed mostly of *function words*. That is, they have little or no lexical meaning (such as pronouns and prepositions) and instead express a grammatical or structural relationship with other words. *Content words,* on the other hand, are words that carry meaning by themselves (such as nouns, verbs, and adjectives). As described in Chapter 3, our eyes tend to fixate on content words when we read and skip over function words. Nonetheless, it is important to give them some attention at the emergent and beginning levels. There are several most common word lists such as Dolch (Dolch, 1936), Fry (Fry, 1998), and Zeno (Zeno, Ivens, Millard, & Duvvuri, 1995). It does not really matter which one you use as they are all relatively similar. The Zeno word list, shown in Figure 8.1, contains the 107 words that students will most likely encounter in texts (Zeno et al., 1995).

Using Most Frequent Word Lists

Attention to sight words should be part of a reading intervention for students reading at the first-grade level and below who are struggling with word identification.

he	you	from	she	said
of	he	had	when	out
and	on	I	an	if
to	as	not	their	some
a	are	have	there	would
in	they	this	her	so
is	with	but	can	people
that	be	by	we	them
it	his	were	what	other
was	at	one	about	more
for	or	all	up	will
into	like	made	way	know
your	could	over	each	little
which	has	see	called	such
do	him	first	did	even
then	how	new	just	much
many	than	very	after	our
these	two	my	water	must
no	may	also	through	
time	only	down	get	
been	most	make	because	
who	its	now	back	

FIGURE 8.1. Zeno sight words.

There are three reasons for attending to sight words: First, recognizing words instantly frees up cognitive space that can be allocated to creating meaning (Tunmer & Nicholson, 2001). Second, words stored in long-term memory can be used to help students recognize and identify words in print with similar letter patterns (Weaver, 2009). And third, having a large store of sight words enhances reading fluency (Jennings, Caldwell, & Learner, 2010).

The approach you use to attend to sight words should be systematic. System instruction means that there is a general plan for introducing the words. As well, some sort of documentation occurs when each word is introduced. Also, the date when students master each word is recorded. To do this, use a simple checklist like the one shown in Figure 8.2. To document when each word is introduced, simply

_____ he	_____ you	_____ from	_____ she
_____ of	_____ he	_____ had	_____ when
_____ and	_____ on	_____ I	_____ an
_____ to	_____ as	_____ not	_____ their
_____ a	_____ are	_____ have	_____ there

FIGURE 8.2. Documenting growth with the Zeno word list.

put the date in front of it. Keep a similar checklist for each student in a three-ring binder. Use this binder to record the date when you notice that students are able to recognize each sight word. This is a form of very direct assessment as you are directly observing authentic reading behaviors. You can do this type of assessment with three students a day, and within 2 weeks you will have very direct assessment with up to 30 students.

Four Quasi-Meaning-Based Sight-Word Activities

Sight-word activities should be brief, briskly paced, and as enjoyable as possible. Games, art projects, and other activities can be used to reinforce these words. An Internet search using the terms *sight-word games* or *sight-word activities* will provide an abundance of ideas. Four quasi-meaning-based activities that you may not encounter in an online search are described below. These activities can be designed using paper, poster, or white board; however, using a PowerPoint enables you to move through them quickly using color to highlight target sight words.

In a meaning-based approach to reading interventions, we want to limit instances where students encounter individual words out of context. This is true even of sight words. In the activities below, the sight words are all found in the context of sentences. Besides reinforcing sight words, the sentences can be designed to reinforce target letter sounds or patterns. For example, the sight-word sentences below were taken from a short-*a* unit. You can also design sight-word sentences that are based on books that students are reading, current events, students' lives and experiences, or things that students are learning in other curriculum areas.

Sight-Word Sentences

These are the steps for designing sight-word sentences: First, introduce three to eight target sight words. Quickly present these using a list, flashcards, or a PowerPoint slide. Go through the target words several times until a degree of fluency has been achieved. And yes, the words are presented in isolation here. We can limit these types of encounters but never totally eliminate them. Next, create a paper sight-word strip with the target sight words printed on them (see Figure 8.3). When working with

the	**in**	**is**	**that**	**was**

FIGURE 8.3. Sentence strip for target sight words.

The cat is here.
<u>**The**</u> cat <u>**is**</u> here.

FIGURE 8.4. Sight-word sentence.

individual students on a computer, this paper strip is laid in front of the monitor. When working with groups, each student (or pair) should have a sight-word strip in front of them. Then, show students a sentence that contains one or more of the target sight words (see Figure 8.4). Read the sentence together. When students see a target sight word, they should point to it on their sentence strip. Finally, show the sentence with the target words highlighted and ask students to read until fluency is achieved.

During an intervention session, use 5 to no more than 10 sentences, each of which has at least one target sight word. This activity should be briskly paced lasting 2 to 8 minutes. Short periods in which students are actively engaged are always more productive for learning than are longer periods of passive exposure.

Sight-Word Inquiry

Sight-word inquiry invites students to look for sight words in the context of a book. First, create a simple tally sheet with some or all of the target sight words on top (see Figure 8.5). (In inquiry learning, this is called a data retrieval chart.) Then give students a book that they have read. This book is reviewed, and tally marks are used to indicate each encounter with one of the sight words. Next, students make a bar graph showing the number of sight words (see Figure 8.6).

This can be used as an inquiry learning project. Inquiry learning is a pedagogical strategy in which students ask a question and then use data to answer the questions (Johnson, 2017). The question here would be, "*What is the most common sight word in* [insert book title]?" This is one of the ways to teach the process of science at the early levels. To extend this, you could compare the sight words found in two different books.

the	in	is	that	was
𝍸	II	IIII	𝍸	II

FIGURE 8.5. Sight-word tally sheet.

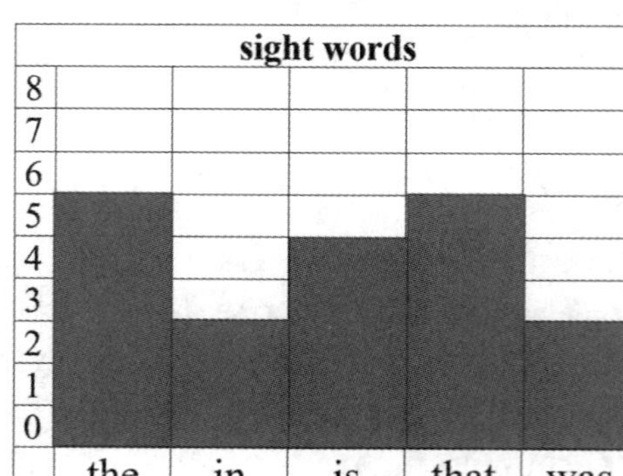

FIGURE 8.6. Sight-word graph.

For early readers, sight-word graphs may need to be a group activity using a big book. It can also be done as a *guided reading* activity in a small-group setting. Guided reading is a small-group strategy for teaching specific skills, including sight words, word identification skills, comprehension skills, and thinking skills using real books (Johnson, 2016b). This strategy is described in the next chapter.

Sight-Word Maze

For this activity, create simple maze sentences using two of the target sight words (see Figure 8.7). The advantage of maze sentences is that they develop the semantic cueing system as you are reinforcing sight words.

Cloze with a Word Box

Here you design simple cloze sentences in which one of the target sight words is the cloze target. To provide scaffolding, include an answer box with three to six target sight words (see Figure 8.8). You could also use a sentence strip for the target sight words. When doing cloze and maze activities, you will often hear students rereading the sentences to see if they make sense (metacognition). This is a mature reading behavior that should be recognized and reinforced.

SCOPE AND NONSENSE CHARTS

The last thing to address in this chapter is the scope and sequence chart. (I would have put this in the last chapter, but that chapter was getting too long.) While the technical name is a "scope and sequence chart," I believe the concept of a scope and sequence chart is utter nonsense—thus, the title, "Scope and Nonsense Charts" for this section. Scope and sequence charts are designed to tell teachers what skills to teach (scope) and in what order (sequence). Figure 8.9 contains a common scope and sequence chart. The thinking is that if children put all these reading subskills together, they will someday be able to read. However, this is nonsense. It represents the Humpty-Dumptian approach to reading instruction that has children putting all these little subskill pieces together. There is no valid research showing that this approach is more effective than a meaning-based approach in helping children create meaning with text.

Pat was [**in** — **had**] the car.
Pat was <u>in</u> the car.

FIGURE 8.7. Sight-word maze.

Jan _____ mad at Sam.
Jan <u>**was**</u> mad at Sam.
the — in — is — that — was

FIGURE 8.8. Cloze with scaffold.

Consonants
(all)

Short Vowels
a, i, o, u, e

Long Vowels
a, i, o, u, e, y

Consonant Blends (front)
sl, st, sp, sn, sc, sw, sk, sm, br, cr, dr, fr, pr, tr, gr, scr, spr, str, cl, fl, pl, bl, gl, spl, tw

Consonant Blends (end)
st, sk, sp, nd, nt, lt, lk, lf, ld, lp, lm, lb, lc, mp, ct, ft, pt

Consonant Digraphs and Trigraphs
sh, ch, tch, th (unvoiced), wh, ck

Double Consonants at End
ff, ss, ll, bb, gg, dd, nn, tt, zz, qu, xx

ng and nk Patterns
ing, ang, ength, ong, ung, ink, ank, unk, onk

Vowel Digraph Syllables
ee (feet), ea (each), oo (boot), ai (bait), ay (stay), oa (boat), ou (out), ow (cow), aw (saw), au (taught), oy (boy), oi (oil)

Endings
silent e (house), es, ed, er, ing, ful, n't

***R*-Controlled Vowels**
ar, ear, er, ir, ur, or (word), ar (warm)

Soft *C* and *G*
c (ice), g (gnaw), gh (through), g (manage), dg (bridge)

Long Vowel with Magic *e* Ending
lake, bike, note, Pete, mute

More Long Vowels
ie (chief), ei (seize), ey (key), y (fly), ie (pie), igh (sigh), oe (toe), ou (soul), old (gold), oll (roll), olt (bolt), ue (true), ew (new), ui (fruit), eigh (eight), ei (vein), ey (hey)

Silent Letters and Advanced
sc (scent), wr (wrap), kn (knee), gn (gnaw), ign (sign), gh (taught), ought (thought), ph (phone), tion (action), sion (mansion), sion (vision), ci (special), ti (patient), ture (picture)

FIGURE 8.9. Common scope and sequence chart.

Scope and sequence charts can be useful in providing a sense of the kind of things you might teach early on, as well as the types of letter patterns you might ask students to begin to notice; however, they simply are not reliable enough to be used in a prescriptive fashion.

To demonstrate the unreliability, I did a Google search using the terms *words with /oa/.* This is one of the vowel diagraph syllables listed in Figure 8.9. When introducing a new letter pattern, the words should be relatively short (five letters or less) so that the pattern is noticeable. The words must also be in students' current lexicon. With this letter pattern I found 27 total words composed of five letters or less that might be in most students' current lexicon (see Figure 8.10). While this is an important letter pattern to begin to notice, spending a great deal of time trying to "master" this letter pattern for 27 words is a waste of precious instructional time. Words containing it are not common enough, and the letter patterns are not

boa, oak, oar, oat, boat, coal, coat, foam, goal, goat, load, loaf, loan, moan, oath, road, roar, soak, soap, toad, bloat, board, coach, coast, float, groan, roast

FIGURE 8.10. Words with /oa/.

Sally went fishing in the old b__ __t.
Wash your hands with s__ __p and water.
Bill heard the loud r__ __r of the lion.
It's cold. Put on a c__ __t.

FIGURE 8.11. Limited use of vowels and vowel diagraphs.

consistent enough to be overly useful. In addition, do a Google search using the terms "*words with long o*" and you will see that many letter patterns produce this same sound. The Humpty-Dumptians would try to enforce children's mastery of all these variations. A meaning-based teacher would ask children to notice the patterns within the texts they are reading.

However, for the sake of argument, let us suppose that there were thousands of words with the vowel diagraph syllable /oa/. Let us suppose as well that it was the only letter pattern in the world that made the long-*o* sound. It would still be of limited use. Even with this very important /oa/ vowel diagraph syllable removed in the words in Figure 8.11, most people are still able to create meaning with the sentences. Go figure.

FINAL WORD

Where does that leave us? Sight words are something to attend to at the emergent and beginning levels. They might be part of a reading intervention for struggling early readers. Scope and sequence charts? Use them only to provide a sense of what letter sounds you might teach early on and what letter patterns you might ask students to notice. They should not be a road map to reading instruction or interventions.

CHAPTER 9

Word Identification Strategies

A QUICK REVIEW

As described in Chapter 4, word recognition and word identification are not synonymous terms. Word recognition refers to seeing a word and automatically knowing what it is. This skill develops over time as children begin to recognize letter patterns and use semantic and syntactic clues. Word identification is a strategy readers must consciously employ to identify a word that is not immediately recognized. This means that the word is in their lexicon, but they do not recognize it.

This chapter focuses on four basic word identification strategies: (1) morphemic analysis, (2) context clues, (3) analogy, and (4) phonics. Direct and explicit instruction related to all four strategies should be included as part of all students' classroom reading instruction. A reading intervention should build on this initial instruction if word identification is a deficit area. You cannot assume that these word identification strategies have been taught. Thus, an intervention may need to include instruction here.

MORPHEMIC ANALYSIS

A *morpheme* is the smallest unit of meaning within a word. Morphemic analysis is a strategy whereby students use prefixes, suffixes, and root words to identify words they do not immediately recognize as they read. Again, they are not using the morphemes to understand new words; rather, they are using them to identify words that they already know.

Teaching the Strategy

When working with students, I call this strategy *prefix–suffix* (vs. morphemic analysis). Figure 9.1 contains the steps for this strategy. Explicit instruction using teacher demonstration with cognitive modeling, guided practice, and independent practice should be used to teach this strategy (see below). Also, a poster with these steps listed should be displayed to use for reference and review.

Prefixes and Suffixes

As part of a reading intervention, you may need to review some basic information related to prefixes, suffixes, and roots words. The 20 most common prefixes, shown in Figure 9.2, account for almost 97% of all prefixed words that students will encounter (White, Sowell, & Yanagihara, 1989). The four most common prefixes account for about 65% of all prefixed words used in school. A review should focus on these 20 prefixes, with special attention given to the first four. A simplified version of Figure 9.2 can be displayed on a bulletin board or word wall (see below) to use as a reference.

Likewise, the 20 most common suffixes, shown in Figure 9.3, account for 93% of the suffixed words that students will encounter (White et al., 1989). The three most common suffixes make up approximately 64% of all the suffixed words used in school. A review should focus on these 20 prefixes, with special attention given to the first three. A simplified version of Figure 9.2 can also be created to use as a reference and review.

Reliability—Not

Prefixes and suffixes are not always reliable in terms of their meaning and spelling. For example, *restart* has an *re-* prefix but *reveal* does not. *Impatient* has an *im-* prefix but *important* does not. *Burial* has an *-ial* suffix but *dial* does not. The unreliability of prefixes and suffixes tells us that a review should focus on helping students to recognize or perceive common letter patterns related to prefixes and suffixes. Only a minimal amount of time should be spent on the meaning of each.

1. Look for clues (prefix, suffix, or root word).
2. Make a guess based on clues.
3. Reread the sentence.
4. See if your guess makes sense.

FIGURE 9.1. Prefix–suffix.

Root words are equally unreliable. Sometimes the roots make sense by themselves and sometimes not. Sometimes the same roots have similar meanings and other times not. For example, the root word *port* is based on the Latin *port,* meaning "to carry," as in *portable.* This meaning holds up in only some of the words listed in Figure 9.4. Thus, minimal time should be spent on the meaning of each root. Instead, the goal should be to help students recognize familiar word parts and letter patterns. Keep in mind that context will also provide clues to meaning along with prefix, suffix, and root clues when using morphemic analysis.

Prefix	**Meaning**	**Example**
un	not, opposite of	unhappy
re	again, back	rebuild, restart, rejoin
in, im, ir, il,	not, opposite of	insecure, immovable, irrational, illegal
dis	not, opposite of, remove	disbelieve
en, em	cause to	empower
non	not, opposite of	nonsense
in, im	immersed	inbound, immerge
over (too much)	too much, above	overstate
mis	wrongly	misjudge
sub	under, lower	subpar
pre	before	pregame
inter	between, among	interpersonal
fore	before	forerunner
de	opposite of, down, remove, reduce	declassify, degrade, deicer, declassify
trans	across, change, through	transatlantic, transact, transition, transparent
super	above, beyond	superman, superimpose
semi	half, partial	semicircle, semiconscious, semiannual, semifinal
anti	against	antipoverty
mid	middle	midlevel, midstream
under	too little, below	underpaid

FIGURE 9.2. Most common prefixes.

Suffix	Meaning	Examples
s, es	plural, more than one	dogs
ed	past tense	jumped
ing	action, process	jumping, singing
ly	characteristic of	friendly, jumpy
er, or (agent)	person connected with	teacher, reporter
ion, tion, ation, ition	act, process, action	connection, election, inflation
able, ible	can be done	enjoyable, edible
al, ial	having characteristics of	historical, facial, social
y	characterized by	jumpy
ness	state of, condition of	happiness
ity, ty	state	gravity, levity, activity
ment	action or process	excitement
ic	having characteristic of	historic
ous, eous, ious	possessing qualities of	curious, hideous, serious
en	made of	wooden, frighten, flatten
er (comparative)	comparative	smarter, bigger
ive, ative, tive	adjective form of a noun	active, attentive, sensitive
ful	full of	joyful, hurtful
less	without	worthless
est	comparative	happiest

FIGURE 9.3. Most common suffixes.

CONTEXT CLUES: THE SEMANTIC CUEING SYSTEM

Valuable data can be garnered by watching the eyes of your students as they are reading. You will notice that expert readers use context clues to identify words as they are reading. If you watch their eyes, you will see them skipping over an unrecognized word, looking for clues on either side of it and then moving back and forth to check for meaning (metacognition). In contrast, struggling readers' eyes tend to move word by word and then stop when they come to an unrecognized word.

By providing instruction in the use of context clues and by including cloze and maze activities in daily sessions (see Chapter 10), you will begin to see struggling readers' eyes jumping over an unrecognized word and making several regressions

portly	pro**port**ion
im**port**ant	**port**ray
s**port**	op**port**unity
air**port**	sup**port**
im**port**ant	pur**port**
portfolio	re**port**
portrait	s**port**y
portage	**port**ico
rap**port**	**port**al
sup**port**	trans**port**
porthole	

FIGURE 9.4. The unreliability of root words.

back before the word. This means they are using context to identify words. This is a mature reading behavior. When working with struggling readers, call attention to this behavior as you observe it. Let them know that this is a good thing, that this is exactly what they are supposed to do.

Teaching the Strategy

Figure 9.5 contains the steps for this word identification strategy. When working with students, I call this strategy *context clues*. Like morphemic analysis, teach this strategy explicitly and create a poster with the steps listed to use for reference and review.

ANALOGY

Analogy is a form of large unit phonics. It is similar to morphemic analysis (above), but instead of familiar prefixes, suffixes, and roots; you are developing students' ability to use familiar letter patterns and word parts to identify words. When working with students, I call this strategy *word parts*. Figure 9.6 contains the steps. Like

1. Look for sentence clues before and after the word.
2. Make a guess based on clues.
3. Reread the sentence.
4. See if your guess makes sense.

FIGURE 9.5. Context clues.

1. Look for familiar word part clues (parts of the word you recognize).
2. Make a guess based on clues.
3. Reread the sentence.
4. See if your guess makes sense.

FIGURE 9.6. Word parts.

1. Look at just the consonants.
2. Sound it out using only the consonants.
3. Make a guess.
4. See if your guess makes sense in the sentence.

FIGURE 9.7. Using consonants.

the strategies above, teach it explicitly, and then display a poster for reference and review.

PHONICS

When working with students, I call this strategy *using consonants* or *sounding out words*. Figure 9.7 contains the steps used. You will notice that students here are encouraged to use only the consonants. Consonants are much more reliable than vowels. Like the strategies above, teach it explicitly; then create a poster for reference and review.

THE BIG PICTURE

Word identification strategies should be taught explicitly using the elements of direct instruction described in Chapter 4: (1) a purpose or purpose statement; (2) input with demonstration, modeling, and examples; (3) guided practice that includes scaffolding; (4) independent practice; and (5) periodic review and practice.

The goal with word identification is to teach word identification strategies so that students can consciously employ them anytime they encounter a word they do not recognize. However, we teach the strategy to develop the skill (automatic word recognition). That is, the goal is to teach the strategy explicitly and practice it so that it becomes a skill that readers employ automatically as they are reading. Put another way, we are teaching the strategy so that the strategy itself becomes obsolete.

CHAPTER 10

Cloze and Maze Activities

SEMANTIC CUEING

A QUICK REVIEW

Eye movement and miscue analysis research shows that expert readers do not attend to every letter (Braunger & Lewis, 2006; Paulson & Freeman, 2003; Weaver, 2009); instead, they use minimal letter clues, along with background knowledge (schemata), syntax, and semantic information, to create meaning with print (Binder, Duffy, & Rayner, 2001; Goodman, Fries, & Strauss, 2016; Hruby & Goswami, 2013; Rayner & Well, 1996) (see Figure 2.3 on p. 20).

This chapter describes two types of strategies for developing the semantic cueing system: *cloze* and *maze*. The theoretical and empirical support for these activities is strong (Ricketts, Davies, Masterson, Morag, & Duff, 2016). Semantic-based activities like these have been shown to enhance students' reading fluency (Berends & Reitsma, 2004), comprehension (Borzabadi, 2011), and word identification (Weaver, 2009). If word identification is a deficit area, cloze and maze activities should be included as one part of the reading intervention.

CLOZE AND MAZE

A *cloze* is a sentence with one word partially or completely missing (see Figure 10.1). The missing word is the cloze target. For low-level or struggling readers, a first letter clue is usually included in the cloze target.

Cloze
Time to **t**___ a nap.
Time to **take** a nap.

FIGURE 10.1. Examples of beginning-level cloze sentence.

Level I
Brad had a [**bat** — **bad**] day at school.
Brad had a **bad** day at school.
Level II
She hit the ball [**hand** — **happy** — **hard**].
She hit the ball **hard**.

FIGURE 10.2. Examples of beginning-level cloze and maze sentences.

A *maze* is a sentence in which students are provided two or three choice options as the maze target. The number of target options is dependent on students' reading level. Figure 10.2 shows examples of maze sentences at two levels.

After using cloze and maze activities for several weeks (duration will vary), you will notice an increasing number of meaningful miscues and self-corrections during students' oral reading (see Chapter 16). The meaningful miscues tell us that students are reading for meaning instead of just sounding out words. The self-corrections tell us that students are using metacognition. Both are mature reading behaviors and should be celebrated.

Designing Cloze and Maze

There are three things to keep in mind when designing cloze and maze: First, the goal is not to try to trick or challenge students; rather, it is to develop their semantic cueing system. As such, the target words should be readily apparent, abundantly clear, and extremely obvious. Second, after the missing word is identified, the complete sentence should be shown to students. This sentence should be read until fluency is achieved. For this reason, PowerPoint is a preferred medium; however, paper can be used here as well. And finally, while cloze and maze are used to develop the semantic cueing system, they can at the same time reinforce literacy subskills and other curriculum concepts. Five examples are presented here:

1. **Letter sounds.** The cloze sentences in Figure 10.3 are designed to reinforce the short-*a* sound. While the cloze target is not always a short-*a* word, there is a short-*a* word in every sentence.
2. **Letter patterns.** The cloze sentences in Figure 10.4 demonstrate how they can be used to reinforce common phonograms. Notice how the answers here are extremely obvious and how an /ay/ phonogram appears in every sentence.

3. **Sight words.** The maze sentences in Figure 10.5 are used to reinforce sight words. With these types of sentences, sight words are used as the maze targets. This invites students to consider each sight word in the context of a sentence.
4. **Morphological maze sentences.** The morphological maze sentences in Figure 10.6 focus on suffixes. Maze targets can also be designed to focus on prefixes and roots.
5. **Curriculum, books, lives, and experiences.** Cloze and maze sentences can also be designed around curriculum areas, books, or students' own lives and experiences (see Figure 10.7).

I had a **b_ _** dream.
I had a **bad** dream.

I am glad to **s_ _** you.
I am glad to **see** you.

She got **m_ _** and went home.
She got **mad** and went home.

The sad boy started to **cr_**.
The sad boy started to **cry**.

FIGURE 10.3. Beginning-level cloze sentences to reinforce the short-*a* sound.

Wh_ _ did you say?
What did you say?

May I go outside and **pl_ _**?
May I go outside and **play**?

I will **st_ _** home today.
I will **stay** home today.

What **d_ _** is it today?
What **day** is it today?

FIGURE 10.4. Cloze sentences to reinforce the /ay/ phonogram.

Pat was in [**the — had**] car.
Pat was in **the** car.

Let go [**of — was**] me.
Let go **of** me.

FIGURE 10.5. Sight-word maze sentences.

Jane [**jump — jumped — jumping**] in the lake.
Jane **jumped** in the lake.

FIGURE 10.6. Morphological maze sentences.

Frogs [**dog — are — has**] amphibians.
Frogs **are** amphibians.

They are born with [**gills — sit — cars**].
They are born with **gills.**

FIGURE 10.7. Maze sentences based on a science curriculum.

PRE- AND POSTREADING ACTIVITIES

Prereading activities are used to provide a scaffold to enable struggling readers to successfully read a text or story that is a little above their independent reading level. Postreading activities are used to enable students to reengage with the text or story (Johnson, 2016b). Maze and cloze activities can be used with both of these.

Story Preview Mazes

A story preview is an overview of the story or text that students are about to read. The preview provides a scaffold for struggling readers by identifying most of the key events of the story or chapter without giving away the ending. Like a good movie preview, the story preview should always end with a hook of some kind to get students to read for purposeful intent. An example of a hook would be: "Read to find out what happens when the bears find Goldilocks in Little Bear's bed."

A story preview maze is a story preview put in a maze format. It usually consists of three to eight sentences that provide an overview of the story, chapter, or text. Figure 10.8 contains a prereading story maze that was designed to be used with the Tom and Ricky Mystery Series, set 1, published by High Noon Books. These are high/low books written at about the second-grade level, but they are of interest to students in grades 3 and above.

Postreading Maze and Cloze Sentences

Postreading maze and cloze sentences are two to five sentences directly related to some aspect of what students have just read. Here, readers must use the text as well as context clues to create meaning with individual sentences. These types of activities develop the semantic cueing system as well as metacognition and comprehension.

The postreading maze sentences in Figure 10.9 are based on a story at the emergent level (Lexile levels 40–150). Notice the difference between the two- and

Chapter 1: The Space Rock

It was night. It was [**thank — run — time**] to go to sleep.

Rickey [**will — was — pack**] in bed. He [**napped — looked — pan**] out his window. He saw a [**falling — of — fell**] star. It landed on an [**funny — old — ran**] farm. The next morning, Rickey and Tom went to [**fall — cat — look**]. They rode their [**bikes — plates — sit**] to the farm. Patches, their dog, went with [**over — sing — them**]. At the farm, Tom found something. Read to find out what Tom found.

FIGURE 10.8. Story preview maze.

Maze Sentences
1. Bongo [**where — woke**] up early.
2. The first [**ever — event**] was running.
3. Bongo wanted to [**where — win**] the race.
4. The Kangaroo [**jumped — just**] the furthest.
5. Bongo swam in the [**pan — pool**].
6. The seal won the [**diving — just**] event
Cloze Sentences
1. Bongo **w**__ __ __ up early.
2. Bongo wanted to **w**__ __ the race.
3. Bongo **sw**__ __ in the pool.

FIGURE 10.9. Beginning-level postreading maze and cloze sentences.

three-word maze target choices. I would recommend starting with two maze targets. The cloze sentences are based on a story at the beginning level (Lexile levels 100–300). When doing these initially, use scaffolded oral reading (ScORe) or choral reading. As the target word is encountered, say *blank*—for example: "Elk *blank* fast." Eventually, students will be able to read maze and cloze sentences with very little scaffolding or support. Maze sentences do not always translate directly into cloze sentences. Since target words must be exceedingly obvious, sometimes sentences need to be rewritten or the target word changed.

Postreading Paragraphs

Postreading maze and cloze paragraphs work best for readers reading at the second-grade reading level and above. These are similar to the maze and cloze sentences above, except the sentences are found within the context of a complete paragraph (see Figure 10.10). To design these paragraphs, first create a six- to eight-sentence paragraph related to the story, chapter, or text. The paragraph can be taken directly from the text, but these generally need to be modified. The first and last sentences in the paragraph should be left complete. Maze and cloze sentences are then created with the sentences between. A reminder again that the maze and cloze targets should be readily apparent.

When presenting these paragraphs, students should first see the maze or cloze sentence and then the complete sentence underneath. Also, students should see the series of individual sentences first. At the end, they should be shown the complete paragraph. The paragraph is then read until fluency is achieved. Again, PowerPoint is the preferred medium here (I usually put two sentences on a slide); however, these can very easily be prepared in paper form.

The Space Rock
It was night. It was [**thank — run — time**] to go to sleep. It was **<u>time</u>** to go to sleep.
Rickey [**will — was — pack**] in bed. Rickey **<u>was</u>** in bed. He [**napped — looked — pan**] out his window. He **<u>looked</u>** out his window.
The night [**sky — fly — grabbed**] was dark. The night **<u>sky</u>** was dark. There were lots of stars in the sky.
The Space Rock It was night. It was time to go to sleep. Rickey was in bed. He looked out his window. The night sky was dark. There were lots of stars in the sky.

FIGURE 10.10. Postreading maze paragraph.

Maze and Cloze Mini-Stories

Maze and cloze paragraphs can also be designed as a stand-alone mini-story unrelated to any chapter or text (see Figure 10.11). Here, a 6- to 10-sentence story is used. These mini-stories are fun to design but take a bit of thinking as the paragraph must be a complete entity.

CLOZE FOR SMALL GROUPS

Cloze can also be used in pairs or small groups. Here, a paragraph or passage is selected that is at students' approximate independent reading level. Words are deleted from sentences in the passage. These words should be content words (vs. function or sight words). Students are told that they are detectives. With this activity, do not include first letter clues or space clues to indicate the length of the word or the number of letters. Instead, students must look for clues found in the text to identify words that make sense in each sentence. They then write (or dictate) a word they think will make sense in each blank. The word students select is not as important as the conversation that takes place as students look for clues before and after the cloze target and in other parts of the paragraph or passage. (You may also have students underline the clues here.) This could also be used as a postreading

The Big Hit
Sam was playing baseball. It was [**his — had — nap**] turn to bat. It was <u>**his**</u> turn to bat.
The pitcher [**threw — man — swam**] the ball. The pitcher <u>**threw**</u> the ball. Sam swung the [**mat — jam — bat**]. Sam swung the <u>**bat**</u>.
He hit [**not — dig — the**] ball hard. He hit <u>**the**</u> ball hard. The ball went [**over — down — sad**] the fence. The ball went <u>**over**</u> the fence.
Sam [**hot — hit — nap**] a homerun! Sam <u>**hit**</u> a homerun! His team won the game.
The Big Hit Sam was playing baseball. It was his turn to bat. The pitcher threw the ball. Sam swung the bat. He hit the ball hard. The ball went over the fence. Sam hit a homerun! His team won the game.

FIGURE 10.11. Maze mini-story.

activity. Here students would also be able to use clues from the selected text to support their word choice.

With this activity, students are able to hear the thinking of other students as they explain and support their thinking. This can act as a form of cognitive apprenticeship as thinking is encountered at the social level first and then gradually internalized. After completing the cloze passage or paragraphs, students select a reader to read it aloud. If there is more than one pair or a small group, it is always interesting to hear how the paragraph or passage differs. You may wish to then show the students the complete passage. Reinforce the idea to students that as long as the passage makes sense, there really cannot be a wrong answer.

TIPS FOR USING MAZE AND CLOZE ACTIVITIES

The most important rule for using maze and cloze activities is that students should never have to stop and sound out words. This is not a sounding-out-words activity.

At the maze or cloze target, say "blank" and finish the sentence. This invites the reader to use clues on both sides of the target. At the lowest level, you may need to read the sentences for students. At the highest level, students will be able to read the sentences independently or with a partner. In between these levels, use ScORe or choral reading to provide as much support as necessary to read the sentences at a fluent rate. If students hesitate in identifying the target, ask, "What word makes sense here?" You may sometimes need to provide some clues. When a word is correctly identified, show the complete sentence and ask students to reread the sentence until fluency is achieved. Then move to the next sentence.

Maze and cloze activities should be briskly paced and relatively brief. You should spend 5–20 seconds on individual sentences. I would recommend that 6–12 sentences be used in daily sessions. The maze/cloze portion of a session should be approximately 6–8 minutes in duration. Keep in mind that you are not teaching anything here. The purpose here is to develop students' ability to use semantic clues to recognize words. You are developing neural pathways and enhancing neural networks so that students will be able to engage these cognitive operations automatically as they read.

As mentioned above, PowerPoint is the preferred medium here as it enables you to move quickly from one sentence to the next. PowerPoint also enables you to show the cloze or maze sentence and then have the complete sentence appear beneath it with the target words highlighted using boldface and color. However, these activities can also be designed on paper. Here you would put your cloze or maze sentences on a single page and use paper to cover it. You would then move the paper down the page as each sentence is revealed.

FINAL WORD

The difference between expert and novice readers is their use of syntax and semantics while reading, not phonics (Braunger & Lewis, 2006). This chapter describes several strategies for developing the semantic cueing system. The next chapter describes activities designed specifically to develop the syntactic cueing system.

CHAPTER 11

Writing for Reading

WRITING FOR SYNTACTIC CUEING

The writing–reading connection has been firmly established (Duke, Pearson, Strachan, & Billman, 2011; Goodman et al., 2016; Goodman & Goodman, 2009; Kuder & Hasit, 2002; Lipson & Wixson, 2009; Parodi, 2013; Pressley, Wharton-McDonald, & Mistretta, 1998; Silliman & Wilkinson, 1994; Strickland, 2002; Weaver, 2009). Writing helps strengthen letter–sound relationships (Weaver, 2002), and it is one of the most effective strategies to use to develop the syntactic cueing system (Parodi, 2013). This is because the writer must attend to grammar, sentence structure, and word order when engaged in the process of thinking and writing. Hence, writing activities like those described in this chapter should be included as part of a reading intervention for students who struggle with word identification.

WRITING ACTIVITIES

The writing activities used in a reading intervention are different from those that occur as part of writing workshops or language arts instruction. Writing activities in a reading intervention should be kept simple and brief. In most cases, these will last between 2 and 8 minutes. And just like the maze and cloze activities described in the last chapter, writing activities can be designed to reinforce or help students notice letter patterns, phonograms, or sight words.

Sentence Mix-Up Activities

Sentence mix-up comes in a variety of forms. With these types of activities, students are given a sentence in which the words are out of order. This sentence could be taken from a language experience activity (LEA), a book students have read or are reading, a topic being studied in other curriculum areas, current events, or from something related to students' lives. Sentences can also be designed to reinforce letter patterns or sight words. Meaning is created by arranging the words in the correct order. Sentence mix-up activities work best for students who are reading at emergent and beginning levels.

Sentence Cut-Up

With this activity, a sentence is written on a large strip of paper so that students can see it. Next, the sentence is cut into individual words. Then, the words are put on a desk or table and mixed up. Students are asked to put them back in order. This activity can be extended by asking students to repeat the activity while timing each attempt to see if they can get faster. Since students always get faster, this helps develop self-efficacy. Analytic phonics instruction can also be used with sentence mix-up activities—for example: "There is a word with the /d/ sound at the end. Can you find it?"; "There is something the same about *the* and *thing*. What is it?"

3″ × 5″ Cards

With this activity, the words from a sentence are written on 3″ × 5″ cards. Here, students do not see the completed sentence before they attempt to put the words in order. If necessary, you can provide clues by either speaking the sentence or providing a single word clue. (Keep in mind that you never want to frustrate students.) And because the dialog that occurs enhances learning, this activity works well in pairs.

Be the Word

This is a small-group activity. Write a sentence as described above. Use letters that are 2″ to 3″ high so that the individual words can be seen from a distance. Cut the sentence into individual words and give a single word from the sentence to different students. Help them to say their word aloud. Then, ask students with a word card to come to the front of the room and arrange themselves in the correct order. Once students are in the correct order, tap them on the shoulder. Students say their word as their shoulder is tapped. Do this several times, getting faster each time. To extend this activity, (1) mix the students up and ask them to find the right order, (2) have students trade cards with a friend who is standing and ask them find the right order, or (3) give their card to a friend sitting down and ask them to find the right order.

With the three activities above, put the words in an envelope when finished. Save them for review and reinforcement on subsequent days.

PPT (PowerPoint) Sentence Mix-Up

The PPT sentence mix-up activity should be designed using PowerPoint. This medium enables you to do four or five sentence mix-up activities in less than 4 minutes. The sentence in Figure 11.1 is an example of a PPT sentence mix-up that is used to reinforce the short-*a* sound. All the words in the sentence appear first on top of the screen out of order. With younger students, include punctuation and capital letter clues. Read through the words together and then ask the students to make a guess as to what the sentence might be. One at a time, words appear below until the students are able to guess the complete sentence. The goal is to try to guess the sentence before the complete sentence is shown. Once the final sentence appears, students reread it until fluency is achieved. You can extend this activity by including simple, quick analytic phonics instruction. An example for Figure 11.1: "Can you find a short-*a* word in this sentence?"

Sentences

The writing activities below are all based on individual sentences. Just like the activities above, these can be taken from or based on a language experience activity, a book students have read or are reading, topics being studied in other curriculum areas, current events, or from something related to students' lives and experiences. Sentences can also be designed to reinforce letter patterns or sight words. Depending on the level of your students, these activities should take 3–10 minutes.

Sentence Dictation

Sentence dictation was described in Chapter 7 as part of word work.

Sentence Combining

Students are shown two sentences (see Figure 11.2). They must combine them while retaining the initial meaning of both. This activity can be done verbally or using writing.

ran away. cat The
The
The cat
The cat ran
The cat ran away.

FIGURE 11.1. Sentence mix-up to reinforce the short-*a* sound.

Jill is fast.
Jill is a runner.
(Jill is a fast runner.)

Jim is in the living room.
Jim spilled his milk.
(Jim spilled his milk in the living room.)

FIGURE 11.2. Sentence combining used to reinforce the short-*i* sound.

Sentence Alteration

With this activity, students are given a sentence and asked to express the same idea (say the same thing) using different words or a different word order (see Figure 11.3). Students can work individually, with a partner, or in a small group. If students are struggling with their writing, the teacher can write students' verbal responses on a white board, poster, or screen. When doing this activity, I always ask for a minimum number of sentences (usually three or four). After you have done this activity several times, students are able and willing to go beyond this number.

When the ideas have been generated and written, read the different versions or ask one student in each group to read the sentences aloud. Ask students to check to see if they make sense and still communicate the same idea. Then have students reread their sentences until fluency is achieved. With this activity, the original sentence should always be visible.

Syntax Sentences

Syntax sentences are similar to daily oral language activities except that these sentences contain only grammar or word order errors (no spelling or punctuation errors). Three sentences are presented on a PowerPoint screen, written on the board or poster, or on a worksheet (see Figure 11.4). Students are asked to identify the grammar or word order error. As the error is identified and corrected, make this a mini grammar lesson. When finished, read the sentence together to see if it makes sense. Eventually, students will be able to work in pairs or small groups for this activity. Again, the conversation that occurs in pairs and small groups always serves to enhance learning.

Sentence Elaboration

Here, students are given a sentence and asked to make it different, better, or more interesting (see Figure 11.5). Students can make it different in any way as long as only one word is changed each time. The changed sentence is written directly below the previous sentence so that the evolution is clear. Unique, creative, humorous, and even silly ideas should be encouraged (as long as they are appropriate).

Jim packed his lunch in a bag.
a. Jim put his lunch in his bag.
b. Jim packed his bag full of lunch.
c. Jim put lunch in his bag.
d. Jim stuffed lunch in his bag.

FIGURE 11.3. Sentence alteration used to reinforce the short-*a* sound.

1. She clap him hands.
2. Did you got a packages?
3. He is back up his car.

FIGURE 11.4. Sentence alteration used to reinforce the short-*a* sound.

The man grabbed some candy.
The big man grabbed some candy.
The big man ate some candy.
The big man ate some prunes.
The big clown ate some prunes.
The crazy clown ate some prunes.

FIGURE 11.5. Sentence elaboration used to reinforce the short-*a* sound.

When finished, students should read the sentences until fluency is achieved. This can be done individually, in pairs, or in small groups. It can also be done as a teacher-directed activity where the teacher records students' ideas on a white board, poster, or screen.

Students' Ideas

The writing activities below ask students to use writing to describe and share their ideas. These are examples of authentic writing activities as they ask students to describe or express their ideas and experiences. They are also a vehicle that enables you to make important personal connections with students.

Language Experience Activities

See Chapter 6 for a discussion of LEA.

One Sentence

Students who are struggling readers are often struggling writers. They can feel overwhelmed when you tell them they are going to write. Reduce this anxiety by telling them up front that they will be writing just one sentence. Initially, you may need to ask questions to help students identify what they want to say (Figure 11.6). If a student says, "I don't know what to say" (which happens frequently in the beginning stages), say, "Okay. Let's write that. 'I don't know what to say.'"

Journal at Beginning Levels and Above

An effective strategy I use when working individually with students is to use a journal as a vehicle for daily writing. At the beginning of each session, I ask them to tell me what is going on in their lives or what they did yesterday: "What have you been doing?" In the beginning, students are often reluctant to write, but once they begin to see that you are really interested in their thoughts and experiences, they

1. What do you want to say today?
2. Did you do anything fun yesterday?
3. What did you see on your way to school?
4. What's something you like to do?
5. What are you going to do this weekend?
6. What are you thinking about?
7. What are you going to do at recess?
8. What are you thinking about right now?

FIGURE 11.6. Questions to elicit one-sentence writing.

become much more motivated to write. They naturally want to get their ideas on paper and express them. This is also a great way to get to know and stay connected with your students.

Figure 11.7 shows an example of a journal entry written by an adult with intellectual disabilities with whom I was working. At the start of every session, he would write about something he had done during the week. This helped improve his reading and writing skills, but just as important, it enabled me to get to know him and to see what was going on in his life. We became friends. It also gave him a vehicle to express and understand emotions and events. He was highly resistant when we first started. The goal then was to write just one sentence. This grew to two. He eventually became comfortable with the process and would write as many sentences as he needed to say what he wanted to say. We would often go back in his journal to see what was going on at earlier periods in his life and to use this to practice reading.

Journal at Emergent Levels and Below

At the emergent level, the student dictates to you what she or he wants to say. Use a computer and word document with 24-point font. Put the computer screen directly in front of the student so that she or he can see the words forming as you are writing. When working with small groups, you will need a screen large enough so that

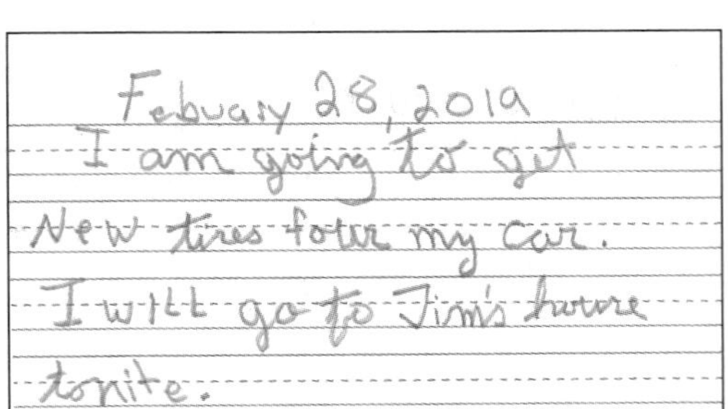
Febuary 28, 2019
I am going to get
New tires fotr my car.
I will go to Jim's howre
tonite.

FIGURE 11.7. Example of a journal.

This is Mickey. He is a pug. He likes to eat. He likes to sleep. We got Mickey from the Humane society.

FIGURE 11.8. Example of a journal.

all students can see it. The advantage of using a computer and Word documents versus poster or paper is that you can insert pictures into the document. In Figure 11.8, I asked a student to bring in pictures. These were put directly into our journal, and we wrote about them. After a couple of weeks, we had a book with pictures. After some edits, I printed it out, put a cover on it, and gave it to the student. Of course, the student was extremely proud of the book he had "written." It gave us something to use to practice reading. He also took a copy home to practice reading.

In using daily journals, I usually ask for a minimum of two sentences for emergent and beginning readers and five sentences for those reading at the second-grade level or above. This routine is of course flexible. Always watch your students. Stop if they become frustrated. After they have finished, students should reread their entry until they have achieved fluency. (Some scaffolded oral reading is often necessary here.) Analytic phonics can be used to reinforce letter sounds and patterns. Journal entries should be dated and saved so that you are able to go back and practice reading things students have written.

Strategies with Structure

I encourage students to write their own entries if they are able. I have found that, for a variety of reasons, most prefer to use a keyboard and computer (see below) instead of a paper and pencil. If possible, give them this option. Again, never frustrate your students. Watch them. Their body language will tell you when they are done writing. Again, it is acceptable to write a single sentence. Keep in mind that these writing activities are just one kind of activity used as part of a reading intervention session. Individual writing activities should last just 3–8 minutes. Also, to be successful, sometimes you will need to provide structure or scaffolding. The activities here can all be used for this purpose.

Speak the Sentence

With some students, it may be effective to have them speak the sentence before writing.

Help Them Edit and Simplify

You often need to help students break longer sentences into shorter ones. For example, a student might tell you, "I am going to Mike's house and we're going to play video games because he got it for his birthday." You would help the student break it into simple sentences: "I'm going to Mike's house. We're going to play video games. He got a new one for his birthday." And if students were to say something that is not grammatically correct, you would simply write the correct version. It becomes a quick, implicit grammar mini-lesson.

A Quiet, Verbal Scaffold

This strategy is most effective for students who are struggling to write one or two sentences. As the student writes, provide very quiet verbal clues (a form of scaffolding) to help that student hear each part of the word. As the student finishes each word, repeat the sentence. This frees up working memory to focus on word order and meaning. These should be quiet, gentle prompts.

A Little Keyboard Help

If using a keyboard, help the student find the letter keys on the keyboard by pointing to the general area where the keys are. Again, this enables the student to focus on meaning without spending valuable cognitive resources looking for keys. When finished, the student should reread the sentence or sentences until fluency is achieved. Also, you can buy keyboards with colored keys and larger, highlighted letters. This makes it easier to find and remember where the letters are on the keyboard.

Facilitated Writing

Facilitated writing can be done individually or in small groups. Again, start this activity by using just one sentence. Ask students what they want to say. As they tell you, write down just the "big" words (content words) on the screen or board. For example, if a student said, "The football game was incredible," you would write, "football, game, incredible" on the board, screen, or paper for them to see. Here you are creating a word box for students to use for their writing. This provides the structure necessary for them to write the sentence or paragraph.

Priming Pictures

Often it is easier for students to write if they can describe something they see instead of writing in the abstract. The priming picture enables this. Here, the teacher presents a picture and then says something like "Use writing to tell us what's going on here," or "Describe what you see," or "What do you want to say about this picture?"

FIGURE 11.9. Priming picture.

Students then write their ideas under the picture (see below). One or two sentences is sufficient here. If students struggle overly much with writing, they can dictate to you. Remember, you never want to frustrate your students. They get enough of that in school already.

For priming pictures, look for a fun, interesting, unique, or relevant picture. If possible, use pictures that include subjects who are about the same age as your students or a little older (see Figure 11.9). You can also find pictures of the community in which students live. You can ask students or their families to send you pictures. Finally, you can take pictures of things at school or in your community. Copy and paste these on a sheet of paper or include them in a Word document so that students can write directly under the picture. You can also put pictures on a PowerPoint or projected screen for small groups.

FINAL WORD

Again, since the focus is on grammar, sentence structure, and word order, all the writing activities above can be used to develop the syntactic cueing system. They can also be used to reinforce letter patterns, phonograms, or sight words. As always, adopt and adapt.

To be an effective reading teacher for struggling readers (or any readers), you do not need to buy expensive programs that are to be implemented with fidelity. You only need to know how humans learn and the process the human brain uses to create meaning with print (neurocognitive model). Once you understand the basic principles, you can design your own activities.

CHAPTER 12

Fluency

WHAT IT IS

The focus of this chapter is on reading fluency. Reading fluency as defined here is the ability to quickly recognize words during the process of reading. It has to do with speed of processing. The ability to automatically recognize words frees up space in short-term memory that can then be used for word identification and comprehension (Rasinski & Samuels, 2011).

STANDARDIZED READING RATES

You can find norm-referenced oral reading rates for each grade that use terms such as recommended, expected, optimal, appropriate, accepted, and even normal. Figure 12.1 contains one such set. However, these sorts of grade-level comparisons should be given limited attention. This is because we read different texts for different purposes and different rates. Let me explain:

The first thing I do every morning is engage in professional reading. One morning I started by reading a chapter from *Literacy Research Methodologies* (Duke & Mallette, 2011). This book described a variety of research methods, some of which were familiar to me, others of which were not. There were also some technical terms of which I had limited knowledge. With the unfamiliar material, I found myself reading very slowly, making regressions within the line, and rereading sentences within the paragraph. This was all done to make sure I was understanding correctly. To help keep my eyes focused, I used a 3″ × 5″ card (see Chapter 13). Although I found the material in the text to be important (I needed to brush up on my knowledge in this area), it was not of high interest to me.

1st grade: 53 WPM
2nd grade: 89 WPM
3rd grade: 107 WPM
4th grade: 123 WPM
5th grade: 139 WPM
6th grade: 150 WPM
7th grade: 150 WPM
8th grade: 151 WPM

FIGURE 12.1. Approximate grade-level fluency norms.

I then switched to a chapter from *Reading Process and Practice* (Weaver, 2002). I have read many of her books and articles. I am therefore very familiar with the content she describes, the vocabulary she uses, and her basic writing style. I also find her work to be fascinating. My reading rate and eye movement were much different here. I seemed to be able to perceive much more text in a single glance. I was able to fly through the pages, using relevant sentences to grasp the meaning of each paragraph, and my comprehension was high.

As I was working on this fluency chapter, I realized that this experience illustrated something important about reading fluency. My reading fluency was different with each text. Had somebody measured my words-per-minute (WPM) rate with the first text, I most likely would have been put in a remedial reading class, given a label, and forced to endure endless phonics instruction. I also would have had few opportunities to read interesting books that I had selected. Had my WPM rate been measured in the second text, I would most likely have been put in the top reading group with little or no skills instruction. I would have had many opportunities to read interesting texts that I had selected.

I exaggerate a bit here to emphasize an important point: Reading rates (as well as word identification and comprehension scores) are highly dependent on the texts being read, students' current knowledge of the content, their word knowledge related to the content, and their interest in the content (Kucer, 2014). As well, good reading is not fast reading. There are times when we want students to slow down and use skills and strategies related to effective comprehension so that they can carefully process and understand the information being described. There are other times (like when reading for pleasure) when it is appropriate to use the least amount of information possible to create an enjoyable reading experience.

This is not to discount norm-referenced reading rates, for they are of some value. They provide a very general sense of the development of students' oral reading fluency. However, students' WPM rates should always be considered in the context of qualitative data that describe the type of material being read, nonverbal behaviors, and reading prosody (see below). A glaring misuse of WPM rates is to expect all students to be reading at a specific norm-referenced WPM rate by the end of a school year. An appropriate use of WPM rates is to use them to identify students' reading rate for baseline data. Goals and benchmarks would then be designed based on this original WPM score. If fluency has been identified as a reading-deficit area, this is what should be part of an individualized education program (IEP; see Chapter 18).

Consider again the two paragraphs from Chapter 3 that are reprinted in Figure 12.2. Read the paragraphs aloud. The first paragraph makes sense; the second paragraph using the same words does not make sense. Notice again how your reading rate changed from paragraph #1 to paragraph #2. Notice also how the quality of your oral reading changed with each paragraph. And if somebody observed your eye movement and nonverbal behaviors, there would also be differences. Simply collecting a WPM score would provide an incomplete picture of your reading fluency.

READING WITH EXPRESSION AND PROSODY

Two terms related to reading fluency need a bit of unpacking: *expression* and *prosody*. Let us first address reading with expression. The Common Core State Standards (CCSS) for English Language Arts for grade 5 (RF 5.4.B) uses this term. It states that students in grade 5 should be able to do the following: "Read grade-level prose

Paragraph #1

Billy was traveling from Minnesota to California. As he was driving through South Dakota, he stopped at a rest stop to stretch his legs and buy a can of pop. When he got out of his car, he saw a herd of buffalo off in the distance. He was very interested. Billy started walking toward the buffalos so that he could take a picture to send to his friend, Molly. Suddenly, there was a loud bang! Somebody at the rest stop had thrown a large firecracker into the air. The buffalos started to stampede toward Billy. Billy ran as fast as he could, jumped in his car, and drove away.

Paragraph #2

Away drove and car his in jumped could he as fast as ran Billy. Billy toward stampede to started buffalo the. Air the into firecracker large a thrown had stop rest the at somebody. Ban loud a was there suddenly. Molly friend his to send to picture a take could he that so buffalo the toward walking started Billy. Interested very was he. Distance the in off buffalo of herd a saw he car his of out got he when. Pop of can a buy and legs his stretch to stop rest a at stopped he Dakota South through driving was he as. California to Minnesota from traveling was Billy.

FIGURE 12.2. Two paragraphs using the same 110 words.

and poetry orally with accuracy, appropriate rate, and expression on successive readings" (National Governors Association Center for Best Practices & Council of Chief State School Officers [NGA & CCSSO], 2010).

Expression

As noted above, the appropriate reading rate will vary depending on a number of variables. As well, accuracy (correct word identification) is different from rate and should not be included in any standard for reading fluency. This is because fluency and word identification are diagnosed, assessed, and addressed differently. However, it is the term *expression* that is of interest here. Unless you are in theater or are doing a dramatic reading, has there ever been a time in your adult life when being able to read with expression was important? When reading a book for pleasure or reading this text, has your reading expression ever been a factor in your ability to create meaning with print? Has there ever been an instance in your life when your success in an academic or a professional endeavor was dependent on your ability to read with expression? Reading with expression is of little importance. Prosody is.

Prosody

The term *prosody* is related to reading fluency. It means oral reading that uses the correct timing, emphasis, inflection, and intonation to demonstrate appropriate recognition of phrases and ideas. In other words, prosodic oral reading sounds similar to how one speaks. Unprosodic reading would be choppy, word-by-word reading, done in a robotic voice without pauses between sentences. A student reading like this is most likely focusing on correctly sounding out words (decoding) at the expense of creating meaning (reading).

NO ROUND-ROBIN READING

During my PhD program at the University of Minnesota, I auditioned for and joined a choir as a way of reducing some of the stress I was feeling (Johnson, 1995). I was surrounded by singers who were adept at reading musical text. We were responsible for practicing and learning our music outside of choir rehearsals. Occasionally, the director would ask one person from each section (bass, tenor, alto, and soprano) to stand and sing a passage in order to see who had learned their music. When I was called upon to do this, I was afraid of looking foolish in front of the whole choir. I experienced a bit of tension and anxiety (I was 36 years old at the time). I found myself with my head buried in the music, singing note by note, without thought to expression or technique. My singing was very mechanical. Using a literacy term, one would call it unprosodic. Upon reflection, I realized that this is exactly what a less able reader feels like when called upon to do round-robin reading.

Round-robin reading, or popcorn reading, is when different students in a class or small group are called upon to read parts of a selection out loud. This approach should not be used (ever) in reading instruction or in a reading intervention at any level for any purpose. Why? First, it does not reflect reality. I have yet to go into a library and see people sitting around a table taking turns reading a textbook or an article out loud. Second, it serves to generate negative emotions (anxiety, tension, humiliation) that interfere with learning and becomes paired with the reading experience. Third, in round-robin reading, creating meaning with print is always sacrificed for decoding accuracy. Fourth, it does not work. It does nothing to improve word identification skills, reading fluency, or comprehension, and it keeps students from real reading practice.

I admit that when I started teaching in 1983, I used round-robin reading. Since I had not read any of my books at the time, I did not know there were any other options. Described below are seven pragmatic options to round-robin reading. None of these strategies should be used exclusively.

Partner Reading

In an approach sometimes called buddy-reading, students are assigned a partner. They find a place in the room and take turns reading paragraphs or sections aloud to each other. The teacher can walk around the room and listen unobtrusively to a large number of students to get a sense of each student's reading.

Silent Reading

Here students read a selection just like most adults do in the real world: silently. Four common questions asked in regard to silent reading are:

- *How do you know if they are comprehending what they read?* A variety of postreading strategies can be used to enable a teacher to get a sense of students' understanding and interpretation of the text (Johnson, 2016b). You do not need to rely on oral reading.
- *How do you know if students are reading the selection?* Watch their eyes.
- *What if they do not read the assigned selection?* Then you should find something else for them to read. If you find the right material, all students will read. If you allow choice and you have a variety of good books and other reading material available that are at the appropriate reading levels, all students will read. Always keep the big picture in mind: Our goal as teachers of reading is to develop students' ability to create meaning with print.
- *What if students need to read an assigned text in another curriculum area such as*

science or social studies? When students read material that is at their instructional level or above, scaffolds need to be put in place such as guided reading notes, outlines, audio-recorded texts, or ERT used in the context of shared reading (below).

Everybody-Read-To

Reading a large amount of text can be overwhelming for struggling readers in any setting. ERT, which stands for *everybody-read-to,* is a silent reading strategy that can be used individually or in groups to alleviate this problem (Johnson, 2016b). Students are told to read to a particular point, usually one to four paragraphs at a time, depending on the level. To be effective, ERT reading activities or strategies need to be carefully planned to create purposeful reading that invites students to read with intention. For example:

- "This section will describe some interesting things about snakes. Read to the second paragraph on page 8. I'll be asking you to identify one interesting or important idea. Look up when you have finished."
- "In this section, Billy seems to be angry. I wonder what made him so angry. Read to the bottom of page 7 to find out. Raise your thumb when you are finished, then we'll talk about it."
- "In this next section, we will discover some interesting things about Maria. Read to the bottom of page 4. We will be creating a comparison chart to compare Maria to Mark."
- "In this next section. we will find out what caused the jar to explode. Read and tell me when you think you know."
- "In the first part of the chapter, Mark discovers a clown in his closet. Read to the top of page 29 to find out what happens. I'll be asking you if you think that Mark did the right thing."

Students then read silently to that spot and wait for your question or activity. If you are using this method with multilevel groups, readers who may not finish are usually able to get enough of the information to participate in the discussion. And what they are not able to comprehend while reading the text, they will be able to assimilate through the discussion that takes place.

Every-Other

Every-other is a form of shared reading. Here the teacher reads a paragraph or section aloud and asks students to read the next paragraph or section silently. Pre- and postreading questions, conversations, or activities should be included to create purposeful reading. For example: "In this chapter, Marvin sees the clown up in a tree. We get to see how Marvin reacts. Let's read this chapter using every-other. At the end, we'll predict what Marvin might do in the next chapter."

Scaffolded Oral Reading

Scaffolded oral reading (ScORe) was described in Chapter 6. This method is designed to provide a scaffold when working individually with students to enable them to read material at their instructional level. This is at the heart of much of my work when working individually with struggling readers. If a student is reading a selection orally and starts to struggle, jump in using ScORe. As stated many times in this book, we never want to frustrate students.

Choral Reading

Choral reading is designed to provide a scaffold for small groups of readers. Here the group reads the text out loud together (see below). The text should be broken into parts with appropriate pre- and postreading questions and activities inserted. This strategy is more appropriate for students at emergent or beginning levels.

Echo Reading

Here the teacher reads a line, and students reread or echo the line (see below). This works best when working with a big book or text projected on a screen, so that the teacher can point to each word as it is being read and reread. This strategy, too, is more appropriate for students at emergent or beginning levels.

WPM VERSUS WCPM: ACCURACY

On some measures of reading fluency, WCPM scores are used instead of WPM scores to assess and document reading fluency. WCPM stands for words correct per minute. However, as described above, when focusing on reading fluency we are concerned only with the rate of word recognition, not the accuracy. Thus, WCPM scores should not be used with reading fluency. There are other places to address and assess word reading accuracy.

The question often asked is this: "What happens if the student just says anything?" Answer: "This rarely happens." But if it does, it slows down the reading process. This is because readers usually pause when they encounter a word they do not recognize. In addition, thinking about and inserting nonsense words takes up more space in short-term memory, requiring more time for a response. Thus, WPM rates should be used to assess and document progress related to reading fluency (below), not WCPM. To assess and document progress related to word identification, other measures are used (see Chapter 16).

FLUENCY STRATEGIES

Automaticity is a term used for automatically recognizing words. Repeated reading activities are one method that can be used to develop automaticity (Kuhn & Stahl, 2013; Samuels, 2013). Here students develop automaticity through reoccurring practice of the same text. Described below are various repeated reading and other fluency activities. If fluency is a deficit area, one of these activities should be included and used as one part of a reading intervention. These activities should last 2–8 minutes.

Repeated Reading Strategies

Adopt and adapt the strategies below to meet your particular needs. These activities can be done individually with students or in pairs.

Words per Minute

Here students are given a piece of text at their independent reading level and asked to read it as fast as they can for one minute. The goal is to read and pronounce as many words as possible. This is done three times. The number of words read is recorded after each attempt. (*Hint:* On the text you use, mark off every 10 words for easy counting.) As described above, we are not concerned about accuracy or comprehension here, just speed. (There are other places to focus on these.) Finally, students record their three WPM scores on a line or bar graph (see Figure 12.3). If one minute is overwhelming, you can use words-per-half-minute (WPHM) scores.

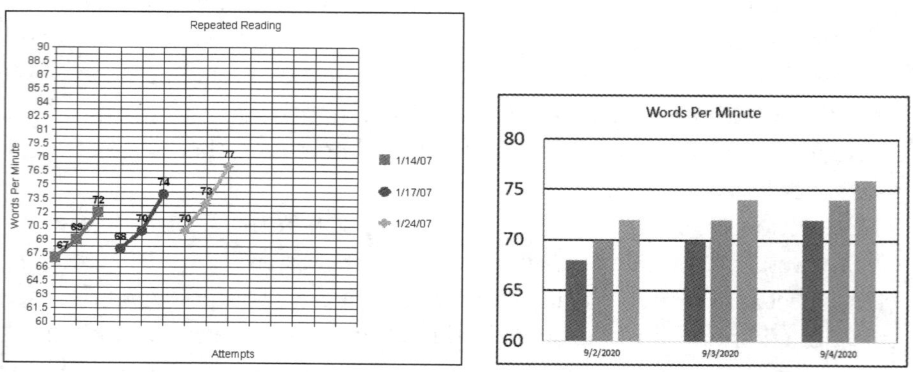

FIGURE 12.3. WPM line graph and bar graph.

The goal of repeated reading activities is to strengthen the neural pathways in order to develop reading fluency. It also is a positive way for students to demonstrate progress in reading. Here students are able to see their progress as their scores go up from their first to their third attempt and over time. This serves to improve their sense of self-efficacy (believing they can accomplish things with effort), which in turn has a positive effect on academic achievement (Schunk & Zimmerman, 2006).

Pairs and Small-Group WPM

WPM can be done with small groups by creating pairs and assigning each student a text. Students in each pair should use texts that are different from those of their partner and are at their independent reading level. On a common signal, one partner reads while the other follows along to make sure every word is read and to help identify problem words. Stop the readers after the allotted time (one minute or half-minute). The nonreading partner counts and records the number of words read. This process is repeated two more times and then the roles are switched. Students then record their times on their fluency graph.

Short-Passage Fluency

Short-passage fluency (SPF) is a repeated reading activity in which students are given a short passage of approximately 50–60 words. The 30th or 40th word is underlined or marked as their target. Depending on students' level, they read to their target mark. Students read the passage aloud three times. The time for each attempt is recorded. Students then record their times for each of the three attempts on a line graph (see Figure 12.4). (Instead of recording the number of words as done in WPM, you are recording times.) When students are consistently able to read the section at approximately 12 seconds, move up to the next target mark or go to a higher reading level.

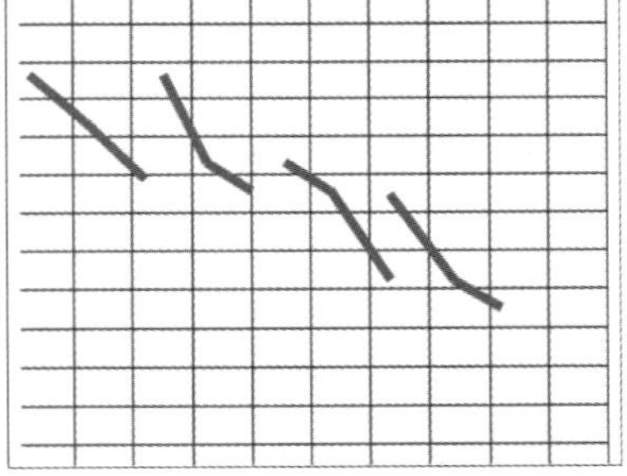

FIGURE 12.4. SPF graph.

For students with severe reading disabilities, I have created a special set of SPF materials called Really Silly Stories (*www.Readocity.com*). These are designed for students reading at the approximate grade 1 or grade 2 reading levels (Lexile 40 to 350). These stories use repetition of words and phrases, repeated characters, sight words, dialog, common language, and common situations to facilitate reading. Each story is divided into 5 to 12 daily sections so that students encounter the same characters and story elements over several lessons. Also, these stories are silly but not childish; thus, they can be used with severely struggling readers in the upper elementary grades.

Scaffolded Oral Reading

ScORe was introduced in Chapter 7 and discussed briefly above. You and the student read the text together aloud, with you acting as a scaffold by reading just a millisecond ahead of the student in order to maintain a steady, comfortable pace. If a student pauses or stumbles, keep reading. The student will rely on your voice to act as a scaffold in identifying words during the process of reading. You should read using a quiet voice, providing just enough structure to keep the pace moving. If the student seems to be reading fluently, provide less scaffolding by sounding out just the beginning sounds of some words or by dropping out completely of others.

Other Fluency Strategies

Replay Analysis

This activity can be used for fluency as well as word identification (see Chapter 7).

Retrospective Miscue Analysis

This activity can be used for fluency as well as word identification (see Chapter 7).

Echo Reading

Echo reading (described above) is where you read a line of text and students repeat or echo it back. When using text on the screen, point to the words as they are being read. If students have their text, they should point to the words as you are reading them.

Reader's Theater

Reader's Theater provides opportunities for students to practice reading their lines many times. Here, a familiar story (one they have read), is broken into parts to

Narrator: One day Billy got on this bus to go to school. His friend Maria said to him:

Maria: Hi, Billy.

Billy: Hi, Maria.

Bus driver: Everybody take your seats!

Narrator: said the bus driver. As they were traveling to school, Maria saw something out her window.

Maria: Look, Billy! Look up in the sky. It's an alien spaceship.

FIGURE 12.5. Reader's Theater script.

create a script (see Figure 12.5). You will have to create the initial scripts here, but eventually students will be able to create their own. Students are assigned to different parts. Use narrator and character parts. These can be audiotaped for use with picture books. (While the words will not match exactly here, the pictures will.)

Conversations

Dialog is familiar to students and is usually easier to read than other types of text. To capitalize on this quality, create your own short conversational dialogs with students. On a word processor, create two characters to have an imaginary conversation. You can use characters from a book, imaginary characters, historical characters, or characters from real life. You can also become a character with the student (see Figure 12.6). Create these dialogs by having a conversation with the student and writing down what that student says. The students should be able to see the screen as you record what they say. Read these dialogs through several times until the student can do the exercise fluently. Save them for future reading practice.

Figure 12.6 contains a conversation I had with Suzy, a second-grade student. As our conversation took place, I wrote down what we said on a computer using 24-point font so that Suzy could see the words appearing on the screen. We read this dialog through a couple of times. I did some analytic phonics instruction here, and then we switched roles. Suzy enjoyed being Mr. Johnson and she liked hearing me do Suzy. We saved this for future reading practice.

Popular Song Lyrics

Song lyrics are excellent sources to use for reading practice with older students. The familiarity of the lyrics provides the scaffolding necessary to enable them to be successful. These can easily be downloaded and used for reading fluency practice. Song lyrics can be used with individual students or groups. First read the song lyric with

March 3, 2019

Mr. Johnson: Good morning, Suzy.
Suzy: Good morning.
Mr. Johnson: What do want to talk about today?
Suzy: I don't know.
Mr. Johnson: Did you have fun at recess?
Suzy: Yes.
Mr. Johnson: What did you do?
Suzy: I was playing kickball with my friends.
Mr. Johnson: That sounds like fun.
Suzy: It was. I kicked the ball really far.
Mr. Johnson: What happened next?
Suzy: Billy threw the ball really hard and hit Melanie in the face.
Mr. Johnson: Oh dear. What did she do?
Sue: She cried.
Mr. Johnson: Oh no. What did you do?

FIGURE 12.6. Conversations.

students using ScORe. Then have students read the lyrics independently until they can read them fluently. Finally, create mini-analytic phonics lessons. Save these for future reading practice.

Wide Reading: The Absolute Best Strategy of All

Wide reading is one of the best cures for most reading problems (Allington, 2012; Krashen, 2004). Reading widely is also a highly effective way to expand conceptual and vocabulary knowledge as well as enhance comprehension, word identification, and fluency. Reading instruction and interventions should include daily reading practice where students are able to read quality books at their independent level or below. Chapter 15 will expand upon the importance of wide reading and describe a variety of strategies to use here.

PROGRESS MONITORING

If fluency is a deficient area, some sort of progress monitoring should be included in an intervention to document students' progress. A couple of pragmatic ideas: First, if you are using WPM or SPF, daily scores can be included here. For more formal measures, use WPM or WPHM scores every 2–4 weeks. Here, students do a cold read with a graded piece of text. A cold read is one in which students have not seen the text or have not engaged in any prereading activity. You can use the same text every 3–4 weeks or use a different text at the same level. As described above, fluency with any text is dependent on the vocabulary, the structure of the text, and the topic. Any WPM scores are general estimates.

FINAL WORD

The fluency activities described in this chapter are one small part of a reading curriculum or a daily intervention session. They should comprise 3 to no more than 8 minutes of any lesson or intervention session. Most importantly, fluency activities should always be put in the context of extensive reading practice.

CHAPTER 13

Comprehension

It bears repeating: Struggling readers are not homogeneous entities (Allington & McGill-Franzen, 2017). Not all struggling readers who have word identification or fluency deficits have comprehension deficits. Likewise, not all struggling readers who have comprehension deficits have word identification and fluency deficits. This chapter focuses on comprehension.

UNDERSTANDING COMPREHENSION

Let us begin by defining our terms: *Comprehension* is creating meaning with print. If this seems remarkably similar to the definition of reading put forth in Chapter 2, it is because it is, in fact, the same. To read is to create meaning. Creating meaning is the whole point of reading in the first place.

Comprehension is not a passive act. You cannot simply run your eyes over the letters on the page and absorb information. To comprehend, you must be actively engaged at some level with the material being read (Almasi, Palmer, Madden, & Hart, 2011; Hoffman, 2017). For example, if you are creating meaning with the text you are currently reading, you are probably doing at least one of the following: (1) checking for understanding, (2) identifying interesting or important ideas, (3) connecting this information to what you already know, (4) pausing every once in a while to see if what you are reading makes sense, (5) connecting the information to your own experiences, (6) going back and rereading previous words or sentences, (7) evaluating the ideas, or (8) thinking about possible applications for this knowledge. These are all examples of *cognitive operations*. A cognitive operation is an act of thinking that operates on or engages with mental content in some form.

Figure 13.1 lists some of the cognitive operations used by effective readers (Brown, Palinscar, & Armbruster, 2013; Learned, Stockdill, & Moje, 2013; Lipson & Wixson, 2009; Tompkins, 2011). The specific ones used are dependent on the purpose for reading and the content of what is read (Kucer, 2014). To enhance students' ability to create meaning with print, we must develop their ability to use these cognitive operations in the context of authentic reading situations (Almasi et al., 2011; Block & Lacina, 2009; Cartwright, 2015; Dole, Nokes, & Drits, 2009; Martin & Duke, 2011).

Too often the instruction and interventions used with students who are struggling readers focus only on low-level skills (Allington & McGill-Franzen, 2017). This makes it highly unlikely that they will develop the cognitive operations necessary to create meaning with print. The intervention activities described in this chapter all focus on developing cognitive processes related to effective comprehension.

TEACH THE PROCESS TO DEVELOP THE SKILL

As stated in Chapter 1, reading interventions should build on effective classroom instruction. However, comprehension tends to be severely undertaught in most classrooms (Allington & McGill-Franzen, 2017). The "comprehension" worksheets included with most basal reading programs do very little (if anything) to enhance students' ability to create meaning with print. In fact, a more appropriate term for these worksheets might be "remembering" worksheets, or "go-back-and-find-details" worksheets, or "show-the-teacher-you-have-read-the-book" worksheets. There is a better way.

Comprehension Strategy versus Comprehension Skill

This is a good place to differentiate between a comprehension strategy (more precisely defined as a study skill strategy) and a comprehension skill.

• compare	• problem-solve	• predict
• respond aesthetically	• analyze	• recognize story grammar
• infer	• evaluate	• reflect, metacognition
• identify important ideas	• make connections	• visualize
• identify supporting details	• order	• question
• identify cause–effect relationships	• perform inductive analysis	• summarize

FIGURE 13.1. Cognitive operations used by effective readers.

Comprehension Strategies

As described in Chapter 4, a strategy is a cognitive process or set of steps that one consciously applies to a situation for a specific purpose. A *comprehension strategy* then would be a set of steps that one consciously applies before, during, or after reading for the express purpose of enhancing comprehension. When reading expository text, especially if the text is difficult or the content unfamiliar, most of us must consciously apply some sort of strategy to enable us to understand what we are reading.

A more precise term for comprehension strategies would be *study skill strategies*. These strategies are used with expository text, the purpose of which is to understand or to construct knowledge. However, the purpose for reading narrative text is quite different. Here the purpose is to read and enjoy the story. Since the purposes for reading are quite different, it follows that the approaches to reading the two types of texts are different. Study skill strategies should be used with expository text, not narrative text. Using a study skill strategy with narrative text would be like going to a movie with a friend and afterward, demanding that the friend identify the main idea and supporting details.

Comprehension Skills

A skill in this context is a cognitive process that has become automated such that you have very little (if any) conscious awareness of it. A *comprehension skill* then would be a cognitive process that is automatically engaged during the act of reading. The purpose of an intervention for reading comprehension is to automatize students' use of one or more of the cognitive operations identified in Figure 13.1 during the act of reading. Thus, we teach the various cognitive operations, not so that students can demonstrate mastery of them but rather, to develop the skill (automaticity).

This is not to imply that study skill strategies should be ignored. These strategies should be explicitly taught to all students every year starting in grade 3. Methods for instruction and types of study skill strategies are described in other publications (Johnson, 2016b). However, the focus here is on comprehension skills.

How You Teach the Process

Comprehension can be improved by teaching the cognitive processes in Figure 13.1 using the elements of effective skills instruction (Allington & McGill-Franzen, 2017; Johnson, 2000). Here the teacher explains and models the cognitive operation, takes students through the cognitive operation using guided practice with a gradual release of responsibility, and then uses independent practice to enable students to practice the skill (see Figure 13.2). When a cognitive operation is introduced in an intervention, these elements should be used to teach it.

Input
1. Define/explain the skill and why it is used.
2. Provide information students need to know to perform the skill.
3. Model and demonstrate the steps.

Guided practice
1. Go through the skill together (whole class).
   a. *Keep all students actively engaged.*
2. Provide scaffolded instruction.
   a. *All students can do the skill with teacher help.*
   b. *Create structure and teacher support up front.*
   c. *Gradually release teacher support (responsibility).*
   d. *Transition toward student independence.*

Independent practice/activity
1. Students reinforce, extend, practice, or apply the new skill.
   a. *Students practice what they have already learned.*
   b. *95–100% success ratio.*
2. Students are able to use new skill independently.

FIGURE 13.2. Elements of effective skills instruction.

COMPREHENSION SKILL ACTIVITIES

This section contains a variety of comprehension skill activities that can be used to develop the cognitive operations that will enhance students' ability to create meaning with print. Adopt and adapt them to meet the needs of the students with whom you work.

Pre–Post Reading Activities to Develop Cognitive Operations

When used as prereading activities, the activities below invite students to read with purposeful intent. These activities help them focus their attention on specific elements within the text. If you only used them as postreading activities, the impact would be severely lessened.

Analyzing Using Pre–Post Confirmations

Pre–post confirmation can be used with narrative or expository text. Create a chart with two to five dualistic statements related to the story or book (see Figure 13.3). A dualistic statement is one for which there are only two possible conclusions: right or wrong (true or false, yes or no). At least one of the statements should be false. As part of the prereading activity, read through each statement on the chart

Which of these is true?

	yes	no	page
Apples are red.			
Apples are yellow.			
Apples are blue.			

FIGURE 13.3. Pre–post confirmations.

with students. Tell them that these are related to the book or chapter they will be reading. Some are true and some are not. This exercise invites students to read with purposeful intent. As students encounter information related to each statement during reading, they classify the statements (true or false) and identify the page number. (Identifying the page number connects students to specific elements within the text.)

For narrative text, dualistic statements can be related to specific content as in Figure 13.3, or they can be based on any of the story's grammar elements (characters, settings, and events) as in Figures 13.4 and 13.5.

Identifying Story Grammar

Story grammar refers to structural elements of a story such as characters, setting, and events. Understanding and recognizing story grammar elements enhances students' ability to comprehend narrative text (Allington & McGill-Franzen, 2017). Before reading, show students a partially completed story grammar chart (see Figure 13.6). Use this chart in the context of a story preview to provide students an overview of the story before reading. Then ask students to identify and record missing elements as they are encountered in the story.

Story grammar charts can be modified for emergent or beginning-level readers by focusing on just two of the story grammar elements (see Figure 13.7) or by listing

Which of these events occur in this book?

	yes	no	page
Biff got a new bike.			
Biff crashed into a tree.			
Billy helped Biff.			

FIGURE 13.4. Pre–post confirmations.

Which of these characters are in this book?

	yes	no	page
Biff			
Molly			
Bopper			
Billy			

FIGURE 13.5. Pre–post confirmations.

Characters	Settings	Events
1. Biff 2. Molly	1. On the sidewalk	1. 2. 3.

FIGURE 13.6. Story grammar chart.

Characters	Events
1. Bopper 2. Sally	1. 2.

FIGURE 13.7. Modified story grammar chart.

Check the events that occur in this story.

Characters	Events
1. Bopper 2. Sally	____ Spilled milk. ____ Missed the bus. ____ Ate lunch.

FIGURE 13.8. More modified story grammar chart.

three or four events and asking students to check the ones that occur in the story (see Figure 13.8).

A story grammar web can also be used in much the same way as pre- and postreading activities (see Figure 13.9). Some students are better able to visualize story grammar elements this way.

Predicting

Predicting is using clues and background information to calculate or deduce what might happen. It is different from guessing. The predict-O-graph in Figure 13.10 can be used to support students' thinking process here. As a prereading activity, give

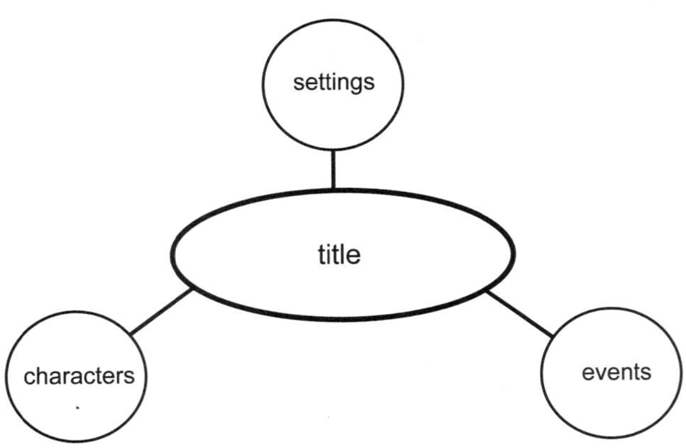

FIGURE 13.9. Story grammar web.

Teacher question: What will Sam and Sally do when the zebra jumps out?
Clues 1. 2. 3.
Student prediction:

FIGURE 13.10. Predict-O-graph.

students a preview of the story and provide them with the prediction question—for example: "In this story, Sam and Sally are walking to school. A zebra jumps out in front of them on the sidewalk. What will Sam and Sally do? There are three clues. Let's read to page 4 and see if we can find them. Then we'll make our prediction."

The clues are then listed on the predict-O-graph as they are encountered in the story. Stop at a point in the story just before the prediction question is answered. Ask students to make their prediction. They then complete the story to see if their prediction was correct. In designing these activities, make sure there are sufficient clues within the text that make the prediction possible. These clues should be abundantly obvious. Also, encourage students to use their background knowledge for clues. The important thing is that the prediction be based on specific clues and not simply be a guess.

Ordering

Here, students put story events in chronological order. Introduce the unordered events as a prereading activity telling students that they will need to put them in the order in which they occur in the story. An ordering chart like the one in Figure 13.11 can be used here. During reading, students put the events in order by numbering them in the column on the right as each event is encountered. You could also

Events	Order
Add cinnamon.	
Mash the apples.	
Cook the apples.	
Cut the apples.	

FIGURE 13.11. Ordering chart.

list the events on individual sentence strips. Here, students would rearrange the sentences in order as each is encountered.

Ranking

Ranking is a variation on ordering. Introduce the events or items and criterion. As part of the prereading activity, tell students they will be ranking each item based on the criterion. This again invites them to read with purposeful intent (see Figure 13.12). The criterion is not important. What is important is the cognitive operation used here. As a postreading activity, students then rank the story events or items based on the criterion. For example: most important to least important, most interesting to least interesting, most scary to least scary, best to worst, funniest to least funny, and biggest to smallest.

Rating

Rating is a variation on ranking. Introduce the events or items and the criterion as part of the prereading activity (see Figure 13.13). Tell students they will be rating each event or item based on the criterion at the end of the story. This again gets them reading with purposeful intent.

Identifying Cause–Effect

In designing these, look for causes in the story or text that have specific effects and effects that have specific causes. Before the story, read the sentences on the cause–effect chart with students as a form of story preview (see Figure 13.14). While reading, complete the chart as students encounter either the cause or the effect. Record the page number here. If students struggle with writing, you may choose to write the students' answers so as not to disrupt the reading flow.

When introducing this cognitive operation, start with one or two causes and have students identify the effects. Then focus on one or two effects and have

Character	Most like me
Biff	
Bopper	
Pat	
Mary	

FIGURE 13.12. Ranking chart.

Character	Rating
Biff	
Bopper	
Pat	
Mary	

Key: 1 = not at all like me, 2 = a little like me, 3 = like me, 4 = a lot like me.

FIGURE 13.13. Rating chart.

Cause	Effect	Page
Bopper lost his socks.		
	The zebra ran away.	

FIGURE 13.14. Cause–effect chart.

students identify the causes. Eventually, include both. The number of causes and effects included will vary dependent on student levels.

Support-a-Statement

As prereading activity, introduce a declarative statement related to some aspect of the story or text. Put the statement in a graphic organizer (see Figure 13.15). Then, ask students to look for and record story details that support that statement as they read.

Inferring

To infer is to make a logical extension or conclusion based on story clues. Effective readers are able to go beyond the descriptions found in the text to fill in some of the details as they are reading in order to understand ideas that are not explicitly stated. Like the prediction above, an inference is not simply a guess. It is a conclusion, assumption, or deduction based on known information.

As part of a prereading activity, present students with a story preview and an inference question. Put the inference question in the context of the infer-O-graph in Figure 13.16. Make sure the inference question is designed so that it can be easily supported by text clues. Again, the clues should be readily apparent. Ask students to identify and list clues that might help them make this inference as they are reading.

Statement: Billy Marble should have stayed home.

Supporting ideas

1. He lost his pants.
2. He was captured by a space alien.
3. He got in a fight with Molly.

FIGURE 13.15. Graphic organizer for making and supporting statements.

Teacher question:
Clues 1. 2. 3.
Student prediction:

FIGURE 13.16. Infer-O-graph.

Comparing and Contrasting

The comparison chart in Figure 13.17 can be used to develop this cognitive operation. This is a more concrete version of a Venn diagram. As part of the prereading activity, use a short story preview to let students know what the story or book is about, then identify the two things you will be comparing. Stating the comparison up front invites students to read with purposeful intent. A variety of things could be compared: characters, entities, objects, events, settings, or conditions at the beginning and end of the story. You could also compare one book to another or a story character to a real-life character. What is compared is not important. Again, it is the cognitive operation that is of importance. The similarities are listed in the middle of the comparison chart, whereas differences are listed under each item on the outsides.

A modified comparison chart can be designed for emergent and beginning readers. To provide a scaffold, include a list of special words in a word box below the chart (see Figure 13.18). Students must decide if the special words apply to one of the comparison items or both.

Comparing Attributes

Attribute charts can also be used to make comparisons. The attribute chart in Figure 13.18 makes the same comparisons as in Figure 13.19. Here, students check the

Item 1	**The same**	**Item 2**

FIGURE 13.17. Comparison chart.

Turtles	Both	Ducks

Special words
4 legs
swims
2 legs
crawls
lays eggs
can fly
shell
breathes air
feathers

FIGURE 13.18. Modified comparison chart.

box that applies to each of the items being compared. The items being compared are listed along the horizontal axis at the top, and the attributes are listed on the left on the vertical access. Like comparing and contrasting above, a story preview and review of attributes should be provided before reading the story.

Attribute charts are effective when comparing more than two items. In Figure 13.20, the items of comparison are listed on the vertical axis on the left, and the attributes are listed on the horizontal axis on the top. After the story preview and review of items and attributes, tell students they will need to decide if the attribute

	Turtles	Ducks
4 legs		
swims		
2 legs		
crawls		
lays eggs		
can fly		
shell		
breathes air		
feathers		

FIGURE 13.19. Attribute chart comparing two items.

	4 legs	2 legs	fins	shell	feathers	scales	skin
Frog							
Turtle							
Duck							
Fish							

FIGURE 13.20. Attribute chart comparing more than two items.

goes with each item. As that item is encountered in the text, students check the attributes that apply to it.

Making Connections

The connecting chart in Figure 13.21 is used to enable students to make different types of connections: between items within the text, between texts, or between text and students' background knowledge. Before reading, provide a story or chapter preview and then go through the list of items on both sides of the connecting chart. Tell students they will be looking for the connections. During reading, students draw a line from the item in Column A to the connected item in Column B. Again, when done merely as a postreading activity, this has little impact. However, when done as a pre- and during-reading activity, it invites students to read with purposeful intent while they are attending to story elements.

Creating Connections with Similes

The is-like chart in Figure 13.22 provides the structure necessary for students to connect what they know to what they are reading by making similes. Before reading, provide a story or chapter preview and go through each item. Tell students that they will be asked to compare items to things they know. To provide an initial scaffold, help students identify characteristics of the item. Then ask them what (or who) else shares some of those characteristics.

A	B
canyon	water
island	hot
mountain	cliff
desert	snow
delta	sand

FIGURE 13.21. Connecting chart.

Item	is like	because
A frog	a scuba diver	Both breathe air, can swim under water, and have webbed feet.
A duck	a goose	
Sam		

FIGURE 13.22. Is-like chart.

Asking Questions

Effective readers ask questions as they read. The question chart in Figure 13.23 works best with expository texts to develop this cognitive operation. At predetermined places in the text, stop and ask students, "What is something you are wondering about?" or "What is a question that you have right now?" We want students to ask questions as they read; hence, the focus is on the question, not the answer. Some questions will not be answered in the text. Unanswered questions become the basis of a future lesson or further reading. Or, as a postreading activity, you can go to the Internet and help students type questions in the search engine to look for answers. This is one way to connect students' reading to the real world.

Read and Pause

When working individually with students, have the student silently read a single paragraph and stop. Ask the student to describe one interesting or important idea and then continue. This can be done in a small group as a form of a reciprocal reading activity. Here students would be paired with a partner and take turns describing an interesting or important idea after each paragraph.

Concept Maps

Concept maps work best with expository text. They enhance students' ability to understand and organize new knowledge and to integrate this knowledge with the existing schema during reading. A concept map is a visual organizer that shows

Question	Not answered	Answered	Page

FIGURE 13.23. Question chart.

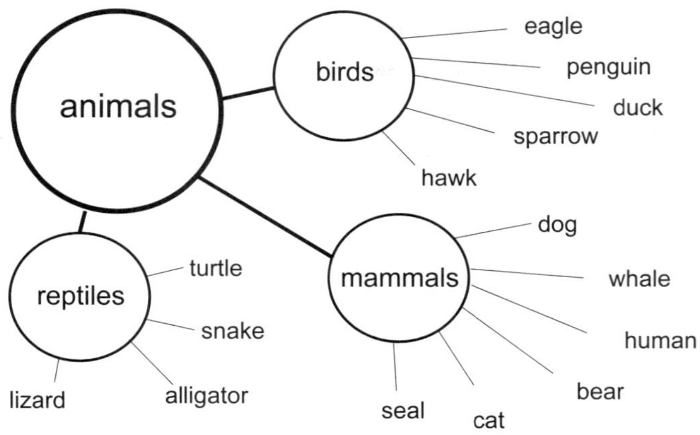

FIGURE 13.24. Concept map.

the relationship between concepts being taught or read (see Figure 13.24). Here, a preview and concept map are presented to students as part of a prereading activity. Scaffolding is provided by using a concept map that is partially filled in. Tell students they will be adding to this as they read. This again gets them reading with purposeful intent. As interesting or important ideas are encountered during reading, students must decide where on the concept map they should be placed, or even if they should be included on the concept map.

Close Reading

Close reading, a strategy that incorporates some of the skills mentioned above, will be described in the next chapter.

Sentence-Level Comprehension Activities

At the emergent and beginning levels, comprehension skills often focus on the sentence level. Metacognition is the specific cognitive operation developed here as students must pause to determine if the sentence makes sense or if a fix-up strategy is needed. Three simple strategies are presented here.

Maze

See Chapter 10 for a description of maze activities.

Sentence Mix-Up

See Chapter 11 for a description of sentence mix-up activities.

1. The rock sinks in the water. 2. The water sinks in the rock. 3. The sinks rock the in water
1. The sinks to the marble. 2. To the in marble sinks. 3. The marble sinks.
1. A float with cork. 2. A cork will float. 3. In cork what float.

FIGURE 13.25. Sentence metacognition.

Sentence Metacognition

This is a postreading activity. Students are shown three sentences related to the text (see Figure 13.25). Only one of the sentences makes sense. The students must read to determine which one makes sense. Like the sentence mix-up activities described in Chapter 11, putting these on PowerPoint is preferred as it enables you to quickly move through a number of these activities.

THREE BIG IDEAS

This chapter ends with three big ideas for using comprehension skills as part of a reading intervention (or reading instruction): First, focus on one comprehension skill at a time. Once students seem to have mastered the skill, move on to another.

Second, most of these activities use graphic organizers to support students' thinking while they are learning these cognitive operations (Johnson, 2017). However, the purpose of these activities is not to learn how to fill in graphic organizers; rather, it is to develop the automaticity of these cognitive operations in order to enhance meaning making during reading. As such, the graphic organizers are only temporary scaffolds needed to support thinking.

And third, you can use the graphic organizers to document and demonstrate. Sometimes teachers are required to demonstrate that students are learning subskills related to reading. Even though they are more appropriately used as temporary scaffolds, graphic organizers can be used to demonstrate and document students' mastery of comprehension subskills (many of which are included in various state standards, including the CCSS for English Language Arts). But again, it bears repeating that the goal of any type of reading instruction is not to master individual subskills. Reading subskills of any kind are always a means to an end, the end of which is to create meaning with print.

CHAPTER 14

Reading Practice (*More, Please*)

We do not teach students how to read. Most students already know how to do this. That is, they understand the process. They know that letters stand for sounds. They know that letters are put together to create words. They know that these words go together to create ideas. They know also that these ideas should make sense. They know how to read. The problem is, they are not very good at it. So, what do you do in your real-world life when you know how to do something, you are not very good at it, and you want to get better? I would assume that you would practice.

READING PRACTICE

Reading practice is incredibly important (Allington & McGill-Franzen, 2017). Extensive reading has been linked to improvement in general knowledge, vocabulary, spelling, verbal fluency, and reading comprehension (Cunningham & Stanovich, 2001; ILA, 2018c, 2019; Krashen, 2004; Springer, Dole, & Hacker, 2017). Also, the amount of reading students do is positively correlated with word identification skills, academic achievement, comprehension, reading fluency, and writing (Cunningham & Allington, 2007; Guthrie, Wigfield, Metsala, & Cox, 2004; ILA, 2018c, 2019). Finally, increasing the time spent reading independently has been shown to be an effective way to reduce the gap between high- and low-achieving readers (Allington, 2012; Krashen, 2004).

So, riddle me this, Batman: If reading practice is so important, why does so little of it occur in schools? Why is free voluntary reading not a mandated part of reading instruction? Why is it not considered an important part of "scientifically based" reading instruction? Why is it not included in lists of "research-based" strategies? Why is reading practice not a central part of reading instruction and intervention programs?

Reading Practice Gets in the Way

One common objection to the inclusion of reading practice for struggling readers is that it gets in the way of all the "research-based" strategies and "scientifically based" reading programs that have been "proven" to work (see Chapter 19). Of course, if all the "research-based" strategies, and "scientifically based" reading programs were actually helping struggling readers create meaning with text, I could have written a much shorter book. It would have been titled *Purchase the Right Reading Intervention Program.* You would not need to be bothered with all the messy thinking and understanding related to reading and the reading process. Designing effective reading interventions would simply be a matter of purchasing the right program and then following the instructions with fidelity. And when that program proves to be ineffective (as it inevitably will), you will then follow the instructions with even more fidelity. And when that does not work, you will purchase a new program or pay a "consultant" to come to your school and tell you how to implement their program with fidelity, and the cycle of for-profit educational life will continue unabated (Altwerger, 2005).

However, there is not a set of "research-based" pedagogical strategies that will make learning magically appear. The assumption that there are such magical teaching strategies represents a simplistic notion of educational research, teaching, and human learning. However, there are a variety of strategies that research has shown to be effective, but their effectiveness is dependent on a multitude of variables such as context, purpose, implementation, and the human entities involved. In other words, the effectiveness of any teaching strategy is dependent on how, how much, how often, why, when, and for whom it is used.

Reading Practice for Students with "Dyslexia"

To illustrate this point and bring us back to free voluntary reading, Roseline Fink (2006) conducted important studies that would not meet the strict definitions of "scientifically based" reading research imposed on the field by the U.S. Department of Education (described in Chapter 22); yet her work offers profound insights into reading instruction and interventions for students with dyslexia. She examined highly successful men and women with dyslexia. Success in her study was defined as preeminence in their fields. Her research participants included 6 people with MDs, 17 who earned a PhD, 19 with a master's-level degree, and 15 bachelor's degree holders. As children, all of these highly successful adults had extreme deficits in their decoding abilities. These decoding difficulties continued into adulthood. (By the way, this is why we develop all three cueing systems and not just the phonological cueing system.)

Despite their difficulties with these low-level reading subskills, all became avid readers, were able to read highly complex material, and made significant achievements in their fields. Yet as adults, they continued to struggle with single-word decoding of unfamiliar words. That is, when presented with a single word out of context or a nonsense word, they had difficulties determining what it was. Given their success, how is this possible?

Fink found that as children, all these successful adults were allowed to immerse themselves and read in their areas of interest. They developed expertise, building their conceptual and vocabulary knowledge. They also became familiar with the schemes and structures of the types of texts found in their field. This background knowledge and familiarity with text structures was more important for facilitating reading accuracy and comprehension than letter clues. That is, marginal decoders used background knowledge, context, text structure, and word order to create meaning with print. Low-level skill mastery was not a prerequisite for comprehension and higher-level thinking.

Implications

Three instructional implications can be taken from Fink's research: First, teachers should help all students discover an area or areas of interest. This is done by presenting a wide variety of topics in classes and class discussions, using book talks in which students talk about books and topics of interest, and having available to students a wide variety of books and other reading material on a wide variety of topics.

Second, children must be able to select and read books and other reading materials that are of interest to them as part of daily reading instruction. Using this material, struggling readers (and all readers actually) must have daily opportunities to practice reading (Allington, 2012). This practice should take place at least 15 minutes a day (ILA, 2019), although 30 to 60 minutes would be ideal. However, if students have not had much experience with independent reading, it may take time to develop the reading stamina necessary to read this for long.

Third, as stated throughout this text, reading instruction and related interventions must include activities to develop all three cueing systems. If one of these cueing systems is weak, the other two can be used by struggling readers to compensate. This maximizes their word recognition efficiency during the process of reading.

READING PRACTICE AS PART OF AN INTERVENTION

High-Quality Books

Reading practice should be one part of a meaning-based intervention for reading. This practice should be built upon the reading practice that occurs as part of an effective, balanced approach to classroom reading instruction. Also, students will read for pleasure if they have something pleasurable to read. This points to the need for having an abundance of high-quality reading material. General education classrooms, resources rooms, and school libraries should have an assortment of interesting and enjoyable books that include both narrative and expository text and encompass a wide range of genres, types of text, and subjects. Also, since most general education classrooms have students reading two to six levels above and below grade level, the books available should be of varying reading levels.

Reading Level for Reading Practice

The books used for reading practice should generally be at a student's independent level or below. One problem often faced by struggling readers in the upper elementary grades and above is that the books that interest them are written at reading levels that are too high for them. And the books that are at their reading level are often written at emotional levels that are beneath them (I call these "ducky books"). I still remember the look of horror on the face of one of the fifth-grade students I was tutoring when I brought out one of the *Hello Kitty* books by Kirsten Anderson for him to use for reading practice. He did not want anybody to see him reading this kind of book. Rule #1 for reading instruction and interventions: Do not embarrass, humiliate, or frustrate your students. Rule #2: Help children fall in love with books.

Two caveats here: First, as indicated in Fink's study, if the topic is of interest and students have sufficient background knowledge, they will often be willing and able to read texts that are above their independent reading level. Second, it is acceptable to read "easy" books. As adults, we do this all the time. (I find young adult literature to be exceptionally well written.) If students read and enjoy "easy" books, they will be able to read more of them. They benefit from encountering a variety of words and sentences in context regardless of the reading level.

High/Low Books

Struggling readers should have a selection of high/low books available to them. These are books that are of high interest but written at a low reading level. High/low books are written to interest students in the fifth through twelfth grades but are written at the second- or third-grade level. High Noon Books is an example of a publisher with a wide selection of high/low books that includes both narrative and expository texts.

High/Very Low Books

Severely struggling readers should have a selection of high/very low books available to them. These are books that are of high interest for students in late elementary to high school but are written at approximately RL 1 (Lexile levels 40–300). Unfortunately, high/very low books are hard to find. I have contacted several publishers of high/low material, urging them to consider high/very low books, but there seems to be little interest in publishing for this market. High/very low books are picture driven with one or two sentences used for each picture and topics that are of interest to students ages 12 to adult. These types of books could be a valuable resource for students with severe reading disabilities, as well as for older students and adults with intellectual disabilities.

Tips for Using Reading Practice in an Intervention

Next are three tips for including reading practice in a meaning-based intervention for reading.

Read at the End

The end of the intervention session is often an appropriate place to include reading practice. Since it is assumed that there will be other places for reading practice during the day (as part of effective reading instruction), this need not be long (2–5 minutes). Choice is an essential element here. Thus, you should have several books or types of reading material from which students can choose.

Scaffolded Oral Reading

Rule #1 tells us we should never frustrate students. If you are working individually with a student, it may be appropriate to use ScORe. If you think the student might struggle, you should ask, "Do you want me to read with you, or do you want to read by yourself?" Also, as stated above, choice is an essential element. This also means choosing to stop reading books that are not of interest. When using ScORe to read with students, after the first page you should ask, "Do you like the book? Should we keep going or find a different book?" This empowers students and reinforces the idea that reading is something that is enjoyable. Always let students know that finding a different book is an option.

Silent Reading or Oral Reading?

For older readers, you would most often use silent reading for reading practice. You can also use a shared reading technique where you read one paragraph or section aloud and the students read the next one silently (see below). For younger or severely struggling readers, you will want to include some oral reading. Decisions to use silent or oral reading should be made on a case-by-case basis. The goal is to keep students engaged in reading practice without frustration.

Teacher Read-Alouds

Teacher-led read-alouds should be part of every classroom experience in some form. They can also be used in a reading intervention for reading practice. For young children, reading-alouds have been shown to enhance vocabulary, listening comprehension, story schema, background knowledge, word recognition skills, and cognitive development (ILA, 2018c). For older students, teacher read-alouds help to build background knowledge and vocabulary, as well as to develop comprehension strategies. Teacher read-alouds also enable the teacher to help students make personal connections to narrative and expository text, and they can become the basis for many kinds of discussions. They can also be a vehicle for cognitive modeling. For example, after reading a sentence aloud, a teacher might say, "I didn't quite understand that sentence. I'm going to read it again," or after a paragraph, "I don't remember what's important. I need to read that paragraph again."

Shared Reading

Teacher read-alouds can be used as a form of shared reading. Shared reading can be used with both narrative and expository text. Here the teacher reads aloud as students follow along or uses the everybody-read-to (ERT) technique described in Chapter 12. The teacher stops at designated places for preplanned questions or activities (Johnson, 2016b). Any of the activities in Chapter 13, as well as the questions in Figures 14.1 and 14.2, can be used for shared reading. As you can see, thoughtful preparation is required for shared reading activities to be effective.

Close Reading

If implemented appropriately, *close reading* is a strategy that can be used to enable students to engage more deeply in texts. The CCSS ELA Anchor Standards (*www.corestandards.org/ELA-Literacy/CCRA/R*) identifies close reading as reading closely. There are a variety of understandings as to exactly what close reading is; however, in its most basic form it is simply a matter of reading a text more carefully. To do this, teacher-directed strategies are used as scaffolds that enable

To check for understanding:
- What is the story about?
- What is the problem?
- What do I want to know more about?
- What do I know about . . . ?
- What doesn't make sense to you?
- What is an important event that has occurred?

To associate:
- What are you thinking about right now? Why?
- What does this story remind you of? Are there events that are similar to another story or to events in your life? (Use the compare-O-graph.)
- Who does this character remind you of? Is this character similar to another character you know in another story or in real life? (Use the compare-O-graph.)

To notice:
- What is an interesting description that you noticed?
- What new or interesting word did you notice?
- What important story clue did you notice?

To elaborate:
- How might you make that sentence more interesting?
- What kind of character would you add to the story?

To problem-solve:
- What is the problem here?
- What are some ideas for solving the problem?
- Which idea do you think is the best?

Means–end analysis:
- What does __________ need to do?
- What are some things that need to be done for this occur?

To predict:
- What's going to happen next?
- What are some important clues? (Use the predict-O-graph.)
- How do you think this story will end?

To infer:
- What does this tell us about that character?
- Based on story clues, what happened before/next?
- How does __________ feel about __________? (Use the infer-O-graph.)

To imagine or visualize:
- What do you imagine this (person, place, or thing) looks like?
- What does this scene look like to you? What are some things you would see if you were there? What picture is painted in your mind?

To summarize:
- What are the important events that have happened so far?
- What's happened so far? Who did what?

To decide:
- What is the decision?
- What do you think __________ should do? (List at least three ideas.)
- What might happen?
- What would you do if you were __________?

FIGURE 14.1. Questions for shared reading: Narrative text.

To preview:
- What do you think this chapter/article is about? What clues do you see in the title or cover of the book?
- What does the title tell us?
- What do the headings tell us about what we will read?
- What are some interesting things you see on the cover of the book?

To check for understanding:
- What is this book, chapter, or article about?
- What are three interesting or important ideas?
- What do you want to know more about?
- What was an interesting or important idea in this paragraph?
- Should we reread the paragraph?

To summarize:
- What do you want to learn more about?
- How is this like ___________?
- How would you explain ___________?
- How would you define ___________?

Questions to ask during reading:
- What is something that is a little fuzzy?
- How else do you think ___________ could be applied?
- How is ___________ like something you know about?
- What are the main parts of ___________?
- How would you compare this to ___________?
- What's an interesting or important idea in this paragraph?
- What do you hope to find out?
- What study skill strategy might I use here?
- What else do you know about ___________?
- What should I record in my notes to help me understand and remember?
- Where should I put this on my concept map?
- What should I add to my concept map?

FIGURE 14.2. Questions for shared reading: Expository text.

students to analyze and interpret a piece of text more deeply. The purpose is to develop the cognitive processes necessary for reading and understanding complex materials.

Close reading can be done individually, in small groups, or as a whole class activity. In most descriptions of close reading, students read the text silently first. They use some strategy (a pencil dot in the text or margins) to indicate important words, words they may not recognize or know, or important ideas. Next, students reread the text as a shared reading activity (above). The teacher then includes questions or activities like those shown in Figures 14.2 and 14.3. The biggest difference between shared reading and close reading is that in close reading, students read the text silently first.

THREE OTHER IDEAS

Here are three other ideas for including reading practice as part of a reading intervention:

Reading Logs

Using a notebook, a file folder, or a Word document, students create a reading log to record the title and date of books read (see Figure 14.3). Students can use this log for books read within the reading intervention, in class, or at home. It can also be used to set weekly goals. Sharing the log with parents is also an effective way to encourage voluntary reading outside of school.

Rating Books

Encourage students to rate the book. This creates good conversations around books. Posters can be created to display the individual book titles and students' ratings. Students are interested in what other students think. You could also include a top 10 list or a worst 10 list.

Reading Time Logs

Students need to practice reading in order to build up their reading stamina. Thus, you might also create a reading time log where students record the minutes spent reading within the intervention session (see Figure 14.4). This, too, can be used to set goals. Also, it can be shared with parents to encourage daily home reading practice. Home reading practice need not be long (10–20 minutes depending on students' level), but it should be consistent.

Title	Date	Rating
1. 2. 3.		

Key: 5 = outstanding, 4 = a good book, 3 = okay, 2 = didn't like it, 1 = stinker.

FIGURE 14.3. Reading log.

Day	Monday	Tuesday	Wednesday	Thursday	Friday
Minutes					

FIGURE 14.4. Reading time log.

FINAL WORD

Of all the research-based strategies for teaching reading, wide reading is perhaps the most effective, most economical, and easiest to implement. Also, if implemented with fidelity, it could be the most impactful. Again, independent reading is an important part of reading instruction. It should be reinforced as part of a reading intervention.

PART III

DIAGNOSING, ASSESSING, AND MONITORING PROGRESS

CHAPTER 15

Standardized Tests

Standardized tests are often used as the sole tool for identifying and diagnosing students with reading difficulties. This chapter focuses on the limitations of standardized tests in diagnosing reading difficulties.

A thought experiment: What would happen if standardized tests were suddenly banned from all schools? How would the education change? Would teachers' daily instruction be different? Would teachers still be able to teach? Would students learn? How would we know if learning occurred? How would we know which schools were the best? How would we know which schools were underperforming? How would we know anything? Would education as we know it cease to exist? Would the educational world suddenly implode from lack of data? Would there be economic chaos? Would there be massive waves of identity crises among the student population because they no longer had numbers attached to them?

STANDARDIZED AND NORM-REFERENCED TESTS

Let us start by defining our terms: A *standardized test* is any published test in which there are mandatory instructions for administering and scoring. It is standardized so that all the testing variables are the same. These tests are usually, but not always, norm-referenced. A *norm-referenced test* compares students to a "normal" population. All the scores are put together and distributed along the familiar bell-shaped curve (see Figure 15.1). The average is established, with half the populations above and the other half below. The term *standardized test* is used in this chapter to indicate standardized tests that are norm-referenced. Standardized tests are good for comparing some students' performance to that of other students in order to determine how far away from "average" they are. The tests can be used as one indication

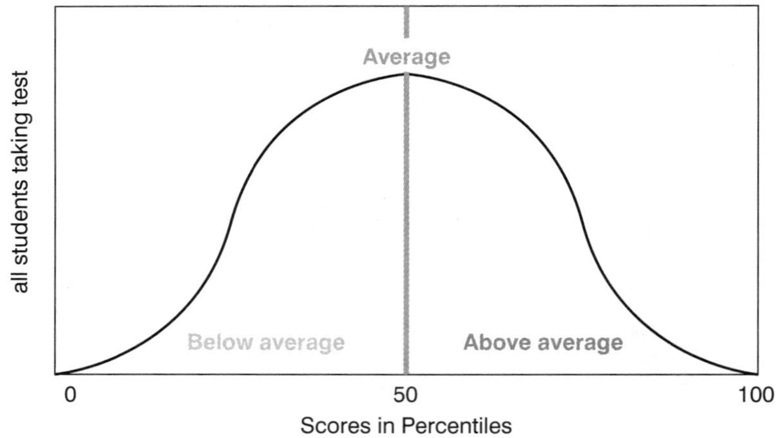

FIGURE 15.1. Bell-shaped curve.

that there might be reading problems. However, they do not tell you exactly what these problems are. They are often inadequate for diagnosing the cause of reading difficulties (ILA, 2017).

AN EDUCATIONAL TOOL

Standardized tests are one tool among many important tools used to evaluate, assess, and document learning. And like any tool, their effectiveness is determined by how they are used. For reading, a misuse of this tool would be to employ them as the sole means of (1) determining students' placement in a program; (2) identifying strengths and weaknesses; (3) measuring students' progress; (4) evaluating teachers, programs, or methods; and (5) diagnosing the cause of a reading disability. An effective use of standardized tests would be to indicate which students might be struggling with reading and might need further diagnosis.

Standardized tests can be helpful in certain situations and for specific purposes, but they are misused and overused in most schools today. There are three reasons:

First, they are quick and easy to use. Their use does not have to be carefully planned. Data do not have to be thoughtfully considered. Environment, sociocultural background, social economic status, individual variables, and context can be ignored. And standardized tests do not even have to be linked to classroom instruction. Instead, you just open the package, read the directions, and administer (much like putting a can of soup in the microwave). They can also be simultaneously given to large groups of students, and all the data can be collected in a single setting. In short, they are simple, quick, and easy to use.

Second, psychometricians, educational psychologists, and the companies that publish standardized tests have convinced people that learning can be quantified and that the numbers generated on these standardized tests mean much more than they do. They promote the false idea that large numbers mean more learning and more effective teaching, while low numbers mean less learning and less effective teaching. Students are then sorted into high-numbered groups and low-numbered groups.

Third, standardized tests serve to further disempower teachers. The only way the educational industrial complex can maintain its hold on the educational system is if classroom teachers are not able to make the decisions that are best for their students. It is the test, not the teacher, that controls what is taught and how it is taught. Disempowered teachers are not able to use their creativity and intelligence to design innovative learning experiences. They must instead implement commercial programs with fidelity and then measure students as directed by entities outside the classroom.

LIMITATIONS OF STANDARDIZED TESTS

Below are some of the specific limitations of standardized tests:

1. **They measure a narrow range of skills.** Standardized tests for reading measure a very narrow range of reading subskills. It is not possible to measure all aspects of being literate in a single setting. They cannot capture or describe the processes used to create meaning with print. Also, there is no room for teacher observation or insight. They do not account for motivation, sociocultural background, or other important contextual factors. And they focus on decontextualized reading subskills. As such, they are blunt instruments at best that provide a very rough estimate of students' possible literacy abilities or potential.

2. **They become the curriculum.** This problem was alluded to above. Since scores on these standardized tests are often misused to identify "achieving" and "underperforming" schools and sometimes even effective and ineffective teachers, there is a natural tendency to teach to the test. As such, the test becomes the curriculum (ILA, 2017b). This means that psychometricians far removed from individual students and the actual teaching situations are making the important decisions about what is taught in any given classroom. The experience, expertise, and insights of teachers are discounted. As a result, less time is spent engaged in authentic literacy experiences or activities that cannot be quantified. Also, little time is spent engaging students in thoughtful conversation and social interaction based on high-quality books. In addition, high-level cognitive processes related to thoughtful literacy are ignored. Instead, focus is put on the kinds of low-level skills that will be measured on the test.

3. **They exclude practitioners' knowledge.** Teachers' observations, insights, ways of knowing, and more authentic assessment methods are delegitimized and

ultimately ignored. Instead, sterilized, for-profit number-generating corporations have been elevated as the epistemologically privileged way of knowing.

4. **They are expensive.** Standardized tests are expensive in terms of time, money, and emotional capital. Imagine if the resources devoted to standardized tests were instead spent on two things that could in fact enhance students' ability to read: good books (see Chapter 14) and teachers' professional development (ILA, 2018b). The teacher is the most significant variable in determining the quality of education and the amount of learning that occurs in any given classroom (Darling-Hammond, 1999; Darling-Hammond, Holtzman, Gatlin, & Heilig, 2005; Darling-Hammond & Youngs, 2002; Marzano, Pickering, & Pollock, 2001). Teachers, like other professionals, such as dentists, nurses, doctors, engineers, and computer technicians, need significant and continued professional development in order to develop expertise and to stay abreast of their field, which is continually changing and evolving.

5. **They lack validity.** There should always be questions related to the validity of any single quantitative score or set of scores derived in a single setting. The scores on standardized tests do not accurately portray the type of literacy real humans use in the real world. They do not reflect the processes that create meaning with print by real humans in the real world. Outside the confines of a school environment, most people have never had to read a paragraph and select the correct bubble to fill in. Also, most people have never been asked to read a list of nonsense words or single words outside a meaningful context.

6. **They do not account for context.** The results from any standardized tests cannot be fully understood outside the sociocultural context in which they were administered and without considering students' motivation and emotional state (Christenbury, Bomer, & Smagorinsky, 2009; Klinger & Boardman, 2011). Thus, to fully understand students' ability to create meaning with print, standardized texts must always be supplemented with data gleaned from other sources such as interviews, surveys, think-aloud protocols, miscue analysis, portfolios, reading logs, response journals, anecdotal records, observations, and story retellings.

7. **They take the focus away from good teaching.** How do we know if students are learning? A more appropriate question to ask is, how do we know if teachers are teaching? Are they using research-based or theory-based strategies? Are they creating the conditions whereby students are actively engaged? Are they responding to the needs and interests of the students whom they teach? Standardized tests do not get to these questions. If more emphasis was placed on effective teaching and less on measuring, there would be more effective teaching and more learning. But more important, students would actually be learning. This again points to the importance of continued and significant teacher professional development. If we know that teachers are using a variety of evidence-based strategies appropriately (not with fidelity) and that students are actively engaged, learning will occur.

8. **They have a so-what effect.** When I review IEPs related to reading, I often see a variety of scores from standardized tests. So what? So, what do you do with that data? Based on the data, what exactly should be done on Monday morning? Knowing that somebody is in the 10th percentile on some score of a reading subskill, what exactly do you do? Standardized tests are not useful in planning for the instruction of individual students (Allington, 1994; Rasinksi, Padak, & Fawcett, 2010). They do little to inform teaching, especially for struggling readers and writers.

9. **They do not diagnose.** Standardized tests do not adequately diagnose the cause of a reading difficulty (see Chapter 16) (ILA, 2017b).

A STORY ABOUT VALIDITY

I was working in a special education resource room with students who were reading at beginning levels. Before I began working with them in the fall, I administered an *informal reading inventory* (IRI) as a diagnostic and to get a sense of their reading levels (see below). For the next several months, daily instruction included LEA, cloze activities, writing activities, word-building activities, short-passage fluency (SPF), and reading practice. For reading practice we used books that students liked. These books had interesting topics with lots of pictures and color, they had appropriate sentence-to-picture ratios, and students could successfully read them. Also, students were given choices about what books they wanted to read.

Observations and progress-monitoring measures indicated that we seemed to be making good progress. Students were enjoying reading, they were reading more fluently and for meaning instead of sounding out words, and they were talking about the books they read. In short, they had become readers. After 3 months, I decided to quantify what I was seeing.

Individually, I pulled students out of the environment we had used for reading and writing, and I took them into a larger room with fewer distractions. For the informal reading inventory, I plopped down a page in front of them that consisted of text with no pictures or color. Then I asked them to perform for me. "Read this," I said.

What is wrong with this picture?

I could tell by their nonverbals (something that would not show up on a standardized test) that students did not want to be there. I had pulled them from an environment in which they felt comfortable, where their friends and teacher were. I asked them to do something that was not fun. The text used in the IRI had no color, no pictures, and was of no interest to them. They were just words printed on a black and white page. Students were not able to use picture clues (like we had taught them to do) to help create meaning. And I became another testing person, making them do things to show what they could not do.

Seeing the negative reactions from the first three students, I shut this process down. The results were disastrous. These students seemed to have become worse readers after all our hard work together.

After a little thinking, I reassessed. I needed to make a change. Instead of using the commercially prepared IRIs, I decided to do miscue analyses with the books we had been using for reading in class for the last 3 months. I recorded the students reading these books in the classroom where they were taught. I also created story-retelling charts based on these books to assess comprehension. And when I was "testing" them, I gave them a choice of two books to read. I asked, "Do you want to read _______ or _______?" It was a choice between only two books, but it was a choice very much like the ones they were used to making.

My readers magically reappeared. I saw an increase in meaningful miscues and self-corrections when compared with the IRI passages we had used for their diagnoses and baseline measures at the beginning of the year. This told me that students were reading for meaning and that improvements were being made in their metacognitive abilities. The scores on the story-retelling charts showed that the students were doing a better job of creating meaning with what they read. Also, the reading fluency and prosody that I had observed during instructional sessions returned. These improvements could have been due to (1) the intervention used, (2) the type of material used for assessment, (3) maturation and increased engagement with authentic literacy experiences, or (4) a combination of all three. The fact was, they were taking important steps in their literacy journey.

FINAL WORD

There are three big ideas you might take from this chapter: First, standardized tests can be a useful tool if used appropriately. This means that they are not the sole tool used to measure, assess, or describe anything. Instead, multiple types of measures are used to fully understand learners (ILA, 2018a). These include measures that incorporate or utilize practitioners' knowledge, expertise, and experience.

Second, when assessment looks different from instruction and practice, you will often get results that underrepresent students' actual ability. Removing a reading event from its meaningful context during assessment creates an artificial, nonreading event. A valid assessment for reading should look, to the greatest extent possible, like real reading (ILA, 2017a).

Third, student assessment of any kind always occurs within the sociocultural, emotional, and experiential context. These variables must be considered when examining results.

CHAPTER 16

Diagnosing the Problem

DIAGNOSTIC READING ASSESSMENT

The term *diagnostic reading assessment* (DRA) refers to an assessment tool that is sometimes identified as an informal reading inventory (IRI). In the hands of a knowledgeable teacher, a DRA provides valuable data that cannot be obtained from standardized tests (Gunning, 2014). Here the examiner is not simply following a formula or a list of sequential steps that some external entity has designed. Instead, the knowledge and experience of the teacher become integral parts of this assessment (Weaver, 2009).

A DRA can provide useful information related to word identification, fluency, and comprehension. It can also be used to find students' approximate reading levels.

In terms of approximate reading levels, grade-level equivalency scores from any type of measure should always be considered a rough estimate of students' actual reading level (Kucer, 2016). This is because the ability to comprehend any given text is affected by one's (1) interest and motivation, (2) conditions and affect, (3) background knowledge, (4) familiarity with the words used, and (5) familiarity with the structure of the text or story.

The Reader

Any reading diagnostic should include the reader's perspective (ILA, 2018a). Could you imagine a doctor diagnosing a patient and not asking that patient to describe his or her symptoms or related conditions? Figure 16.1 includes examples of the types of questions that could be included as part of a reading diagnostic, and Figure 16.2 is an example of a reading attitude survey. Both of these figures present

1. Tell me about your reading.
2. What do you do when you get to a word you don't recognize?
3. What do you do if you don't understand what you are reading?
4. What makes reading hard for you?
5. What would you like your reading teacher to know or do?
6. What kind of things do you like to read?
7. What topics would you like to learn or read about?
8. What kinds of things do you like to read?
9. What would you like to read about?

FIGURE 16.1. Understanding your reader.

examples of the types of items that provide valuable insight and information when used as part of a reading diagnostic. Both can also be used for progress monitoring. That is, they can be used along with other measures to indicate change over time. When using questions and surveys for this purpose, I would recommend that there be at least 6–8 weeks between data collection.

Basic Elements of a DRA

A DRA usually consists of three elements: (1) word lists used to get a very rough estimate of students' possible reading level, (2) graded or leveled passages used for miscue analysis (described below), and (3) comprehension questions or story-retelling charts to get a sense of students' level of comprehension. There are a variety of commercial DRAs from which to choose. Figure 16.3 contains a list of some of these assessments. However, you can also create and implement your

____ I enjoy reading.
____ I am able to read.
____ I understand what I read.
____ Books can be interesting.
____ I know most of the words on the page.
____ I know what to do when I don't know a word.

Key: 5 = strongly agree, 4 = agree, 3 = don't know, 2 = disagree, 1 = strongly disagree.

or

Key: 5 = always, 4 = often, 3 = sometimes, 2 = seldom, 1 = never.

FIGURE 16.2. Reading attitude survey.

- *Qualitative Reading Inventory, 7th Edition* (Leslie & Caldwell, 2017)
- *The Flynt/Cooter Comprehensive Reading Inventory, 2nd Edition* (Couter, Flynt, & Cooter, 2013)
- *Classroom Reading Inventory, 12th Edition* (Wheelock, Campbell, & Silvaroli, 2011)
- *Basic Reading Inventory, 12th Edition* (Johns, Elish-Piper, & Johnson, 2016)
- *Analytical Reading Inventory, 10th Edition* (Woods & Moe, 2015)
- *Ekwall/Shanker Reading Inventory, 7th Edition* (Shanker & Cockrum, 2019)
- *Informal Reading Inventory, 8th Edition* (Roes & Burns, 2011)

FIGURE 16.3. Common DRAs.

own reading diagnostic based on the material that students are reading in their classrooms. This makes it a more accurate and valid assessment of their reading strengths and deficits.

Next, I describe the two most important elements of a DRA: the miscue analyses and retelling charts.

MISCUE ANALYSES

A *miscue analysis* (MA) is used to analyze and document the types of miscues a reader makes while reading. A *miscue* is when what the student reads does not match what is on the page. A miscue analysis provides valuable diagnostic information for reading interventions. The six steps for using a miscue analysis are described here.

Step 1: Collect Data

1. Find a graded passage that is slightly above the student's independent reading level. This would be a passage or book in which the student can identify approximately 92–97% of the words (see Figure 16.4). This could be a narrative text, a textbook, a passage, or a leveled passage that is part of a DRA.

2. Give one copy to the student. Make a second copy for yourself; this will be the data collection copy. If you are using a picture book, type the entire text on a single sheet of paper.

3. Ask the student to read aloud. Record the session with an audio recorder. This will be used later to analyze the types of miscues made by the student (see below).

4. As the student is reading, underline words that are miscued. Do not try to do any analysis of miscues at this stage.

5. If the student is able to correctly identify 98% or more of the words (independent level), move to a higher-level passage. If the student seems to be struggling and is getting frustrated, move to a lower-level passage.

- **Independent level.** At this level students can read unassisted. They are generally able to identify 98% or more of the words. Comprehension scores are 90% or higher. When students read independently for pleasure, you want them to be reading at this level or below.
- **Instructional level.** At this level students can read with some assistance. They are generally able to identify 90–97% of these words. Comprehension scores are between 75 and 89%. This is the level of reading material that should be used for reading instruction. Here you will need to provide some assistance such as a story map, vocabulary help, scaffolded oral reading, or a story preview.
- **Frustration level.** At this level students cannot be successful even with a lot of the teacher's help. They are able to identify 89% or fewer of these words. Comprehension scores are less than 75%. Avoid any type of reading at this level. Challenging students with frustration-level material will NOT help them progress faster. Reading at this level results only in frustrated students who learn that they can't learn to read and that they don't like reading.

FIGURE 16.4. Independent, instructional, and frustration levels.

Step 2: Listen to the Audio

1. Listen to the audio recording of the graded passage to identify the types of miscues being made. You usually need to listen to the recording two or three times to accurately identify the types of miscues.

2. On the data collection copy (Figure 16.5), put a line through the miscued words and write down exactly what the student said on top of the word.

3. Indicate the types of miscues on the data collection copy (see Figure 16.6).

Step 3: Analyze the Miscues

1. Use page 1 of the MA analyzing sheet (Figure 16.7) to record miscues. For each miscue, write the target word found in the text in the first column and what the student said (miscue) in the second column.

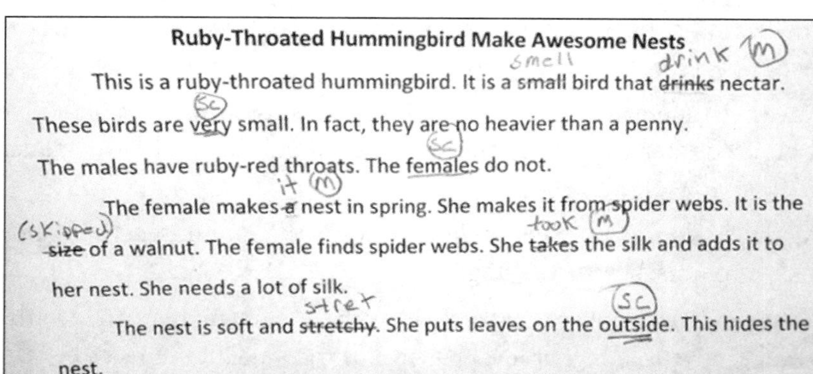
Ruby-Throated Hummingbird Make Awesome Nests

This is a ruby-throated hummingbird. It is a small bird that drinks nectar. These birds are very small. In fact, they are no heavier than a penny. The males have ruby-red throats. The females do not.

The female makes a nest in spring. She makes it from spider webs. It is the size of a walnut. The female finds spider webs. She takes the silk and adds it to her nest. She needs a lot of silk.

The nest is soft and stretchy. She puts leaves on the outside. This hides the nest.

FIGURE 16.5. MA data collection copy.

Meaningful miscue. A meaningful miscue (MM) is one that does not change the fundamental meaning of the sentence. For example: If the student said, "The dogs run down the road" instead of "The dogs ran down the road," this would not change the meaning of the sentences. Write a large "M" with a circle around it to indicate that it was a meaningful miscue. On the analysis form, these will be counted as half of a miscue.

Meaning-disrupting miscue. A meaning-disrupting miscue (MDM) changes the meaning of the sentence or does not make sense within the sentence. For example, if the sentence was "The dogs ran down the road," suppose a student said, "The dogs rammed down the road," or "The dogs rode down the road." One point is deducted for every such meaning-disrupting miscue.

Self-correction. If the student makes a miscue but goes back and corrects it, it is not counted as a miscue. This is a self-correction. On your scoring sheet write "SC" with a circle around it on top of the word. SCs represent mature reading behaviors (metacognition). No points are deducted here.

Skipped words. If a student skips a word, circle it and write "skipped" in parentheses. Note whether the skipped word was an MM or MDM miscue.

Grammatically correct miscue. A grammatically correct miscue (GCM) is one that has the same grammatical function as the target word. It can be an MM or MDM. These GCM's tell us that the reader is using the syntactic cueing system. While they are of interest, they are not usually noted or recorded in a miscue analysis.

FIGURE 16.6. Types of miscues to record for the MA.

2. If a student skips a word, write the target word in the first column, and write "skipped" in parentheses in the second column.

3. In the last two columns, put a check to indicate whether it was a meaning-disrupting miscue (MDM) or a meaningful miscue (MM). Having the target words and miscued words displayed this way enables you to easily recognize common miscue patterns.

4. Add up the points to determine the total miscue points.

Note: There is a debate as to whether any points should be deducted for meaningful miscues. Studies by Stephen Kucer have repeatedly demonstrated the limitations of word accuracy in determining students' ability to comprehend and create meaning with text (Kucer, 2013, 2016, 2017). In examining the relationship between reading miscues and comprehension, Kucer found that students' comprehension was significantly better on passages in which there were meaningful miscues when compared to (1) passages containing no miscues or (2) passages containing meaning-disrupting miscues. This was because meaningful miscues indicated students were processing the text at deeper levels for meaning compared to surface-level accuracy. For now, I deduct half a point for meaningful miscues, but Kucer's research made me question this.

Student: ______________________ **Date:** ___________ **Level of passage:** __________

Target word	Miscue	MDM*	MM*
	Totals**		

***Key:** MDM = meaning-disrupting miscue; MM = meaningful miscue.

****MDM = 1 miscue point; MM = half of a miscue point.**

Total miscue points:_______

FIGURE 16.7. Page 1 of an MA analyzing sheet.

When I do a miscue analysis, I also like to record the number of grammatically correct miscues (GCM) on the MA analyzing sheet. (Most others do not.) I simply put a "G" in parentheses next to the word in the miscue column. These are of interest to me because they provide solid evidence as to the existence of the syntactic cueing system being used. They are also helpful in noting change over time. Here I note changes in the percentage of GCMs to indicate increased use of the syntactic cueing system.

5. On page 2 of the MA analyzing sheet (Figure 16.8), record the number of self-corrections. Self-corrections are good as they indicate metacognition. This is a mature reading behavior. Then, record the number of meaningful miscues. Meaningful miscues represent mature reading behaviors and also indicate that the reader is creating meaning with print while using syntactical and semantic clues.

Student: ______________________ **Date:** __________ **Level of passage:** __________

Totals

Number of self-corrections	
Number of meaningful miscues	
Fluency (words per minute)	

Miscues

Total number of miscue points	
Total number of words minus miscue points	
Total number of words	
Percentage of nonmiscued words	%

Observations and recommendations:

FIGURE 16.8. Page 2 of an MA analyzing sheet.

An increase in meaningful miscues can indicate movement away from word-by-word reading to reading for meaning.

Step 4: Identify Fluency Rate (Words per Minute)

1. Record the time it took for students to complete the passage.

2. Divide the time (in seconds) by 60. For example, if Pat read a passage in 90 seconds, you would divide 90 by 60: 90 ÷ 60 = 1.5 minutes.

3. Divide this (1.5) by the total number of words. If Pat read a total of 119 words in 1.5 minutes, you would divide 119 by 1.5: 119 ÷ 1.5 = 79 WPM.

4. Record WPM.

Step 5: Record the Percentage of Nonmiscued Words

1. Record the total miscue points.

2. Subtract total miscue points from the total number of words in the passage to find the total number of nonmiscued words.

3. Record the total number of words in the passage.

4. Divide the total number of nonmiscued words by the total number of words to find the percentage of nonmiscued words the student read in the passage.

Step 6: Record Your Observations and Recommendations

1. Record relevant observations related to students' nonverbal language, behaviors, affect, demeanor, circumstances, or any other data you feel may be significant. (Some teachers prefer to record observations as the student is reading.)

2. Record any relevant observations related to word identification. The questions in Figure 16.9 can be used to guide you.

3. Record your observations related to fluency. The questions in Figure 16.10 can be used to guide you.

4. Finally, based on the data and your analysis, describe the types of instruction and activities that you would recommend for the student (see the example in the Appendix at the end of this chapter).

COMPREHENSION

The MA above provides data related to word identification and reading fluency. A different type of measure should be included to get a sense of students'

1. What does the student do to identify words?
2. Does the student use context clues?
3. Does the student recognize word parts?
4. Does the student use onsets to identify unknown words?
5. Does the student overuse phonics?
6. Does the student self-correct?
7. Are the miscues schema-related?
8. What types of miscues does the student make?
9. Does the student recognize and use morphemes (prefixes, suffixes, and roots)?
10. Does the student correctly identify the onset or beginnings of miscued words?

FIGURE 16.9. Listening for word identification strategies.

1. Is the reading choppy, word by word?
2. Is the reading choppy, letter by letter?
3. Does the student pause at the end of sentences? (prosody)
4. Is the inflection appropriate to the sentence or passage? (prosody)
5. Does the student pause to check for understanding? (metacognition)

FIGURE 16.10. Listening for reading fluency.

comprehension levels. (Again, comprehension and word identification levels can differ.) Two options for assessing reading comprehension are described below: (1) retelling charts and (2) a maze.

Retelling Charts

Retelling charts are one type of measure that can be used to get a sense of students' ability to create meaning with print. These are individually administered measures. Retelling charts are designed by the teacher and should be based on the types of reading material with which students are familiar. Different types of charts should be used for narrative and expository text.

Story-Retelling Charts

A story-retelling chart is used for narrative text. This chart is designed by identifying the important characters, settings, and events within a graded piece of narrative text (see Figure 16.11). Here a student reads the story and is then asked to recall these story elements. Points are earned for prompted and unprompted responses.

Name: ________________________ Grade: __________ Date: __________

Story Title: ________________________ Reading Level: ________________

Context: Story read by: child silently ____, orally ____ Story read to child ____

	UNPROMPTED	PROMPTED
CHARACTERS: 2 points each.		
1.		
2.		
3.		
4.		
5.		
SETTING: 2 points each.		
1.		
2.		
3.		
EVENTS: 2 points each.		
1.		
2.		
3.		
4.		
5.		
6.		
TOTAL POINTS: ____/____ = ____%	____/____	____/____

Key: *Unprompted* = 2 points; *Prompted* = 1 point.

Note: The number of characters, settings, and events will vary depending on the story. You may need more or fewer numbers of rows than are on this chart. Please adjust your story-retelling chart accordingly.

Independent reading level = 90–100% accuracy
Instruction level = 75–89% accuracy
Frustration level = 74% or lower

FIGURE 16.11. Story-retelling chart.

Nonfiction Retelling Charts

A nonfiction retelling chart is used for expository text. This chart is designed by identifying the important concepts or big ideas within a graded passage of expository text (see Figure 16.12). Critical supporting details are listed below the idea or concept. After reading, identify the important concept or idea, then ask the student to explain or tell you about it. The expository-retelling chart is scored in the same way as the story-retelling chart.

The Illusion of Objectivity

Is there a bit of subjectivity in designing and interpreting story-retelling charts and retelling charts? Yes. However, subjectivity exists in all measures of comprehension simply in terms of the passages selected and the questions that are asked. Also, as illustrated by the top-down flow of information in the neurocognitive model of reading, how one constructs meaning and what is remembered are highly influenced by one's background knowledge. Think about your own recall or understanding when reading a news article, journal article, or textbook. The elements that you attend to are highly influenced by your beliefs, interests, and background knowledge.

Maze

A maze is a validated measure for comprehension that can be given simultaneously in large or small groups (Deno & Marston, 2006; Vaughn & Fletcher, 2012). A maze uses a graded reading passage consisting of 125 words or more. After the first sentence, every fifth (or seventh) word is deleted. Students are supplied three choices: the correct target word, an incorrect word that has the same grammatical function as the target word, and an incorrect word that has a different grammatical function (see Figure 16.13). You can purchase commercially prepared maze materials; however, you can also create your own using graded passages that represent the types of material with which students are familiar.

FLUENCY

The final diagnostic area to consider is reading fluency. Listening to students read aloud should provide you all the data necessary to determine if fluency is a problem area. The questions in Figure 16.10 above can be used as a guide here. You can quantify your observations by using WPM (words per minute) rates with graded passages as described in step 4. But keep in mind that fluency, like word identification and comprehension, is affected or influenced by what one is reading.

Name: ______________________ Grade: __________ Date: ____________

Story Title: ______________________ Reading Level: ______________________

Context: Story read by: child silently ____, orally ____ Story read to child ____

	UNPROMPTED	PROMPTED
TOPIC:		
CONCEPT:		
•		
•		
•		
CONCEPT:		
•		
•		
•		
CONCEPT:		
•		
•		
•		
TOTAL POINTS: ___/___ = ___%	___/___	___/___

Key: *Unprompted* = 2 points; *Prompted* = 1 point.

Independent reading level = 90–100% accuracy
Instruction level = 75–89% accuracy
Frustration level = 74% or lower

FIGURE 16.12. Nonfiction retelling chart.

The mouse came out. He was hungry. He [**when — was — dog**] looking for some cheese [**to — wet — in**] eat. He ran across [**then — sat — the**] floor.

Prairie dogs are small, burrowing rodents. They live in short-grass [**prairies — oceans — big**] and the high plains [**said — in — of**] the western USA and Mexico. [**Her — They — Up**] will eat all sorts [**of — it — many**] vegetables and fruits.

Levels

Independent level = 85% and above
Instructional level = 50–84%
Frustration level = 49% or less

FIGURE 16.13. Examples of maze passages.

FINAL WORD

An effective reading diagnostic should provide data about students' performance in the three reading deficit areas: comprehension, word identification, and fluency. This data should inform instruction. That is, based on the data collected, you should have specific ideas as to the types of strategies to use. I have not found an instrument better able to do this than some form of a diagnostic reading assessment or informal reading inventory.

The Appendix that follows is the report I wrote after giving a DRA to a fourth-grade student, Pamela Brown (not her real name). This report was sent to her classroom teacher and reading specialist. At this time, Pamela had not been formally identified as needing special education services. The goals and benchmark ideas provide suggestions that could be used for an individualized education program (IEP), but that was not the intended purpose here.

APPENDIX: REPORT

Pamela Brown is in the fourth grade. On Friday, September 10, 2019, I had the opportunity to meet Pam at Minnesota School. I asked her the following questions:

Q: Tell me about your reading.

A: Sometimes I don't know the words.

Q: Is reading sometimes hard for you?

A: Yeah.

Q: What makes reading hard for you?

A: When there's a lot of it.

Q: What do you do when you come to a word you don't know?

A: I kind of sound it out.

Q: What kinds of things do you like to read?

A: I like to read chapter books kind of.

Q: Is there any particular book you like?

A: *Baby Mouse* (*very enthusiastically*).

I did an analysis of her reading using a DRA. Pam was asked to read a word list at the pre-first-grade level. She correctly identified 20 out of 20 words. I then moved up to a word list at RL 1. She was able to identify 15 out of 20 words. Based on these results, I asked Pam to orally read a passage at RL 1.

Out of 250 words in this passage, she correctly identified 245 or 98% of the words. All the miscued words fit grammatically within the sentence. For example, she substituted *when* for *then*. This is good news. This tells us that Pam is using syntax (grammar and word order) to help her create meaning with print. This is a mature reading behavior. Also, this indicates that her word identification level is at the second-grade level.

I was very pleased to see two self-corrections. First, Pam paused when she realized the miscued word did not make sense in the sentence. She then corrected her miscue. This tells us that she is using metacognition (she is monitoring her comprehension). This is mature reading behavior. Second, four of Pam's miscues were meaningful miscues. This means that she inserted a word that still made sense within the sentence. This is good news. It indicates that she is using context and word order to make sense of what she is reading.

Pam's oral ready was slow and choppy. She made many pauses and seemed to get frustrated at times. Her reading rate was 55 WPM. This indicates that we need to work on reading fluency.

Pam scored 94% on her comprehension measure. This also is good news. It tells us that Pam is reading for meaning instead of just trying to sound out words.

Word Identification

- **Recommended annual goal:** Pam will consistently identify 90% or more of the words in passages at RL 3.
- **Recommended benchmarks:**
  1. Identify 98% at RL 2.
  2. Identify 50% at RL 3.
  3. Identify 80% at RL 3.
- **Recommended measures:** Word identification will be measured using a running record on graded passages of 250 words or more.

Fluency

- **Recommended annual goal:** We would like to see Pam consistently reading 66 WPM at RL3.
- **Recommended benchmarks:**
  1. 75 WPM at RL 2.
  2. 40 WPM at RL 3.
  3. 66 WPM at RL 3.
- **Recommended measures:** Fluency will be measured using WPM rates on graded passages of 250 words or more.

Recommendations for Home

1. Daily reading practice. Even 10 minutes of reading practice a night will be helpful. Keep it fun. It is imperative that we not frustrate Pam. Find books that are at her independent level or below (first or second grade). Encourage her to select books that are of interest and that have plenty of pictures. If Pam seems to struggle, read aloud with her, pointing to words on the page.

2. Read to Pam. This will help her develop a sense of sentence structure and grammar as well as increase her vocabulary.
3. Create a chart at home to keep track of the books read. Celebrate every three books or five books read. Set goals for the week. Celebrate meeting weekly goals as well.

Instruction and Intervention Activities

It would be effective to have extensive overlap between classroom instruction and a reading intervention. It is recommended that Pam have a minimum of three 30-minute reading intervention sessions each week (five is better) consisting of the activities below. (Not every activity should be used each day.) Each is briefly described, as follows:

- **Language experience activities (LEA).** Each intervention session will include an LEA. There must be a minimum of five sentences. Pam will reread her daily entry until she achieves fluency. The paragraph/story is then used for analytic phonics mini-lessons.

- **Word-building activities.** The word-building activities are presented on PowerPoint and based on the target vowel sounds. The target onset-rimes are found within the context of a sentence. Sight words are reinforced here.

- **Cloze activities.** Cloze activities are presented on PowerPoint and used to reinforce the target vowel sound. After completing the cloze, students should reread this sentence until fluency is achieved.

- **Maze activities.** Maze activities are presented on PowerPoint and used to reinforce the target vowel sound. After completing the maze, students should reread this sentence until fluency is achieved. This activity should be briskly paced and relatively brief, lasting just 3–8 minutes.

- **Fluency activities.** Included are a series of Really Silly Stories (RSS) divided into sections. Students are to read one section every day. In each section, 30- and 40-word increments are designated with boldfaced type and underlines. Students read to their designated target three times. Each attempt is timed, and results are recorded on a graph.

- **Sentence mix-up.** A mixed-up sentence appears on top of the PowerPoint. Students are presented clues, one word at a time. Sentences are used to reinforce target vowel sounds. Students are shown additional clues until they can identify the mix-up sentence.

- **Reading practice.** Five to 10 minutes of reading practice will be included in every intervention session. This will build on the reading practice in the classroom and at home. Reading practice enables students to practice newly learned skills in authentic reading contexts. Also, students' LEA stories can also be used to practice reading.

CHAPTER 17

Progress Monitoring

WHAT IT IS

Progress monitoring is the process used to assess and document the progress that students are making in any given area. With any reading intervention, you are looking to assess students' responsiveness to the types of strategies used as well as to document their progress. You are asking questions such as: Is the intervention working? What sorts of things have been effective? What is not working? What changes need to be made? How much progress has been made? Are we meeting the defined benchmark? Using the data collected as part of progress monitoring to answer these types of questions is an example of *data-based decision making* (see Chapter 21).

Progress monitoring involves collecting small bits of data along the way, not massive amounts of data all at once. It is recommended that data generally be collected every 2 to 4 weeks. This means that the measures used need to be pragmatic in terms of implementation and scoring. This chapter describes some simple progress monitoring measures used for word identification, comprehension, fluency, and student attitude and perception.

WORD IDENTIFICATION

Noting the differences between word identification and word recognition described in Chapter 4, we use the term *word identification* here because that is the term used most often to describe students' ability to recognize and identify words while reading. For word identification, two basic approaches are described here. The first one documents students' ability to identify words while engaged in a more authentic reading activity (running records). The second approach documents students' ability to identify words with specific letter sounds and letter patterns.

Running Records

Running records and miscue analyses have similar elements but are slightly different. Whereas a miscue analysis examines the types of miscues students make, a *running record* (see below) simply documents the number of words correctly identified on the oral reading of a graded passage. This provides a general sense of students' reading level as it pertains to word identification. The directions are as follows:

1. Select a graded passage that is at students' independent level. Here they can identify at least 98% of the words. The three levels for word identification are presented in Figure 17.1. If you are unsure, estimate low.
2. Students read the passage aloud. These sessions are not audio recorded. You should have a copy of the text students are reading to use for documentation. Just like the miscue analysis, you can type the text on a single sheet of paper or make a copy of the book or passage.
3. Underline the words that are incorrectly identified. Miscues are not analyzed here. Divide the number of correctly identified words by the total number of words to find the percentage of words correctly identified (see Figure 17.2).
4. Move up until you find students' instruction level. Here, they would be able to recognize 97% of the words or less.

Running records provide a general sense of students' independent and instructional levels for word identification. And because running records enable students to use the semantic, syntactic, and phonological cueing systems, it is a more valid measure when compared to word identification measures in which students are asked to identify words in isolation. Two ways to use running records—(1) pre–post measure and (2) change over time—are described below.

- **Independent level:** Students are able to identify 98% or more of the words.
- **Instructional level:** Students are able to identify 90–97% of these words.
- **Frustration level:** Students are able to identify 89% or fewer of these words.

FIGURE 17.1. Reading levels for word identification.

SALLY'S ICE CREAM

Dick was sitting in a chair. He was reading a book. Dick liked to read books. Sally came into the room. She had a bowl of ice cream. She walked over to Dick and dumped the bowl of ice cream on his head.

Dick looked up "Oh Sally! What have you done?"

"I've dumped a bowl of ice cream on your head," she answered.

"But why?" asked Dick. "Why did you dump ice cream on my head?"

Sally said, "Because we don't have any milk."

"Oh," said Dick. "That makes sense."

"Yes it does," said Sally.

Just then Jane came into the room. "Hello Dick. Hello Sally," she said.

"Hello Jane," Sally and Dick both said.

Jane looked at Dick and said, "Did you know you have ice cream on your head?"

"Yes I do," said Dick. "We're out of milk."

"Oh," said Jane. "I see." She turned to leave and said, "Goodbye Dick. Goodbye Sally."

"Goodbye Jane" they both said.

158/162

RL 2 – 162 words
157 words correct or above = independent level
149 to 156 words correct = instruction level
148 words correct or below = frustrate level

FIGURE 17.2. Example of a running record.

Pre–Post Measure

The first method for using running records for progress monitoring is to look at change over time using the same text. Here, a passage is read to get an initial baseline score for word identification. This passage should be at students' instructional level. Then, 2 to 4 weeks later the same passage is read. Changes are recorded (see Figure 17.3). Using the same documenting sheet for both reads will enable you to note specific changes.

Student: ______________________________

Title: ____________________ Reading Level: ____________________

Assessment Date:

Number of words correctly identified	Total number of words	Percentage

Assessment Date:

Number of words correctly identified	Total number of words	Percentage

FIGURE 17.3. Pre–post for running record.

Date							
Level							
Number of words correctly identified							
Total number of words							
Percentage							

FIGURE 17.4. Change over time for running record.

Change over Time

The second method for using running records for progress monitoring is to look at change over time using different texts. Here you would not use the same passage but would instead have students reading different passages, moving up when they are able to consistently read at the independent level. The date and the level of the passage used are recorded (see Figure 17.4).

Documenting Letter Sounds and Letter Patterns

Because of program requirements, it may sometimes be necessary to focus on specific reading subskills related to letter sounds or letter patterns. Two options are presented here: (1) maze sentences and (2) pre–post word lists.

Words in a Maze Sentence

To use maze sentences for progress monitoring, design simple sentences in which the maze target contains three exemplars of words with target letter patterns (see Figure 17.5). Students will be able to use semantic and syntactic clues here as well as letter–sound and letter–pattern clues to identify the correct word. And since this is how they will encounter these words in real-life contexts, it is a more valid measure than presenting the words in isolation. As well, maze sentences are fairly pragmatic to use since students can complete them independently.

Maze sentences can be used as a pre–post measure like the running record above or to document students' ability to identify words with specific letter sounds and patterns.

1. She was [**mad — mat — flag**].
2. Please come [**back — pan — fan**] here.
3. Sit on the [**call — tap — mat**].
4. Grab the [**sank — call — ball**].

FIGURE 17.5. Assessment for word identification for short *a*.

Pre–Post Word Lists

The last method described here for progress monitoring for word identification is the least desirable in terms of validity and pragmatics. Here you present a student with a list of words containing one or more of the target letter sounds or letter patterns. The student is then asked to read the list (see Figure 17.6). Check marks are used to indicate words incorrectly identified. The same list is then used as a post-unit measure to indicate growth. As stated previously, when reading real texts in the real world, we rarely (if ever) encounter single words in isolation. Words are always found in a meaningful context. Letter clues are always used in conjunction with semantic and syntactic clues.

COMPREHENSION

The maze described in Chapter 16 is the simplest and most pragmatic method to use to monitor progress related to comprehension. Just like measures above, the same maze passage can be used as a pre–post measure (see Figure 17.7). Also like the measures above, different maze passages of similar levels can be used to document progress over time (see Figure 17.8). The retelling charts described in Chapter 16 can be used in similar fashion.

Pre–Post: Short *a*

Student: ______________________

Preassessment date: ______________________

Short *a*

____ mad	____ map	____ flat	____ ram
____ back	____ sank	____ rat	____ tap
____ pan	____ flag	____ ball	____ grab
____ glad	____ mat	____ call	____ fan

Postassessment date: ______________________

Short *a*

____ mad	____ map	____ flat	____ ram
____ back	____ sank	____ rat	____ tap
____ pan	____ flag	____ ball	____ grab
____ glad	____ mat	____ call	____ fan

FIGURE 17.6. Pre–post for words in isolation.

Comprehension: Maze

Student: ____

Title: ________________________ Reading Level: __________

Assessment Date:

Percentage

Assessment Date:

Percentage

Levels
Independent level = 85% and above
Instructional level = 50–84%
Frustration level = 49% or less

FIGURE 17.7. Pre–post for maze.

FLUENCY

Daily SPF or WPM fluency scores are of some interest (see Chapter 12). But for progress monitoring, you will get a more accurate sense of students' fluency gains by using cold reads of graded passages. Here you provide a graded or leveled passage and ask the student to read for 1 minute. The number of words is recorded.

As described in Chapter 15, the focus here is only on reading rate, not word recognition accuracy. Thus, WPM scores are used, not WCPM scores. And like

Comprehension: Maze

Student: ____

Date										
Level										
Percentage										

Levels
Independent level = 85% and above
Instructional level = 50–84%
Frustration level = 49% or less

FIGURE 17.8. Change over time for maze.

the above, the same passage can be used as a pre–post measure (see Figure 17.9). You can also use passages at the same levels to show change over time (see Figure 17.10).

STUDENT PERCEPTION/ATTITUDE

The last area for progress monitoring is one that is often excluded: student attitude and perception. For progress monitoring, use a rating survey chart similar to those described in Chapter 16; however (see Figure 17.11), here you would include a score total. Total scores are recorded to show change over time. You can also record changes in each element of the rating scale (see Figure 17.12).

Fluency

Student: ______________________________

Title: ______________________ Reading Level: __________

Assessment Date:

WPM

Assessment Date:

WPM

FIGURE 17.9. Pre–post for fluency.

Fluency: WPM

Student: ______________________________

Date										
Level										
WPM										

FIGURE 17.10. Change over time for fluency.

____ I enjoy reading.
____ I am able to read.
____ I understand what I read.
____ Books can be interesting.
____ I know most of the words on the page.
____ I know what to do when I don't know a word.

____ Total

Key: 5 = strongly agree, 4 = agree, 3 = don't know, 2 = disagree, 1 = strongly disagree.

FIGURE 17.11. Rating scale to document attitude and perception.

Date							
Enjoyment							
Ability							
Understanding							
Interest							
Word recognition							
Word identification							
Total							

FIGURE 17.12. Attitude and perception change over time.

FINAL WORD

As you start recording these scores for progress monitoring, beware of the allure of numbers. Attaching a number to something does not make that thing any more real. Scores should be used to document what you already know to be true. That is, you are a kid watcher using scores to document what you are seeing as you interact with readers. To really document the progress of readers, I would also recommend using portfolio assessment that includes authentic forms of assessment. However, this is the topic for another chapter in another book.

PART IV
INDIVIDUALIZED EDUCATION PROGRAMS

CHAPTER 18

Individualized Education Programs for Reading

Individualized education programs (IEPs) are plans developed for students with disabilities to ensure that (1) they have educational goals germane to their specific needs, (2) there is a plan for achieving these goals, and (3) there are measurable benchmarks to make sure they are making progress toward these goals. Figure 18.1 contains four IEP elements required by IDEA 2004 that pertain to reading interventions: (1) present level of performance, (2) measurable annual goals, (3) benchmarks and assessment, and (4) special education and related services. These elements are addressed in this chapter.

INDIVIDUALIZED EDUCATION PROGRAMS

To be of any use, an IEP must be simple, clear, pragmatic, and purposeful. It should also address five basic questions:

1. What is the student's current state?
2. What is the student's desired state?
3. How do we get there?
4. Are we getting there?
5. How do we know when we have arrived?

How each of these questions is addressed in the context of an IEP is described.

1. A statement of the child's present levels of academic achievement and functional performance including:
   a. How the child's disability affects the child's involvement and progress in the general education curriculum (i.e., the same curriculum as for nondisabled children) **or**
   b. For preschool children, as appropriate, how the disability affects the child's participation in appropriate activities.

2. A statement of measurable annual goals, including academic and functional goals designed to:
   a. Meet the child's needs that result from the child's disability to enable the child to be involved in and make progress in the general education curriculum.
   b. Meet each of the child's other educational needs that result from the child's disability.

For children with disabilities who take alternate assessments aligned to alternate achievement standards (in addition to the annual goals), a description of benchmarks or short-term objectives.

3. A description of:
   a. How the child's progress toward meeting the annual goals will be measured.
   b. When periodic reports on the progress the child is making toward meeting the annual goals will be provided such as through the use of quarterly or other periodic reports, concurrent with the issuance of report cards.

4. A statement of the special education and related services and supplementary aids and services, based on peer-reviewed research to the extent practicable, to be provided to the child, or on behalf of the child, and a statement of the program modifications or supports for school personnel that will be provided to enable the child:
   a. To advance appropriately toward attaining the annual goals.
   b. To be involved in and make progress in the general education curriculum and to participate in extracurricular and other nonacademic activities.
   c. To be educated and participate with other children with disabilities and nondisabled children in extracurricular and other nonacademic activities.

FIGURE 18.1. Required elements of an IEP under IDEA 2004. Retrieved from *https://sites.ed.gov/idea/topic-areas/#IEP.*

PRESENT LEVEL OF PERFORMANCE

Present Level of Academic Achievement and Functional Performance

This first part of an IEP is usually referred to as simply present level of performance (PLOP). PLOP addresses the first question above: *What is the student's current state?* PLOP data for reading should include students' approximate reading grade level. A grade-level descriptor should be used instead of some other leveling system such as Fountas and Pinnell, Lexile level, or percentile ranking. This makes the information more accessible to parents. Reading grade levels provide a starting point and enable comparisons to be made throughout the year and from year to year.

PLOP for reading should also include information relative to the three deficit areas for reading: fluency, word identification, and comprehension. This is why data gleaned from a DRA are essential here as they enable you to create goals that target the specific deficit area. Data for each of the deficit areas should be reported in the context of a specific grade level. For example, on a passage at the second-grade level, Sam read 78 WPM (fluency). He identified 248 out of 251 words or 98% (word identification). His comprehension score was 100% (comprehension).

Federal regulations related to IDEA require multiple measures to be used to determine eligibility for special services. Often, standardized test scores are overrepresented in describing students' PLOP. But using more than one type of standardized test does not necessarily mean you are using multiple measures. Instead, you are using the same type of measure multiple times. To use the analogy of the blind men and the elephant, you would be feeling the same part of the elephant multiple times (see Figure 18.2). Instead, including multiple types of data provides a more complete picture. Data here could include things such as (1) informal measures, (2) running records, (3) formative assessments, (4) classroom observations–anecdotal records, and (5) work samples (Minnesota Department of Education, 2013).

FIGURE 18.2. Using only standardized test scores.

Qualitative Data

Qualitative data, such as those described above, provide context for the quantitative standardized test data included in an IEP. Besides those already identified, you could also include things such as observations related to reading fluency and reading prosody, reading behaviors, types of things the student likes to read or had read, general demeanor and attitudes, observations related to strategies used to identify words or comprehend text, student interview data, metacognitive behaviors, nonverbal behaviors, anecdotal records, or anything else deemed relevant to that student as a reader. Keep in mind that students' strengths as well as areas to work on should be described. This enables instruction to build on students' strengths in addressing deficit areas.

General Education Curriculum

Also described in the PLOP should be how the disability affects involvement and progress in the general education curriculum. For reading, this description should include how the disability affects progress in the reading curriculum as well as other curriculum areas where reading is used.

MEASURABLE ANNUAL GOALS

Measurable annual goals (MAG) addresses the second basic question: *What is the student's desired state?* In other words, where would you like the student to be by the end of the year? Establishing appropriate goals based on PLOP is the most important part of an IEP. Yet this is the part of the IEP that is most often done incorrectly with struggling readers.

A Wrestling Analogy

As a once-upon-a-time wrestling coach, let me first offer a wrestling analogy: Like reading, wrestling has three main elements: (1) taking an opponent down, (2) turning the opponent or pinning moves, and (3) escaping from the bottom. If we were to design a wresting IEP, just like a reading IEP the focus would be on the deficit area. One could be strong in one or two of these areas; however, weaknesses in the others would be detrimental to winning matches. Thus, if take-downs was a deficit area, it would be silly to spend additional practice time working on pinning moves. Just like an IEP for reading, an IEP for wrestling should have a goal specifically related to the deficit area: in this case, take-downs.

Let us say that Sally is a high school wrestler. In her matches, her ability to escape from the bottom and turn opponents is good. However, she has a hard time taking opponents down to the mat. In her previous year of wrestling, she was only able to score 14 take-downs. An appropriate annual wrestling IEP goal for Sally would be to score 25 take-downs. An inappropriate annual goal would to include things related to pinning or escapes. It would also be inappropriate for the goal to focus on individual take-down moves or parts of moves (this would be analogous to reading subskills). The goal is not to learn individual moves; rather, it is to be able to use those moves in a match to take opponents down to the mat. There are wrestlers who know just a few take-down moves, but they perform them so well that they are able to be successful in authentic wrestling situations. Likewise, there are wrestlers who know a great number of moves, but in authentic wrestling match conditions, they are not able to put them together to take opponents down to the mat. The focus should always be on the macro, not the micro. Micro goals, while sometimes helpful, do not address the macro goal, which is to be a wrestler who wins matches and/or a reader who creates meaning with print under authentic conditions.

Focus on Deficit Area or Areas

To be of any practical use, reading IEP goals need to be directly related to the deficit area identified by the diagnostic assessment. This again illustrates the importance of good diagnostic data. For example, if fluency has been identified as a deficit area, there should be an IEP goal directly related to fluency (see below). If there are deficits in all three areas (i.e., fluency, word identification, and comprehension), there should be a separate goal for each area. As stated previously, this is because the methods used to address each area are different. In the same way, if one or more of the three areas is not problematic for a student, that area should not be included in any part of the IEP.

Anything not related to reading (such as behavior, writing, or spelling) should not be included in an IEP goal for reading. Even if a bothersome behavior in reading class interferes with learning, a behavior problem requires a behavioral goal, not a reading goal. (Problem behaviors are often a result of frustration and humiliation caused by the wrong type of instruction. With appropriate instruction, inappropriate behaviors may diminish or disappear.) As well, even though writing is an important part of instruction and interventions for reading (see Chapter 11), it should not be included in a goal for reading. If writing is a deficit area, it should have its own goal. This is where many IEPs for reading get it completely wrong. A MAG is not a place for dumping. To be effective, a MAG IEP goal should be directly related to the deficit area and *nothing* else.

Goals versus Standards or Subskills

Allow me to clear up a common area of confusion: Reading standards or reading subskills are *not* appropriate goals. Yes, federal law requires goals to be aligned with a state's academic content standards (below), but this is much different from replicating a standard as a goal. For example, the goals in Figure 18.3 are all based on Grade 2 Common Core State Standards (CCSS). While these may be appropriate elements to

- Pat will be able to distinguish long and short vowels when reading regularly spelled one-syllable words.
- Pat will be able to decode words with common prefixes and suffixes.
- Pat will be able to use context to confirm or self-correct word recognition and understanding.
- Pat will be able to compare and contrast the point of view from different stories.
- Pat will be able to determine the theme of a story and summarize the text.
- Pat will be able to read grade-level text with accuracy and expression.

FIGURE 18.3. Examples of inappropriate IEP goals for reading.

include in a reading curriculum, they are a means to an end, not an end. Mastering the distinction between long and short vowel sounds tells me nothing about a student's ability to (1) identify words in an authentic reading situation, (2) create meaning in an authentic reading situation, or (3) read fluently in an authentic reading situation.

As stated previously, IEP goals should always focus on the macro. Reading standards or subskills may be helpful in achieving the macro, but not always. Academic standards can be helpful (see below), but not always. Again, an academic standard replicated as an IEP goal is ineffective in helping students become better readers.

Alignment with Academic Content Standards

In 2007, the U.S. Department of Education issued an update to IDEA 2004 that stated, among other things, that the goals for an IEP should be aligned with a state's academic content standards (U.S. Department of Education, 2007). This ruling was clarified again in a November 16, 2015, letter from the U.S. Department of Education Office of Special Education and Rehabilitative Services:

> Ensuring that all children, including children with disabilities, are held to rigorous academic standards and high expectations is a shared responsibility for all of us. To help make certain that children with disabilities are held to high expectations and have **meaningful access to a State's academic content standards**, we write to clarify that an individualized education program (IEP) for an eligible child with a disability under the Individuals with Disabilities Education Act (IDEA) must be **aligned with the State's academic content standards** for the grade in which the child is enrolled. Research has demonstrated that children with disabilities who struggle in reading and mathematics can **successfully learn grade-level content and make significant academic progress** when appropriate instruction, services, and supports are provided. Conversely, low expectations can lead to children with disabilities receiving less challenging instruction that reflects below grade-level content standards, and thereby not learning what they need to succeed at the grade in which they are enrolled.

There is much to unpack here:

Inclusive Education Model

This regulation states that students with disabilities (behavioral, learning, physical, or other) should have meaningful access to a state's academic content standards in all content areas. For reading, this means that they should not be subjected to instruction that overemphasizes direct instruction of low-level skills. Neither should they be segregated and given a slowed-down, simplified curriculum that would impede their progress in learning important academic concepts and skills. To do so would be to write a prescription for low achievement. (Yet this is what too often occurs in remedial or special education services.) Instead, the regulation states that all students are to have access to challenging curriculums (U.S. Department of Education, 2007).

However, a challenging curriculum is different from a frustrating curriculum. Students who are struggling learners should not be dumped into a general education curriculum without accommodations or modifications of the curriculum. As stated above, instruction must be appropriate. One way to do so is to use an inclusive education model (Peterson & Hittie, 2010). Here, the same content is presented to all students but is differentiated to meet the varied needs of all learners. Strategies such as universal design for learning (UDL), tiered assignments, shared reading, and contract learning are just some of the pedagogical strategies that can be used to differentiate a common curriculum in a multilevel inclusive education classroom. For literacy, two instructional models support multilevel instruction: Four Blocks™ and Reading Workshop. Both involve an emphasis on self-selected reading, authentic writing, discussion, direct instruction, and flexible grouping for skills work. As stated in the letter excerpt above, struggling learners can successfully learn grade-level content and make significant academic progress; however, this only occurs when the instruction is appropriate.

Alignment, Not Replication

An IEP must be in alignment with a state's academic content standard; however, alignment does not mean replication. Alignment in this context means that it addresses a state's academic content standard; however, the goal related to the standard should be "restricted in scope or complexity" in order to make it "ambitious but achievable."

To illustrate, the IEP goal for comprehension in Figure 18.4 is aligned with two fourth-grade CCSS related to reading literature, yet it has been modified so that it is reasonable and achievable. It addresses the more global purpose, which is to identify story grammar elements, but it does so in a way that is appropriate for Sam. In this way, Sam might actually benefit from it. Imagine that.

The IEP goal for word identification in Figure 18.5 is aligned with four fourth-grade CCSS related to reading foundational skills. It has also been modified so that it is reasonable and achievable.

IEP Goal:

On a graded reader (RL 3) using narrative text, Sam will identify major characters, events, and settings with at least 90% success.

Aligned Standards:

CCSS.ELA-LITERACY.RL.4.3

Describe in depth a character, setting, or event in a story or drama, drawing on specific details in the text (e.g., a character's thoughts, words, or actions).

CCSS.ELA-LITERACY.RL.4.10

By the end of the year, read and comprehend literature, including stories, dramas, and poetry, in the grades 4–5 text complexity band proficiently, with scaffolding as needed at the high end of the range.

FIGURE 18.4. Example of a goal for comprehension aligned with the CCSS.

IEP Goal:

On a graded reader (RL 3) with at least 200 words, Sam will correctly identify 90% of the words.

Aligned Standards:

CCSS.ELA-LITERACY.RF.4.3

Know and apply grade-level phonics and word analysis skills in decoding words.

CCSS.ELA-LITERACY.RF.4.3.A

Use combined knowledge of all letter–sound correspondences, syllabication patterns, and morphology (e.g., roots and affixes) to read accurately unfamiliar multisyllabic words in context and out of context.

CCSS.ELA-LITERACY.RF.4.4.C

Use context to confirm or self-correct word recognition and understanding, rereading as necessary.

CCSS.ELA-LITERACY.RF.4.4

Read with sufficient accuracy and fluency to support comprehension.

CCSS.ELA-LITERACY.RF.4.4.B

Read grade-level prose and poetry orally with accuracy, appropriate rate, and expression on successive readings.

FIGURE 18.5. Example of a goal for word identification aligned with the CCSS.

IEP Goal:

Sam will read 75 WPM at RL 3.

Aligned Standards:

CCSS.ELA-LITERACY.RF.4.4

Read with sufficient accuracy and fluency to support comprehension.

CCSS.ELA-LITERACY.RF.4.4.B

Read grade-level prose and poetry orally with accuracy, appropriate rate, and expression on successive readings.

FIGURE 18.6. Example of a goal for reading fluency aligned with the CCSS.

The IEP goal for fluency in Figure 18.6 is aligned with two fourth-grade CCSS related to reading foundational skills. It has been modified so that it is reasonable and achievable.

Alignment, Not Grade-Level Performance

This ruling does *not* say that IEP goals should have students performing at the grade level in which they are presently enrolled. This is a common misunderstanding. For example, if a fifth-grade student was reading at the second-grade level, this ruling does not require IEP goals for reading to have this student reading at the fifth-grade level by the end of the year. To ask a student to improve three reading grade levels in a single year would most likely present an unattainable goal as well as a cruel one. The only outcomes of such a goal would be feelings of failure, frustration, and humiliation.

Humpty Dumpty

A quick note about academic standards: A few carefully defined academic standards are good. They provide teachers with a general sense of the skills and concepts that can be taught at specific grade levels. But this does not mean that more academic standards are better. Having too many academic standards creates a splintered, unfocused curriculum. In addition, many of the academic standards for literacy developed by state or national organizations actually impede students' ability to create meaning with print. The underinformed assumption associated with overreliance on academic standards is that if students master each of the little standards, they will be able to put them all together to achieve reading mastery relative to that grade level. This Humpty Dumptian thinking is built upon the fallacy of reductionism (Poplin, 1988).

Teachers must always use their professional knowledge and expertise as well as their understanding of the students with whom they work to make professional decisions about which academic standards to attend to and which to dance lightly upon. Abdicating our professional responsibility in this regard is not in the best interest of our students or society. We are teaching students, not standards. We are getting students ready for life outside the classroom, not the next classroom. We want students who are able to perform well in reality, not on standardized tests. The macro goal: We are helping human beings achieve their full potential so that they are able to succeed in and contribute to society.

BENCHMARKS AND ASSESSMENT

The benchmarks and assessment on an IEP are the measurable part of a measurable annual goal. They answer the fourth question: *Are we getting there?* Benchmarks are the baby steps that lead to the annual goal. They also answer the fifth question: *How do we know when we have arrived?* This refers to the method or methods of assessment (the measure) used to measure the annual goal. It tells us if the goal has been met.

Benchmarks and assessment for each goal should be simple and specifically reflective of the goal. Also, each of the measures must provide quantitative data that enable you to easily determine if the annual goal has been met. Toward these ends, they should be as simple as possible. More complexity does not mean more rigor or more learning.

Fluency

If reading fluency is a deficit area, you will need a MAG, a set of benchmarks, and a type of measure specifically for this area (and nothing else). They would look something like those in Figure 18.7.

Word Identification

If word identification is a deficit area, you will need a MAG, set of benchmarks, and type of measure specifically for this area (and nothing else). They would look something like those in Figure 18.8.

Comprehension

If comprehension is a deficit area, you will need a MAG, set of benchmarks, and type of measure specifically for this area (and nothing else). They would look something like those in Figure 18.9.

Goal—Fluency:

Pat will read 100 WPM at RL 4.

Benchmarks:

1. Pat will read 100 WPM at RL 3.
2. Pat will read 60 WPM at RL 4.
3. Pat will read 80 WPM at RL 4.

Measuring Progress:

Progress will be measured using timed readings with graded readers.

FIGURE 18.7. Goals, benchmarks, and measurements for fluency.

Goal—Word Identification:

On a graded reader (RL 4) with at least 200 words, Pat will correctly identify 90% of the words.

Benchmarks:

1. Pat will correctly identify 90% of the words on a graded reader (RL 3).
2. Pat will correctly identify 50% of the words on a graded reader (RL 4).
3. Pat will correctly identify 70% of the words on a graded reader (RL 4).

Measuring Progress:

Progress will be measured using running records on graded readers.

FIGURE 18.8. Goals, benchmarks, and measurements for word identification.

Goal—Comprehension of Narrative Text:

On a graded reader (RL 4) using narrative text, Pat will identify major characters, events, and settings with at least 90% success.

Benchmarks:

1. On a graded reader (RL 3) using narrative text, Pat will identify major characters, events, and settings with at least 70% success.
2. On a graded reader (RL 4) using narrative text, Pat will identify major characters, events, and settings with at least 90% success.
3. On a graded reader (RL 4) using narrative text, Pat will identify major characters, events, and settings with at least 70% success.

Measuring Progress:

Scores will be measured using a story-retelling chart.

FIGURE 18.9. Goals, benchmarks, and measurements for comprehension.

SPECIAL EDUCATION AND RELATED SERVICES

A statement of the special education and related services is the part of the IEP that addresses the third question: *How do we get there?* This is a global description of the needs, interventions, supports, type of education, or kinds of services that will enable the student to achieve the annual goal or goals. This does not describe the particulars of the services or instruction; rather, it states in general terms the types of services or instruction necessary to enable students to achieve their goal.

In the example of Sally the wrestler above, special education and related services would be something like this: Sally will spend 15 minutes every night before practice working on take-downs with the assistant coach. This tells us in general terms the kind of special educational services Sally will receive, but it does not tell us exactly what take-down moves will be taught or how they will be taught. Since the IEP is essentially a contract, a global statement does not lock us into a particular type of instruction or a particular set of skills or subskills. This is because wrestlers are different, and conditions change. What works with one wrestler may not work with another.

So it is with reading. Special education and related services for a student who is a struggling reader could include things such as (1) in-class remediation provided by a paraprofessional under the guidance of the teacher or reading specialist, (2) individual or small-group instruction outside the classroom, (3) instruction outside the classroom provided by a reading specialist, (4) instruction in a special education resource room, (5) individual tutoring after school or outside the school setting, or (6) other. A statement reflective of this would not lock us into a specific program, strategy, method, or set of skills. For example: "Pat will go to the reading specialist four times a week for interventions related to word identification and reading comprehension." Another example: "Molly will be provided with a supplemental reading intervention with the reading specialist 30 minutes every day."

The IEP should also not identify a specific program or curriculum because, as stated throughout this book, there is no one-size-fits-all program or curriculum. Thus, knowledgeable teachers who have a wide variety of pedagogical tools at their disposal are essential in providing appropriate special education and related services to students with special learning needs. This again points to the importance of continued and ongoing professional development and academic learning opportunities for teachers. It is not possible to create finished teaching products in four semesters of any teacher preparation program.

Peer-Reviewed Research, Autonomy, and Pragmatism

Services should be based on peer-reviewed research to the extent practical. Peer-reviewed research is the topic of the next chapter. However, two things stand out here. First, educators have professional autonomy and responsibility in determining the types of services that are based on peer-reviewed research. Second, the phrase "to the greatest extent possible" means that services need to be pragmatic. For example, the ideal type of service for a struggling reader might be to have a reading specialist provide individual tutoring sessions for 2 hours every day. However, this is most likely not feasible in most public school settings, for a variety of reasons.

EIGHT TIPS FOR DESIGNING EFFECTIVE IEPs

Poorly designed IEPs have real-world consequences. They impede rather than enhance students' progress in literacy. Conversely, well-designed IEPs with appropriate goals, benchmarks, and assessments can ensure that struggling readers receive the type of instruction that will enhance their ability to create meaning with print. Toward this end, this chapter ends with eight tips for designing effective IEPs.

1. **Valid diagnostic data.** IEP goals and benchmarks must be based on valid diagnostic data. Some form of a DRA provides this kind of data for reading (see Chapter 16).
2. **Focus.** IEP goals should focus on the specific deficit area and nothing else. For reading, the goals should always be word identification, comprehension, and/or fluency.
3. **Separate goals.** Each reading deficit area requires a separate goal. This is because word identification, comprehension, and fluency are each addressed differently.
4. **Macro versus micro.** MAG should focus on macro goals. Macro goals related to reading would be to identify words, create meaning, and read fluently. As such, academic standards and reading subskills are not appropriate for reading IEP goals.
5. **Simple.** Keep the goals simple. More complex does not mean more learning.
6. **Communicate.** IEPs should be as clear and understandable as possible. Jargon, acronyms, and test data should not be used because they can be confusing. The goal is to communicate to parents, to explain things in ways that a parent without a background in education or assessment can easily understand.
7. **Useful, pragmatic, and effective.** The IEP should be something that teachers and educators can actually use. The plan should be able to be easily implemented by busy teachers. It should also be effective in moving the student forward.
8. **Individualized.** IEPs by definition are individualized. Thus, they should focus on the individual's specific needs.

CHAPTER 19

Peer-Reviewed Research

As shown earlier in Figure 18.1, an IEP states that special education services (instruction and interventions) should be based not just on any old type of research, but rather on *peer-reviewed research*. This short chapter explores the mystery of peer-reviewed research (PRR). Chapter 21 will examine an equally mysterious term, *scientifically based research* (SBR).

BLIND PEER REVIEW

In order for research to be scientifically based research, it has to be peer reviewed. According to the U.S. Department of Education (2006), peer-reviewed research "generally refers to research that is reviewed by qualified and independent reviewers to ensure that the quality of the information meets the standards of the field before the research is published" (p. 46664).

The Process of Peer Review

Peer review (or *blind peer review*) refers to the process used to evaluate the quality of research. This is how it works: Once a study has been conducted, researchers write an article describing what they did and what they found. This article is sent off to an academic journal for consideration for publication. The editor of the journal selects reviewers who are considered to have expertise in the field. These reviewers evaluate the study without knowing who conducted it (hence the term *blind* peer review). Reviewers consider things such as the clarity of the research question, the theoretical context in which the research question was set, the adequacy of the methodology, the analysis of the data, the interpretation of the data, the validity of the conclusions, and the quality of writing (see Chapter 24). They then have four options: (1) recommend it for publication, (2) recommend it for publication with revisions, (3) suggest specific revisions be made and that it be resubmitted for consideration, or (4) recommend the article be rejected.

Peer review simply denotes a process; the quality or rigor of this process varies. Reviewers and editors of highly prestigious academic journals use a process that is rigorous and very selective. These journals have low acceptance rates and tend to have considerable influence on the field. Other journals have a less rigorous review process and higher acceptance rates. However, all are still considered peer-reviewed journals.

Once published, the research is examined by researchers and practitioners within the field as well as the general public. Here it is further analyzed, evaluated, critiqued, debated, and embraced and/or rejected. Journal articles are then written supporting or denouncing the findings of the original research. Other research is carried out to replicate, reinforce, extend, or refute the findings. Tenure and promotion are earned, grants are awarded, fellowships given, books written, and guest appearances made. This all leads to new questions and new research. Thus, the cycle of research life continues.

The Reviewers

But who reviews the reviewers? One of the concerning factors with peer review is the possibility of a skewed composition in the selection of members (Zirkel & Rose, 2009). It is possible that the reviewers are overrepresented by individuals (1) who have a singular research paradigm, (2) whose strong adherence to a singular theoretical model renders them data-resistant, (3) who have a strong political or ideological bias, or (4) who might profit financially (directly or indirectly) from a certain type of research publication. An example of a skewed composition that results in reviewer bias will be illustrated in Chapter 22.

A Panel of Experts

Also included in a definition of peer-reviewed research by the U.S. Department of Education would be studies that are reviewed by a "panel of experts." This is a loosely defined construct. For example, each of the groups in Figure 19.1 has at various times been considered to be a panel of experts related to education or reading instruction. However, based on their experience, expertise, and world view, it is very likely that the people in each group would have vastly differing views on both research methodology and effective reading instruction. You can see then that the views and the subsequent recommendations made by any given panel of experts vary greatly and are highly dependent on who is doing the selecting and who is selected.

- Professors in the area of special education
- Professors in the area of literacy
- Elementary reading specialists
- Experienced teachers
- Business leaders
- Researchers who have published research in the area of reading
- Researchers who have expertise in a singular scientific method that utilizes randomized controlled trials
- Teachers and scholars who have reviewed a great deal of research related to literacy
- People who have written books about literacy or education
- Groups selected by recognized and established literacy learning organizations such as the International Literacy Association (ILA) or the National Council of Teachers of English (NCTE)
- Well-known or recognized figures in education
- Political appointees to state and national education departments
- Appointees selected by political appointees
- People from the National Institute of Child Health and Human Development (NICHD)

FIGURE 19.1. Panels of experts.

The National Reading Panel

To illustrate what can go wrong with a panel of experts, in 1997 Congress asked the National Institute of Child Health and Development (NICHD) to work with the U.S. Department of Education to establish a National Reading Panel (NRP). The task of this panel of experts was to evaluate existing research related to reading instruction in order to find the best ways of teaching children to read. Congress perhaps had never heard of two prominent organizations devoted to doing just this: the International Literacy Association (ILA) and the National Council of Teachers of English (NCTE). These organizations are composed of thousands of teachers, researchers, scholars, and other educational professionals. At the time this panel was put together, these organizations had been studying reading instruction for over 40 and 80 years, respectively. Instead of utilizing the expertise, experience, and accumulated knowledge of these organizations, the NICHD selected 14 people and gave them 18 months to review selected reading research (see Figure 19.2).

And how was this 14-member panel selected? The director of the NICHD (who was a physician) consulted with the secretary of education (who was a lawyer with a degree in accounting). They selected a physicist to chair this panel of

Organization	Number of individuals	Time frame	Research models considered
NRP	14	18 months	Randomized controlled experiments
NCTE	77,000	Over 80 years	All
ILA	300,000	Over 40 years	All

FIGURE 19.2. Empirical data related to the National Reading Panel.

experts. They put together a 14-member panel that included a physicist, a certified public accountant, a sociologist, a pediatrician, a school administrator, and six people from psychology or educational psychology.

To be fair, some members of this panel had made significant contributions to the field of reading instruction; however, clearly excluded from this panel were those who did not adhere to a simple view of reading represented by the phonological processing model. Also excluded were those who did not embrace controlled experimental research as the exclusive, epistemologically privileged way of determining causality and making claims as to what constitutes knowledge. It is fairly obvious that this panel of experts was overrepresented by those with a singular theoretical perspective and research paradigm. In short, the panel of experts was put together to find a predetermined answer. However, real science does not start with the answer.

In 2000, the panel issued their 500-page report (National Reading Panel, 2000). While this report contained some useful information, none of it was new or groundbreaking (Allington, 2002). However, because it started with a definition of reading as merely sounding out words, it should not be surprising that the conclusions described a rather narrow and parochial view of what effective reading instruction was.

IMPLICATIONS

So what? What might you take from this very short chapter? Four things: First, if you did not fully understand the peer-review process before, hopefully you now have a better understanding of it. It is not a perfect process, but it is a process, and this process is important.

Second, the process is not without bias or flaws. Peer review does not magically make research unbiased or pure. It is not possible for human beings to have a completely objective, unbiased view of anything. Peer review is simply another filter to try to remove some of the impurities related to bias, methodology, theoretical context, applications, and conclusions.

Third, you as an educator are the ultimate filter. You are the most important peer reviewer. In this respect, you must always ask, Does the strategy or approach work with the students in front of you? Does it enhance their ability to create meaning with print? Does it move them forward, unimpeded, in their journey to achieve their full literacy potential? It does not matter if a strategy or approach demonstrates significant results with a large sample size if it does not work with your sample size.

Fourth, the federal government has many significant roles to play in enhancing the betterment of our society and improving the lives of all people. However, identifying effective reading instruction is not one of them.

PART V
DESIGNING READING INTERVENTIONS

CHAPTER 20

Response-to-Intervention Particulars

This chapter illustrates how everything described in this book thus far fits into a response-to-intervention (RTI) context. It puts meat on the bones of the structure that was described in the Introduction.

ASSESSMENT AND INTERVENTION

As described earlier, RTI is an integrated assessment and intervention program that is designed to provide immediate instructional help for students who struggle to read, write, or do math without them having to be formally identified for special education programs. Students are provided different levels of instructional help based on how they respond to classroom instruction and interventions.

RTI proposes that three tiers of intervention be used for students who are struggling with reading, writing, or math: (1) Tier 1 includes high-quality classroom instruction, screening, and group interventions; (2) Tier 2 includes targeted instruction; and (3) Tier 3 includes intensive interventions and comprehensive evaluation. Strategies for each tier are described below as they apply to reading.

TIER 1

Tier 1 interventions take place within the general education classroom. They include high-quality classroom instruction, screening, and group interventions.

High-Quality Classroom Instruction

As described in the Introduction, successful RTI programs for reading are dependent on having teachers who are experts in reading instruction (IRA, 2010; Wixson et al., 2014). Expert reading teachers do not simply use variations of the same direct instruction technique to teach a predetermined list of reading subskills in a predetermined order in a predetermined way. Rather, expert reading teachers have a variety of pedagogical tools in their teaching tool boxes that they use as needed. They understand the processes the brain uses to create meaning with print. Based on this and their students' specific needs, they adopt and adapt. Expert teachers teach students, not curriculum or programs.

Screening

Screening in Tier 1 is used to see if students are responding appropriately to the instruction found within the general education curriculum. Screening consists of establishing a baseline, setting goals or benchmarks, and monitoring progress (Averill et al., 2014).

Establishing a Baseline

The baseline is a measure of students' current level of reading performance. Since it is administered in large groups, any type of measure used here must be simple and pragmatic. It also needs to be a valid indicator of students' ability to create meaning with print. A maze is an economical, practical, and effective method used to establish a quantifiable baseline (see Chapter 16). It has also been shown to be a valid and reliable indicator of students' ability to create meaning with print (Graney, Martinez, Missall, & Arick, 2010). A maze can also be used to determine students' independent, instructional, and frustration reading levels. Because the vocabulary and concepts contained in the text of a maze can create variabilities in difficulty, it is recommended that at least two mazes be used to establish an initial reading baseline.

Goals

RTI goals are different from individualized education program (IEP) goals. RTI goals are essential benchmarks that identify where you think students should be at various times during the year (Wixson & Valencia, 2011). RTI benchmark goals should be set at three (maybe four) points during the year. Since the maze measure was used to establish a baseline, this type of measure should also be used to determine if students have met the identified benchmark goals. Keep it simple.

Monitoring Progress

If screening shows that students are not making adequate progress toward established benchmark goals or if they are currently performing below grade-level expectations, a Tier 1 intervention is used. This is where a progress monitoring system is implemented to check students' progress at shorter intervals. Progress monitoring strategies are described in Chapter 17.

Group Interventions: In-Class Supplemental Instruction

Tier 1 interventions involve supplemental instruction that occurs in the general education classroom. Small-group, in-class supplemental instruction is usually used here. And because a classroom teacher is still responsible for teaching the general education curriculum, Tier 1 interventions must be simple, pragmatic, and effective. It is recommended that variations of six elements be included:

1. **Daily sustained silent reading of books at students' independent level and below.** The goal here is reading volume. Reading volume has been shown to enhance comprehension, fluency, vocabulary, and word identification (Allington, 2012; Cunningham & Stanovich, 2001; Krashen, 2004). Strategies for reading practice were described in Chapter 14.
2. **Daily writing.** Writing is one of the best strategies for developing the syntactic cueing system as well as letter–sound relationships (Parodi, 2013). Writing activities need not be long, but they should be authentic. That is, students should be writing and sharing their ideas. These strategies were described in Chapter 11.
3. **Guided reading lessons.** Guided reading lessons are used to teach specific reading skills to students in small, flexible groups using authentic reading materials (Johnson, 2016b; Lipson & Wixson, 2009). The skills taught here are usually related to word identification (see Chapter 9) and comprehension (see Chapter 13).
4. **Word work.** Word work is instruction related to letter sounds or letter patterns (Cunningham & Cunningham, 2002; Erickson & Koppenhaver, 1995). This work would include analytic, synthetic, and large unit phonics instruction (see Chapter 7).
5. **Cloze and maze activities.** Cloze and maze activities are used to develop the semantic cueing system (Paulson & Freeman, 2003) (see Chapter 10).
6. **Fluency work.** Fluency work usually involves some form of repeated reading (Kuhn & Stahl, 2013) (see Chapter 12).

As stated in the Introduction, RTI interventions at all tiers must be coordinated with classroom instruction (Allington, 2011; Averill et al., 2014; IRA, 2010; Scanlon, 2011; Wixson et al., 2014). They should reflect and reinforce the types of research-based instruction and activities used with the general education reading curriculum. Struggling readers need consistency, not fragmentation.

TIER 2

Students not meeting Tier 1 benchmark goals are identified for a Tier 2 intervention. Tier 2 interventions are most often done in small groups outside the general education classroom. The type of instruction students receive here should be more intense versions of the instruction received in Tier 1.

Data-Based Decision Making

RTI calls for data-based decision making to be used throughout (Averill et al., 2014; IRA, 2010; Wixson et al., 2014). This means that the reading intervention for each student in Tier 2 should be based on solid, diagnostic data (Foorman & Connor, 2011; Wixson & Valencia, 2011). This diagnostic data should indicate students' approximate reading grade level (or Lexile level) and students' strengths and weaknesses in each of the three reading deficit areas: word identification, fluency, and comprehension (Spear-Swerling, 2013; Valencia & Buly, 2004). Chapter 16 described methods and measures to use here.

Decisions about the intervention should also be based on data collected as part of progress monitoring. As described in Chapter 17, progress monitoring is used to assess and document the progress that students are making with the reading intervention. It indicates students' responsiveness to the types of strategies used, and it documents their progress.

Targeted Instruction

Tier 2 instruction should be targeted. Targeted instruction does not mean simply implementing a program, curriculum, or strategy with fidelity. Instead, targeted instruction in a reading intervention means that it specifically addresses or at least emphasizes each student's deficit area or areas. This again points to the importance of having good diagnostic data. It is also why teachers must have a variety of strategies and be able to adopt and adapt these strategies to meet individual needs.

Frequency and Duration

To have an impact, Tier 2 intervention groups need to meet a minimum of 3 days a week. Depending on the age and level of the student, the duration for these sessions should be anywhere from 15 minutes a day for younger students to no more than 45 minutes a day for older students. Shorter sessions in which students are focused are much more effective than longer sessions in which students are not actively engaged.

Strategies used in Tier 2 are similar to those used in Tier 1. Variations and combinations of these strategies should be included depending on students' needs. Sessions should be briskly paced, consisting of four to eight of these strategies. Each strategy should be 3–6 minutes in duration.

Progress Monitoring

The progress monitoring strategies used should reflect the intervention, which reflects the deficit area, which in turn reflects the original diagnostic measure.

TIER 3

If students are not making adequate progress in Tier 2, they are targeted for a Tier 3 intervention. Tier 3 should build upon Tier 2 instruction to the greatest degree possible. The main difference between Tier 2 and Tier 3 is that Tier 3 should be more frequent and intensive (Swanson & Vaughn 2011). Students not making the desired level of progress in response to the Tier 3 intervention should then be referred for a comprehensive evaluation to see if they are eligible for special education services under the Individuals with Disabilities Education Improvement Act (IDEA) of 2004 (National Center for Learning Disabilities, 2014).

Tier 3 is often synonymous with special education; however, RTI was specifically designed to avoid special education labels and services. IDEA calls for Tier 3 interventions to be delivered primarily in a general education setting by a general education teacher and additional staff. If special educators do become involved at this level, the International Literacy Association (IRA, 2010) recommends that literacy/reading specialists and coaches provide leadership in every aspect of the RTI. There must also be careful planning and continued communication with all parties in all phases.

The final point here in regard to special education is this: Tier 3 is where students need the most highly qualified reading teachers. In special education settings, students rarely get improved access to expert, intensive reading instruction

(Allington, 2011). That is, special education teachers often do not have the expertise in all aspects of reading instruction that reading specialists and elementary education teachers have. As a result, students rarely experience accelerated reading achievement once they begin special education services (Allington, 2011; Bentum & Aaron, 2003; Denton, Vaugh, & Fletcher, 2003; Scanlon, 2011). Thus, if special education teachers become involved as part of Tier 3, it should occur only under the guidance of a reading/literacy specialist.

FINAL WORD

One of RTI's strengths is its flexibility (IRA, 2010). It is expected that there will be wide variation in how these regulations are interpreted and implemented. However, to be successful, any RTI plan must be (1) economical, (2) practical, and (3) effective. The meaning-based plan described in this book meets these criteria. Also, RTI plans for reading call for evidence-based pedagogy to be used in each tier (Averill et al., 2014). However, evidence-based pedagogical strategies are much different from a specific program or method. As stated previously, there is no single evidence-based program, research-based curriculum, or scientifically based teaching strategy that works best for all students (Allington, 2012; Wharton-McDonald, 2011). Thus, RTI plans for reading must comprise several research-based strategies that enable teachers to flexibly apply them in ways that best meet the needs of their students.

CHAPTER 21

Scientifically Based Research

As stated in Chapter 20, RTI can be used as an assessment mechanism to identify students with learning disabilities who might be eligible for special education services. Here we identify students by how they respond to interventions that are supported by *scientifically based research* (see Figure 21.1). Exploring and explaining this concept will be the focus of this chapter.

> Statute/Regs Main » Regulations » Part B » Subpart D » Section 300.307
>
> **Specific learning disabilities.**
>
> (a) General. A State must adopt, consistent with §300.309, criteria for determining whether a child has a specific learning disability as defined in §300.8(c)(10). In addition, the criteria adopted by the State—
>
> (1) Must not require the use of a severe discrepancy between intellectual ability and achievement for determining whether a child has a specific learning disability, as defined in §300.8(c)(10);
>
> (2) Must permit the use of a process based on the child's response to scientific, research-based intervention; and
>
> (3) May permit the use of other alternative research-based procedures for determining whether a child has a specific learning disability, as defined in §300.8(c)(10).
>
> (b)Consistency with State criteria. A public agency must use the State criteria adopted pursuant to paragraph (a) of this section in determining whether a child has a specific learning disability.

FIGURE 21.1. Identifying students with specific learning disabilities.

RESEARCH, SCIENCE, AND METHODOLOGY

Research in its most basic form is simply a matter of asking questions and using data to answer those questions. We do this in varying forms every day. For example: "What is the temperature today?"; "What is the strange noise in my car engine?"; "Why is Johnny not learning?"; "What is the most effective approach to use to teach this skill?"; "Was my lesson effective?"; "How should I teach reading to students who are struggling readers?" Asking and answering these questions are all forms of research (or *re*-search—to search again).

Scientific research is a process that uses systematic methods to collect data to answer questions. These systematic methods come in a variety of forms. Meaning that there is really no such thing as *the* scientific method; rather, there are methods of science. In contrast, the U.S. Department of Education has determined that only a single type of research methodology can be used to ask and answer questions in the field of education (see Figure 21.2). They have ironically labeled this

(37) SCIENTIFICALLY BASED RESEARCH—The term "scientifically based research"—

(A) means research that involves the application of rigorous, systematic, and objective procedures to obtain reliable and valid knowledge relevant to education activities and programs; and

(B) includes research that—

- (i) employs systematic, empirical methods that draw on observation or experiment;
- (ii) involves rigorous data analyses that are adequate to test the stated hypotheses and justify the general conclusions drawn;
- (iii) relies on measurements or observational methods that provide reliable and valid data across evaluators and observers, across multiple measurements and observations, and across studies by the same or different investigators;
- (iv) is evaluated using experimental or quasi-experimental designs in which individuals, entities, programs, or activities are assigned to different conditions and with appropriate controls to evaluate the effects of the condition of interest, with a preference for random-assignment experiments, or other designs to the extent that those designs contain within-condition or across-condition controls;
- (v) ensures that experimental studies are presented in sufficient detail and clarity to allow for replication or, at a minimum, offer the opportunity to build systematically on their findings; and
- (vi) has been accepted by a peer-reviewed journal or approved by a panel of independent experts through a comparably rigorous, objective, and scientific review.

FIGURE 21.2. A definition of scientifically based research. Retrieved from *www2.ed.gov/policy/elsec/leg/esea02/pg107.html#sec9101.*

scientifically based research (SBR). However, can anything be said to be truly scientific if it ignores or invalidates an abundance of data?

In identifying scientifically based research for use in education, the problem is not with the type of research methodology described in Figure 21.2. This has been and continues to be an invaluable research tool. The problem is with the exclusive use of this type of research methodology to the exclusion of all others. This methodological peephole creates a very narrow and unrealistic view of the very educational reality it seeks to examine. Yet, the federal government (not the source I would use to understand research methodology in any field) has mandated that this is the only type of research that can be used to evaluate reading instruction.

To be clear, people who were not reading researchers, who had spent little (if any) time reading research related to reading instruction, determined that the only type of reading research that can be used to evaluate reading instruction is that which meets the narrow parameters described in Figure 21.2. They decreed that the same research methods used to study the physical world in the artificial confines of a controlled laboratory setting are the only research methods that can be used to study and make causal assertions about human beings in real-world educational settings. Hence, the only data that count in coming to understand educational reality are data that are collected using one specific research method. This method is said to be "the gold standard."

THE GOLD STANDARD

To understand the limitations of the gold standard, we must first get a sense of what it is. The gold standard, sometimes called experimental research, quantitative research, or randomized controlled trials (RCTs), will be referred to here as *controlled experimental studies* (CES).

Controlled Experimental Studies

The purpose of CES is to determine a causal relationship between one thing and another. To do this, conditions are created (experiments) in which all the variables are controlled or isolated except the independent and dependent variables.

The Independent Variable

In educational research, the *independent variable* (IV) is most often the treatment or condition being imposed on one or more *subjects* in an *experimental group*. The subjects in educational research are most often students. The independent variable has been made independent of all other things. That is, it is the only thing given to or made to happen to the subjects in the experimental group. This isolation enables the researcher to clearly see if the thing (IV) has an effect on the subjects.

The Dependent Variable

What happens to the subjects as a result of the treatment or condition (the end state) is the *dependent variable* (DV). This end state is dependent on the treatment. In other words, if it were not for the independent variable (treatment), the change from the beginning state to the end state would not have occurred. Researchers using CES try to isolate independent and dependent variables so that the only thing that happens to subjects in the experimental group is the treatment. This enables researchers to say with confidence that one thing (the IV) caused another thing (the DV) to occur.

Control Groups

To provide more confidence in this causal relationship, a *control group* is often used. This group is similar to the experimental group in every way except the subjects here do not get the treatment (IV). If the difference in end states between the experimental and control groups is *statistically significant* (greater than could occur by chance), the researcher can say with even more confidence that one thing (the IV) caused the other thing (the DV) to occur.

True Experiments

To be a *true experiment*, the subjects of the experiment must be randomly selected from the general population and assigned to either control or experimental groups. Random selection ensures that the groups being compared are relatively similar. In this way, the research does not end up comparing apples and oranges. Random selection also makes it more likely that the subjects in an experiment represent the general population. Finally, random selection prevents researchers from selecting subjects who may respond more favorably to the treatment versus others.

Quasi-Experiments

In most schools and classrooms, random selection is not possible (see below). In this case, *quasi-experimental design* is used. This is experimental research in which there is no random assignment of subjects to groups. Other methods must then be used to ensure that the groups being compared are relatively equal. Two methods commonly used for this are pretests and matching.

Pretests

In using *pretests*, a pretest measure is given to a comparison group based on the dependent variable being examined. If the groups are relatively similar, the research proceeds. If there is a significant difference between groups, there are three options: (1) find another group to compare, (2) reconfigure the existing groups so that they match, or (3) take the dissimilarity of groups into account when describing the results and conclusions.

Matching

Matching is also used to create groups that are relatively similar. Here again a pretest measure is given to the subjects based on the variable that is being examined. Based on the test results, subjects are matched with another subject with a relatively similar score. Groups are then created by putting matched subjects in separate groups. For example, one would go in the experimental group and the other would go in the control group.

The description above is a very basic overview of what the U.S. Department of Education would call scientifically based research. For a more complete description of various types of research design used in education, see *A Short Guide to Action Research* (Johnson, 2012).

Limiting What We Might See

As stated above, the limitations of the gold standard are not in the methodology itself; rather, they are in the exclusive use of that methodology to understand educational reality and make causal assumptions. Causal relationships can be determined using a variety of methodologies. Here are two illustrating examples:

Silt and Broken Ribs

One summer I was riding my bike down a hill. I was riding fast because I wanted to get in a hard ride before the weather conditions changed. It had been raining the day before and a fine silt had seeped onto the bike trail. When I hit the silt patch the wheels flew out from under me. I was projected through space and landed in such a way that I broke two ribs.

I did not need to conduct a controlled experimental study to determine a causal relationship between my broken ribs and the silt. Clearly, the silt on the trail caused me to fall off my bike and break my ribs. However, there were other variables at play as well, which included the moisture content of the silt (really wet), the speed at which I was riding (much too fast), the density of the silt (extremely fine and slippery), the quantity of the silt on the trail (a lot), the placement of the silt on the trail (all over), the grade of the hill on which the trail existed (really steep), the surface covering of the trail (pavement), and my inability to perceive the silt (fogged glasses). These factors, combined with my lack of silt knowledge, my age, my health, and the way I landed, all contributed to my broken ribs.

Despite the lack of gold-standard data collection and analysis, I was able to identify a causal factor. It was the silt on the trail. However, there was a variety of important data that I would be foolish to ignore simply because gold-standard research was not used. All these data were useful in enhancing my existing theory about bike riding and trail conditions and added a few more data dots to my theoretical model of trail conditions and bike riding. As a result, the next time I encountered similar or related conditions, I would have a more complete understanding of the situation, and I would also be more inclined (hopefully) to take the appropriate action (slowing down).

Had I been limited to the gold standard to isolate a variable, I would have had a very restricted view of the causal relationships between silt and broken ribs. Silt does not always cause broken ribs. Other things besides silt can cause broken ribs. However, it is reasonable to conclude that under certain conditions, with certain people, doing certain things, a certain type of silt on a bike trail can lead to broken ribs (or worse).

Fifth Grade

One day when I was teaching fifth grade in Grantsburg, Wisconsin, one of my students (Pat) came in from noon break. He had a tear in his shirt, scrape marks on his arms, and a bruise on his face. I did not need to rely on the gold standard to establish a causal link to his condition. That morning Pat and Sam had exchanged angry words. In the lunchroom right before the noon break, the two had engaged in a shouting match and Pat said, "I'll see you at recess!" Several students told me exactly what happened. Putting all the data bits together, I was able to establish, with a great deal of confidence, the causal factor related to Pat's condition: Pat and Sam had gotten into a fight. Even though I had not directly observed the event or had not isolated any variables, I knew exactly why Pat's condition was as it was. The gold standard was not needed here to establish a causal link.

The Joy of Petri Dishes

If the students with whom we work were all homogeneous elements existing within the confines of a very large petri dish where all variables could be isolated and experimental treatments could be implemented with fidelity, then the exclusive use of the gold standard to establish causal factors would indeed be appropriate for evaluating reading instruction and other educational variables. However, this is not the case. Human beings are wonderfully complex, multidimensional entities existing in social worlds that are incredibly varied and extremely uncontrollable. These human beings interact with other human beings, all of whom have a diverse array of abilities, motivations, dispositions, values, life situations, and other forces acting upon them. As such, it is unlikely that causal certainty could ever be achieved with any type of scientific method (Heshusius, 1994; Iano, 1987; Poplin, 2011). In the world of educational research, certainty is never achieved. At best, the gold standard can be used to reduce uncertainty.

INSTRUCTIONAL PRACTICES

The gold-standard mandate imposed by the U.S. Department of Education reflects a simplistic view of science and how it is used to understand phenomena (Seriven, 1994). This in turn has led to a simplistic view of "research-based" strategies. One result of these simplistic views is that cause–effect relationships have been converted into stimulus–response instructional techniques in which students are manipulated into producing predetermined behaviors that represent measurable learning objectives. Learning is said to have occurred only when students display the appropriate behavioral response to an instructional stimulus. While this approach is appropriate for mice in a Skinner box, it is remarkably inappropriate for human beings in a classroom.

Also, the strategies designated to be "research-based" by gold-standard research standards include a troubling amount of direct instruction. While direct instruction has been shown to be effective for learning low-level skills, it is extremely ineffective for developing high-level thinking, understanding complex concepts, and acquiring sophisticated skills (Eppley & Dudley-Marling, 2018). The subsequent problem is that students who are struggling readers are often force-fed an interminable array of mind-numbing lessons that use direct instruction to teach low-level concepts and skills. As a result, they have few opportunities to participate in activities that would enable them to develop complex thinking and deeper understandings of the world. You do not have to control any variables to understand that if only low-level skills are taught, only low-level learning occurs.

EDUCATIONAL WONDERLAND

If gold-standard research were truly the answer to all problems related to teaching struggling readers (as proponents claim), why have these problems not been solved? The Education Science Reform Act was passed in 2002. Surely with all the gold-standard researchers clamoring for tenure, promotion, grants, and book contracts, all the problems related to reading instruction would have been solved by now. To help struggling readers, we would simply need to identify the "breakdowns" in the educational machinery or find the "impaired" educational products and then insert the correct research-based widgets into the educational machinery. Teachers would simply implement the correct research-based widget with fidelity and keep the products moving down the conveyor belt. Simple and tidy, neat as that. We would be living in an educational wonderland, a utopia where all children would be reading books at or above grade level.

But this is not the case. Why? Because the educational world is much more complex and multidimensional than can be contained in or controlled by any set of variables. For the field of education to evolve, it must allow the research method to be determined by the question and not the other way around. It must be able to escape from the choke hold put on it by the reductionist gold-standard paradigm that restricts the flow of new information.

CHAPTER 22

When the Gold Standard Is Un-Golden

A REVIEW OF TORGESEN ET AL. (2009)

UN-GOLDEN GOLDENALITY

Just because a study meets all the criteria of the "gold standard" outlined in the previous chapter (see Figure 21.2) does not mean that the resulting data are always valid, reliable, useful, or meaningful. In fact, some studies meet all the criteria of the gold standard and still manage to be significantly un-golden. I reviewed a variety of studies that illustrate this point and ultimately selected a study by Torgesen, Wagner, Rashotte, Herron, and Lindamood (2009) titled "Computer-Assisted Instruction to Prevent Early Reading Difficulties in Students at Risk for Dyslexia: Outcomes from Two Instruction Approaches."

I selected this study for four reasons: First, the work of the lead author, Joseph Torgesen, is widely cited in books and articles related to reading instruction for struggling readers. Second, the focus of the study was related to the content of this book. Third, I have analyzed previous studies conducted by Torgesen and found them to be a bit "creative" (Torgesen, 2009; Torgesen et al., 1999, 2001; Torgesen, Wagner, & Rashotte, 2012). And fourth, this study meets all the criteria of the gold standard.

THE ILLUSION OF OBJECTIVITY

As described in Chapter 21, the gold standard is said to rely on "the application of rigorous, systematic, and objective procedures" to obtain reliable and valid knowledge (see Figure 21.2). There are three things to unpack here in regard to objectivity: First, neither total objectivity nor lack of bias in any type of research-based endeavor is possible (Code, 1993; Harman, 1994). The idea of a neutral, emotionless spectator detached from the research in order to obtain an untainted view of reality is an illusion perpetuated by the gold-standard research paradigm. Subjectivity seeps into all research influencing decisions such as what questions get asked, what gets compared or examined, what data are collected, how those data are analyzed, and how the data are interpreted.

Second, two of the authors of this study (Lindamood and Herron) developed and had financial ties to the intervention products used in this study (Lindamood Phoneme Sequencing Program for Reading, Spelling, and Speech [LIPS] and Reading, Writing, and Typing [RWT]). In other words, they stood to benefit financially if the results of this study turned out a specific way. Although the authors of these two programs were cited by name within the article, a blind peer review would not have revealed the authors' connections to the interventions. In addition, there was no disclosure statement anywhere in this article about these connections. Also, at the time of publication, Joseph Torgesen, Richard Wagner, and Carol Rashotte were all part of the Florida Center for Reading Research (FCRR) out of Florida State University. FCRR heavily promotes LIPS and other for-profit programs focusing on the direct instruction of reading subskills. (Calls to both FCRR and Lindamood to determine the exact nature of the relationship were not returned.) It should not be surprising, then, that this study produced results that the researchers interpreted as favorable to the two approaches compared.

Third, according to Chapter 21, gold-standard research is that which "has been accepted by a peer-reviewed journal or approved by a panel of independent experts through a comparably rigorous, objective, and scientific review." This article appeared in the *Annals of Dyslexia*, a journal that is published by the International Dyslexia Association (IDA). According to the IDA, dyslexia is of neurobiological origin (a brain disorder), the symptoms of which are difficulties in word recognition, spelling, and decoding while reading (see Figure 22.1). IDA prescribes a specific type of treatment for this "neurobiological" condition, a treatment that is remarkably similar to the types of treatment used in the Torgeson et al. study.

In looking at the IDA website and reviewing their material, it becomes evident that this organization uses the phonological processing model to understand reading and dyslexia. Thus, we can assume that the reviewers selected to review articles for the *Annals of Dyslexia* shared this theoretical construct. Any articles submitted for publication would be viewed and evaluated through this theoretical lens. And because the IDA has already determined that only a specific type of instructional treatment is suitable, any outcome at odds with this conclusion would likely not be tolerated in an article submitted for peer review. It is doubtful that any research not in alignment with the theoretical parameters of this organization would be accepted for publication. In this sense, the peer review process used with this journal acted as a filter, not for quality (as is apparent by this study) but for theoretical compatibility.

IDA definition of dyslexia

Dyslexia is a specific learning disability that is neurobiological in origin. It is characterized by difficulties with accurate and/or fluent word recognition and by poor spelling and decoding abilities. These difficulties typically result from a deficit in the phonological component of language that is often unexpected in relation to other cognitive abilities and the provision of effective classroom instruction. Secondary consequences may include problems in reading comprehension and reduced reading experience that can impede growth of vocabulary and background knowledge.

IDA recommendations for students with dyslexia

In public school settings where many teachers are not knowledgeable about this condition, students with dyslexia may be considered stupid or lazy. Parents who have children diagnosed with dyslexia should seek out reading instruction that is based upon a systematic and explicit understanding of language structure, including phonics. This reading instruction goes by many names: Structured Literacy, Orton–Gillingham, Simultaneous Multisensory, Explicit Phonics, and others.

FIGURE 22.1. IDA definition and recommendations.

As stated in Chapter 19, blind peer review speaks to a process, but the process itself is not necessarily an indicator of the quality of the study.

THE ABSTRACT

The abstract provides an overview of the study and offers insights into some of its problems:

> The relative effectiveness of two computer-assisted instructional programs designed to provide instruction and practice in foundational reading skills was examined. First-grade students at risk for reading disabilities received approximately 80 hours of small-group instruction in four 50-minute sessions per week from October through May. Approximately half of the instruction was delivered by specially trained teachers to prepare students for their work on the computer, and half was delivered by the computer programs. At the end of first grade, there were no differences in student reading performance between students assigned to the different intervention conditions, but the combined-intervention students performed significantly better than control students who had been exposed to their school's **normal reading program. Significant differences** were obtained for phonemic awareness, phonemic decoding, reading accuracy, rapid automatic naming, and reading comprehension. A follow-up test at the end of second grade showed a similar pattern of differences, although only differences in phonemic awareness, phonemic decoding, and rapid naming remained **statistically reliable.** (p. 40)

There are three things to note: First, even though the term *dyslexia* appears in the title of the article and is listed as a keyword search term, it is noticeably absent in the abstract.

Second, an inference is made that the interventions were more effective than the "normal" reading program in producing a certain result (hearing sounds and naming symbols very quickly). This point is not at all related to the title of the article or the stated purpose of the study.

Third, the authors use the term *significant differences* in this abstract to describe differences between the intervention and control groups at the end of first grade. This is a bit of semantic sleight-of-hand that confuses *significant* with *statistically significant*. There are important (significant?) differences between these two terms. *Significantly* in the previous sentence of the abstract is an adverb used to denote something that one believes to be important or noteworthy. *Statistically significant* differences or differences that were "statistically reliable" in the next sentence describes a relationship between two or more variables that statistical analysis has determined to be caused by something other than chance. Gold-standard research relies on *statistical significance* to establish causal connections, not authors' subjective feelings about what they believe to be important.

These three elements provide a bit a foreshadowing. Each is elaborated below.

THE RESEARCH QUESTIONS

We turn now to the three research questions. Research questions are important, as they guide the research process. Everything that follows should be directly related to these questions.

• **Research question 1: Are there reliable differences in instructional impact between these two approaches to early intervention?** Both the title and statements in the beginning of this article give the impression that the primary purpose of this study was to compare two computer-based intervention approaches (RWT and LIPS) for students with dyslexia (or students "at risk" for dyslexia). The authors state, "By including two computer-based approaches that both addressed critical instruction needs for students with dyslexia but did so in slightly different ways, we hoped to determine whether the variation in emphases of the programs made a difference in their effectiveness for students who enter school delayed in the development of reading-related phonological skills" (p. 43). This is a bit misleading.

While research question 1 clearly focuses on the differences between the two interventions (LIPS and RWT), little attention is actually given to this comparison. In fact, only two sentences in the 16 pages of this article addressed research question 1. "None of the contrasts between the two treatment groups was statistically significant at the immediate posttest" (p. 48). And, "As with the immediate posttest, none of the differences between treatment groups was statistically significant at the 1-year follow-up" (p. 50). As will be shown below, the primary focus of this article was the comparison made in research question 2.

- **Research question 2: Do students receiving supplemental instruction using the RWT and LIPS programs show more rapid growth in early reading skills than students who do not receive the instruction?** In other words, is something better than nothing? A control group was included in this study so that it could be compared with the two intervention groups. Most of the space in the Results and Discussion sections of this article was used to describe this comparison. It is important to note, however, that the two intervention groups received reading instruction in their general education reading class *as well as* 84 hours (LIPS) and 80 hours (RWT) of additional specialized instruction outside the general education classroom. This instruction was provided in small groups by specially selected and trained teachers. In contrast, the students in the control group did not receive additional specialized instruction outside the standard reading class and did not have specially selected and trained teachers working with them in small groups.

And just to be clear, the authors of this study compared two groups of students who received specialized instruction outside the classroom to a group of students who did not. There is an old research adage: Anytime you compare a group that received something to a similar group that received nothing, the group that received something will always score higher on measures of something than the group that received nothing.

- **Research question 3: What proportion of students receiving the computer-based instruction remained significantly impaired in reading skills following the intervention?** This question is meaningless, for it assumes that students in the study were in fact "impaired." In this study, "impairment" was never defined or established. It also reveals the hubris of the authors who are willing to use the term *impaired* with these human beings. If a student enters first grade with inadequate instruction and little experience with text, or if a student lives in an environment in which the words and language structures sound much different than the measures used for assessment, it is highly likely that the student will show up as "impaired" (Gee, 2012)—which leads to the fallacy of dyslexia described below.

PREVENTING EARLY READING DIFFICULTIES IN STUDENTS AT RISK FOR DYSLEXIA

There is no universal agreement as to what dyslexia is or even if it exists. According to the International Literacy Association (2016a), "There is no empirical basis for the use of the term dyslexic to distinguish a group of children who are different from others experiencing difficulty in acquiring literacy" (p. 8). Some see the term as merely a designation for those on the lower end of the reading continuum (Elliot & Grigorenka, 2014; Stanovich, 1994) or simply as another name for poor reading (Protopapas & Parrila, 2018). (Dyslexia will be examined in Chapter 24.) However, for the sake of this chapter, we will proceed with the assumption that dyslexia is a viable concept and that it is of "neurobiological" origin (a brain disorder; see Figure 22.1) as the IDA claims.

"At Risk" for Dyslexia

The title of this article indicates that two computer-assisted intervention programs were used with students who were "at risk" for dyslexia. The term *at risk for dyslexia* is a curious one. The only place I have encountered it is in research articles related to dyslexia. Why is that? What exactly puts one "at risk" for dyslexia? Can students catch dyslexia from other students? Can you really determine dyslexia *risk factors* from the three identifying measures described below?

The subjects for this study were selected from 812 pre-first-grade students in three elementary schools. Students were screened before the school year on a test that measured letter–sound knowledge. Those scoring in the bottom 35% were screened a second time on three measures: (1) phoneme elision—students had to supply the missing sound in a word; (2) serial naming of numbers—students had to say the names of numbers on a timed test; and (3) the vocabulary subtest of an IQ test. (The validity of these measures will be examined below.) Using scores from these three measures and eliminating any students with an IQ below 75, 112 of the 812 pre-first-grade students were determined to be "at risk for dyslexia." However, the authors were careful (sneaky?) in how these students were described within the article. They referred to them as "students with the highest probability of reading difficulties" (p. 43). This of course is much different from students with dyslexia or even students "at risk" for dyslexia, whatever that might be.

At Risk for Statistical Insignificance

There is very little to indicate that any of the 112 students in this study met the IDA definition of dyslexia. They were simply a group of students about to enter first grade, who scored poorly on tests measuring sounds, quick number naming, and vocabulary. Poor performance here could be due to a variety of factors including inadequate instruction in preschool and kindergarten, poverty, environmentally induced chronic stress, little experience with or exposure to books and other print material, deficits in language experiences, and cultural and linguistic backgrounds that did not mirror the majority culture or language or the measures used. These factors have all been shown to impact scores on standardized tests (Gee, 2012; Jensen, 2009). The impact of these extraneous factors is reflected in the data in

Figure 22.2, showing the overrepresentation of students from minority and low socioeconomic status (SES) populations in the three participating schools.

The 112 students identified here as being "at risk" for dyslexia represent approximately 14% of all the first-grade students at these three elementary schools. This percentage is at odds with common estimates suggesting that 3–5% of all students have dyslexia or a severe reading disability (Snow, Burns, & Griffin, 1998; Ziegler & Goswami, 2005). (Interesting aside: The IDA claims that up to 20% of all students have "symptoms" of dyslexia. Apparently, any student who does poorly sounding out words or spelling has a symptom of dyslexia. Imagine that.) A more representative sample size for this study would have been 24– 40 students, not the 112 who were identified. This means that 72–88 students of the 112 students in this study (64–78%) most likely did not have dyslexia as defined by the IDA. Thus, it is reasonable to conclude that many more students without dyslexia than with dyslexia were included in this study. So why was the term *dyslexia* used here? (*Hint:* To get this article published in a dyslexia journal?)

The term *at risk for dyslexia* seems to have been created for research purposes. Dyslexia (or severe reading disabilities) is a low-incident condition. This means sample sizes in most studies related to this group will be small. Accurate comparisons of small groups in different settings is problematic in gold-standard research because of the many confounding variables unique to each setting. This also explains why gold-standard research related to dyslexia often involves students in the first grade. These are students who have not yet been entered into the educational system and formally assessed; thus, researchers can use the creative but not very accurate term *at risk for dyslexia*. Using this term creates larger sample sizes and more favorable results. With larger sample sizes, gold-standard researchers will have a greater chance of finding statistical significance even if the population being studied is not exactly the population identified as being studied. (Creative, no?)

Figure 22.3 shows the numbers used in this study compared to numbers that would depict a more accurate view of reality. However, including only 24–40 students would have disrupted the statistical analysis, making generalization to larger populations even more invalid.

The very *quasi-kinda-maybe-dyslexic* makeup of the subjects included in this study is illustrated by a sentence the authors included in the very last paragraph of

	Male	Minority	Low socioeconomic status
School average	50%	15%	17%
Study average	55%	33%	33%

FIGURE 22.2. Makeup of the subjects in this study.

	In this study	Representing reality
Percentage with dyslexia	14%	3 to 5%
Number with dyslexia	112	24 to 40
Experiment group size	36 and 40	8 and 13

FIGURE 22.3. Reality versus this study.

this article: "Although students were identified for the study because of poor performance on tests that are typically used to diagnose dyslexia, it is very likely that not all students in the current sample had neurobiologically based dyslexia" (p. 54). Exactly how many students is "not all"? The very last sentence of this article then states, "Thus, the use of the term 'dyslexia' in the title of this study needs to be qualified by the fact that we used only language and cognitive measures to identify the study participants, and we allowed general verbal ability to vary across a relatively wide range." Gosh. Ya think?

EQUIVALENCY AND VALIDITY

Were the groups being compared the same? Were the measures used valid?

Equivalency

To determine the equivalency of the two intervention groups, students were given 16 pretest measures. However (funny thing), the students in the control group were given no pretest measures other than the ones used to identify them for inclusion in the study (elision, digit-naming, and vocabulary). The authors' claim of equivalency was based solely on random selection. In other words, because students were randomly assigned to the intervention and control groups, we are asked to assume that the groups were equal.

There are two things to consider here: First, because of the small sample sizes of the groups (36, 36, and 40), it is very difficult to make the case for equivalency without pretest measures. Having one or two students in any of the groups scoring on the extreme ends of the measures used for comparison would impact the statistical analyses.

Second, given the many "creative" elements found in this gold-standard research project, it is logical to assume that claims of random selection to groups might be equally "creative." The equivalency between the intervention and control groups was never established. Hence, we have another old research adage: You cannot compare things that are not comparable (Bracey, 2006).

Validity

Validity in a research context is the extent to which the data you are measuring truly represent the phenomenon you are claiming to measure. In this case we must ask, were the measures used in this study valid assessments of students' reading ability?

A Simple View of Reading

In this article, the authors defined reading as decoding or sounding out words (the phonological processing model). If reading is understood this way, some of the measures used in this study might be valid sounding-out-word measures. However, as described throughout this book, reading is creating meaning with print using an interacting set of cognitive processes. The low-level reading subskill tasks in Figure 22.4 are not representative of the more complex interactive cognitive processes the brain uses to create meaning with print. As well, since these measures enable students to use only one of the three cueing systems (the phonological cueing system), they can hardly be accurate or valid assessments of students' ability to create meaning with print (reading) under authentic reading conditions.

Establishing Validity

The three instruments used here were the Gray Oral Reading Test (GORT-3; Wiederholt & Bryant, 1992), the Comprehensive Test of Phonological Processing (CTOPP; Wagner et al., 1999), and the Woodcock Reading Mastery Tests (WRMT; Woodcock, 2011). In reviewing these three testing instruments, the validity of each was established by comparing them to similar instruments of similar questionable validity. Does comparing an invalid instrument to another invalid instrument make it a valid instrument? (In determining validity, do two negatives make a positive?) To establish validity for reading, the question that should be asked is this: Do these instruments measure or predict students' ability to create meaning with print under authentic reading conditions? Do they quantify students' literacy potential?

It is very possible that pre-first-grade students scoring higher on the measures in Figure 22.4 may indeed get higher scores on later reading achievement tests. Children come to school with vastly different degrees of exposure to language and literacy experiences. Those with greater exposure will score higher; those with less will score lower. However, it is not students' ability to quickly name letters or single digits in 45 seconds that predicts future literacy achievement. Rather, it is their exposure to language and literacy experiences. But since these things are much more difficult to quantify, they are seldom included in gold-standard research.

Phoneme Things

- Elision—a word is pronounced with a missing sound; the student identifies the missing sound.
- Blending—students put discrete sounds together to create words.
- Segmentation—students break word into component sounds.

Nonsense Things

- Rapid naming of letters and numbers—students were timed to see how many letters and how many single-digit numbers they could identify in 45 seconds.
- Individual words—students were asked to read individual words presented out of context.
- Rapid identification—students were asked to identify as many words as they could in 45 seconds.
- Nonsense—students were asked to sound out nonsense words.
- Errors—students were asked to read a paragraph, and the number of "errors" was recorded. (This comes closest to a measure of word recognition. However, the types of "errors" [miscues] students make is important. Some "errors" represent mature reading.)

Comprehension Things

- Passage comprehension—students were asked to read a sentence or short passage and supply the key missing word.
- Reading comprehension—students were asked to read passages while the administrator timed and marked errors. The student answered five multiple-choice questions read by the administrator. Score was determined by time and accuracy of reading as well as correct responses.

Spelling

- Spelling—the ability to correctly arrange letters has nothing to do with creating meaning with print.

FIGURE 22.4. Tasks in the pretest–posttest measures (CTOPP, WRMT, GORT-3).

Phoneme Things

Phonemic awareness is the ability to hear and manipulate sounds within words. The ability to hear sounds within words and break words into sounds (phonemic awareness) is often a result of children's early exposure to language and literacy experiences (Gee, 2019). While phonemic awareness may be related to later sounding-out-word measures, a causal connection linking phonemic awareness activities to creating meaning with print is at best weak (Weaver, 2009).

Nonsense Things

Asking children to name as many numbers, letters, and nonsense words as they can in 45 seconds may be related to the ability to quickly process symbols, but it is unclear how this exercise is supposed to measure or predict their ability to create meaning with print. Again, children coming from environments in which there was little exposure to numbers, letters, and nonsense words typically have more difficulty identifying them, and even more so when asked to do so in 45 seconds. But the bigger question is: When in your adult life have you been asked to identify nonsense words with somebody sitting next to you holding a stopwatch?

The measures in Figure 22.4 focus on words parts, nonsense words, and decontextualized individual words—not meaning. They are abstract and meaningless tasks. As such, they are highly inauthentic. Moreover, they keep students from using the two most powerful cueing systems needed to recognize words (semantics and syntax). These timed measures of the subparts of reading subskills might be predictive of scores on early sounding-out-word measures, but a strong causal connection to creating meaning with text under authentic reading conditions has not been clearly established.

Comprehension Things

In one of the comprehension measures used here, students were asked to read a passage out loud. They were timed (fluency), their reading errors were counted (word identification), and their responses to multiple-choice questions were assessed. However (as has been described in the previous chapters), fluency, word identification, and comprehension all influence each other; but each is a different and distinctly separate deficit area for reading. Each is assessed differently, and each requires a different type of instruction and intervention. In the measure above, they are all jumbled up together.

How valid are these inauthentic tasks in assessing students' ability to create meaning under authentic reading conditions? In the real world, we read silently. We are usually able to select what we read and how we read. We are able to read at our own pace, review passages that we do not quite understand, attend to only those passages we find interesting or important, and stop reading things we find boring or irrelevant. These are mature reading behaviors. How well would you fare if you were asked to read aloud a passage from a text that somebody else had selected, your word recognition errors were noted, you were timed in the reading of the passage, and then you were asked to respond to multiple-choice questions?

RESULTS

Welcome to the world of gold-standard research where all the variables are controlled and all the students are manipulated so that absolute laws governing teaching and learning can be discovered and generalized to students everywhere. The point of this chapter was not to disparage experimental research studies, but to illustrate an important point: Just because a study meets all the requirements of the U.S. Department of Education's definition of scientifically based research does not mean that it is an accurate, valid, and unbiased account of the bit of reality it attempted to study. The academic world is filled with bad gold-standard research projects related to reading instruction. These projects are usually based on a limited understanding of reading, conducted by researchers far removed from the teaching experience, and used to justify educational practices that are effective only in certain instances for specific purposes.

It should also be noted that there is no such thing as the perfect research study. Every research project has confounding variables or limitations. These are usually identified and discussed at the end of the research article. (Curiously, the gold-standard research study examined in this chapter did not do this.) Besides the limitations already described above, there are four last things to consider:

First, the 72 students in the intervention groups spent 80 hours outside the general education reading class engaged in literacy-related activities, some of which included reading and writing. The question to consider is this? What would have been the result if these students had instead spent 80 hours enjoying and talking about good books and engaged in authentic writing and sharing experiences? One of the reasons why a gold-standard experiment of this kind is not carried out by literacy researchers to "prove" the effectiveness of authentic literacy experiences is that we know their importance in the development of students' literacy skills as well as their intellectual, social, and emotional development. It would be highly unethical to withhold this type of "treatment" from any group of students simply for the sake of getting an article published in the *Annals of Dyslexia*.

The question that my gold-standard colleagues usually ask at this point is this: *How can students read good books if they don't know how to read?* Therein lies the crux of many of the issues surrounding gold-standard reading research: It is conducted by people who are expert gold-standard researchers, but who lack extensive knowledge of literacy learning and instruction. Just because one does not know of something does not mean that that something does not exist. Likewise, just because one does not know how a thing works does not mean that that thing does not work. Developmentally appropriate meaning-based instruction and activities have been successfully used for years to enable young children at the emergent and beginning levels to develop their abilities to create meaning with print (Krashen, 2004). Authentic literacy activities may not produce the instant bump in meaningless measures related to reading subskills, but in the long term, they help develop the type of cognitive skills that transfer to real-life literacy activities and life outside the classroom.

Second, as described above, this study had very little to do with dyslexia. The term *at risk for dyslexia* was used to create the illusion that it was a study about dyslexia so that this article would be published in a peer-reviewed dyslexia journal. It is doubtful that a study of this quality would be accepted for publication in any of the leading literacy research journals.

Third, this study was supported by a grant from the NICHD. What would have happened had they found absolutely nothing of significance? (Which was actually the case here.) In order to justify the grant, they had to find something to report, and it had to be reported in a peer-reviewed journal. If this study concluded, as it should have, that there was really nothing to see here, it would have jeopardized the flow of research dollars and put future sales of their "research-based" products at risk. Thus, it can logically be assumed that the outcome of this study was determined long before the first variable was ever identified. The authors simply had to determine the best way to get there. The real gold-standard research question to ask would be: Who stood to gain from this project?

And fourth, who reads the *Annals of Dyslexia*? Will the results of this study be challenged by anyone other than a little bald man (me), sitting in his basement, writing a book about reading interventions, with a completely different set of epistemological and ontological assumptions, and using a different theoretical construct to understand literacy and literacy research? When you wade through all the jargon, fancy words, and statistical analyses, you find that this study was little more than an infomercial presented under the guise of academic research. Yet this study will be used as "evidence" to prove that LIPS and RWT are research-based entities and should be purchased by parents and school districts.

CHAPTER 23

Evaluating Research

As this book was evolving, it became clear that a chapter on evaluating research was necessary. This chapter provides some basic tips for evaluating the research used to inform reading instruction and interventions. Many of the ideas presented here are taken from my book *Academic Writing: Process and Product* (Johnson, 2016a).

FIVE GENERAL POINTS RELATED TO RESEARCH IN EDUCATION

The world of reading interventions is heavily populated with people making claims that things are research-based or that research has shown a particular thing to be true. Just because somebody says "research-based" does not always make it so. And just because a strategy is "research-based" does not mean it is effective or, as we saw in the last chapter, that the research is valid, reliable, or generalizable. Before looking at specific tips for examining and evaluating reading research, the following five general points need to be made about research and research-based strategies.

Multiple Studies, Perspectives

No single study should be the final word on anything. When looking at any topic within the field of education, many studies need to be reviewed to get a true sense of the topic. Reviewing multiple studies from a variety of perspectives is necessary to provide context for the topic and to act as a check on extreme or outlier positions. Using only a single study to come to a conclusion about anything is like trying to identify a dot-to-dot picture by looking at a single dot.

Research Can Be Misused

There is an old adage that claims that research can be used to say anything you want it to say. This is not quite accurate. Research can be misused to make any point you wish to make. That is, you can find an outlier study, a study that has not been peer-reviewed, or a set of data that somebody has collected to support an outlandish idea. You can also overinterpret or misinterpret research results to make any point you wish to make. This is a misuse of research. You will often see this done by those with a vested interest in a particular conclusion. However, when you look at a body of peer-reviewed research from a variety of perspectives, you can clearly see general trends develop. By the way, this is why academic writers conduct a review of the literature and not a review of the single study when writing a book, a chapter, or an article.

Research Does Not Prove Anything

In an academic setting, research finds evidence to support a hypothesis or to state that a hypothesis is true with varying degrees of certainty. Research can also find there to be no evidence to support a particular hypothesis. But research in the social sciences does not prove anything. It does not arrive at universal truth. Truth is a philosophical or metaphysical concept. Absolute proof exists only in the sterile world of mathematics where outside variables do not exist. Instead, research supplies evidence to support theories. Theories are then used to explain phenomena occurring in the natural world.

Again, research supports and provides evidence, but it does not prove anything with absolute certainty. Even in the most controlled experimental research there are far too many uncontrolled variables, many of which the researcher is unaware, to conclusively state that something is proven true for all times and in all situations. As such, there may be research-based practices, validated practices, practices that are supported by empirical evidence, and evidenced-based practice, but there are no practices or strategies that research has proven to be effective.

Research-Based Strategies

To sell products, some may suggest that there are research-based strategies or methods that have been proven to work. I sincerely wish this were true. All we would need to do then would be to plug these research-proven strategies in a teaching algorithm and sit around and wait for those test scores to start rising. But this is not the case.

Effective for Whom?

A research study may indeed indicate that a strategy, practice, or approach is effective, but we must always dig deeper. The questions to ask are: Effective for whom?

For what purpose? Under what conditions? When, how, and how often? (Dudley-Marling, 2011). Research can be used to justify a particular strategy or approach, but the final word should always be the students in front of you. For reading, we ultimately want to know if the strategy or approach enhances the ability to create meaning with print with the students you work with every day.

One Thing versus Another

We must be most wary of any research that "demonstrates" or "proves" that one thing is more effective than another. The effectiveness of any strategy is determined by how it is used. For example, John Hattie and Gregory Yates (2014) used gold-standard research to compare discovery learning with direct instruction and concluded that direct instruction is effective and discovery learning is not. Their conclusion demonstrates only their considerable lack of knowledge related to teaching, learning, and pedagogy: Direct instruction and discovery learning are both pedagogical strategies used for different purposes. Neither of these strategies should be utilized exclusively as the sole means of instruction for teaching anything for any population in any circumstances. There are instances when each is the most effective strategy to use. Moreover, it is not an either/or assertion. Often discovery learning and direct instruction are included in the same lesson.

EVALUATING RESEARCH

There is no such thing as a perfect study. All research has strengths and limitations. Five elements— researcher credibility, literature review, research question or purpose, integrity, and validity of the results or conclusions—will enhance your ability to become a critical consumer of educational research.

Researcher Credibility

Does the researcher's degree or current position indicate adequate knowledge in the particular field of research? Background knowledge is necessary to guide all phases of the inquiry. Expertise enables one to know what questions to ask, to see how new knowledge connects to existing knowledge, and to determine what is relevant and irrelevant. Being an expert research methodologist in another field does not provide an adequate background for research in reading.

Literature Review

New knowledge builds on existing knowledge. The research study you are evaluating should begin with a review of related literature. This literature review should provide a solid theoretical context and research support for the research question or purpose of the study. It should also make a case for why the study you are examining is important.

Research Question or Purpose

The specific research question or study purpose should flow directly from the literature review. As well, the research question or study purpose should be clearly stated and easy to understand. Everything that follows should be directly related to this question or purpose. At the end of the study, you should be able to answer yes or no as to whether the question has been answered or whether the purpose of the study has been achieved.

Integrity

It is impossible to be totally objective. Subjectivity occurs simply in deciding what questions to ask, what data to collect, and what measures to use to collect data. However, any obvious subjectivity, bias, or conflict of interest should be stated up front by the researcher. Questions to ask here: Does the study appear to be free of bias or hidden agendas? Are there groups that might benefit from a particular result? Is the researcher connected with a group that has a particular agenda or point of view? Does the researcher start with the answer and then look for data to support the answer? Is the study published in a journal that considers a variety of perspectives, data, and research methodology?

Validity of the Results or Conclusions

The conclusions, recommendations, or applications made at the end of an article should be confined to whatever can be supported by the data collected and described in this study. That is, they should come directly from and be supported by the data. Also, data should not be overinterpreted to mean something they do not; neither should they be generalized to populations that may not be represented in the study.

QUANTITATIVE RESEARCH

These five elements should be considered when evaluating any type of research. We turn now to specific elements to consider when evaluating quantitative and qualitative research.

Quantitative research focuses on collecting numerical data and isolating variables in order to explain, predict, and/or control phenomena of interest. This includes experimental research as well as correlational and causal–comparative research. The elements below pertain to research in the social sciences, although the concepts can be applied to research in other areas as well. As you examine them, you cannot help but reflect on the last chapter.

Unequal Samples

You cannot compare things that are not comparable. If comparisons are being made, the groups in a study must be similar in terms of demographics, ability, age, size, or other characteristics or variables. If not, the interpretation of the results should be questioned. For example, if you are comparing public schools to private schools, you must control for variables such as ability, socioeconomic status (SES), parents' education level, and class size in order to make reasonable comparisons.

Sampling or Selection Bias

This kind of bias occurs when the types of subjects included or excluded in the study influence the results. For example, one group will always outperform another if low-performing subjects are underrepresented or high-performing individuals are overly represented in one group or another. Sampling bias systematically favors some outcome over another. Randomized selection to groups is the best way to avoid selection bias.

Unequal Treatment or Conditions

If comparisons are being made related to a treatment or condition, there should be no significant differences other than the independent variable you are examining. For example, if a study was comparing Method A to Method B, and Method A was implemented sporadically, for shorter durations, and by less qualified people than was the case with Method B, the interpretation of the results should be questioned.

Size and Scope of the Subject Sample

Is the subject sample representative of the population to which it applies, or is it generalized? For example, if you did a study examining the effects of Treatment A on 25 elderly people in a small town, it may be difficult to generalize to larger populations. The results could be germane to just elderly people, rural environments, the particular sample, or some other unaccounted variable. This does not mean that studies with limited subject samples are useless or invalid. Rather, they are limited in the types of generalizations that can be inferred from them.

The Mistaken Assumption of Homogeneity

You cannot assume that because two groups or populations share a single variable they are similar. For example, it would be difficult to make reasonable comparative conclusions between gun owners in Boise, Idaho, and gun owners in inner-city Los Angeles, California, because of the differences in environmental factors and myriad other uncontrolled variables. In the same way, it would be difficult to make comparative conclusions about reading instructional methods in a first-grade class in Blackwater, Arizona, and a first-grade class in Apple Valley, Minnesota. There are simply too many unaccounted-for variables. Research studies that generalize to larger groups based on single-variable comparisons between groups should always be questioned.

Clearly Described Population

You should be critical of any research in which the researcher does not clearly describe the populations or samples involved. This description should include adequate pretest data.

Statistical Significance

As described in Chapter 22, statistical significance means that the difference between two groups is more than could happen by chance. If the difference between groups is slight, the difference could simple be a matter of chance. Thus, for small groups you need to see large differences and for large groups you can see smaller differences. Always look to discern whether the differences in groups or results are statistically significant. As we saw in Chapter 22, having differences that are just considered significant are differences based on the author's subjective inner state. These kinds of differences should not be used to reach any conclusions in a quantitative study.

Validity of the Measure

Do the measures used for the dependent variable actually account for whatever it claims to measure? Is it a valid measure of that trait or attribute? For example, you can get very accurate and reliable data pertaining to people's ability to run 100 meters, but this would not be a valid measure of their ability to play tennis or football. In education, the question of validity often arises when scores on achievement tests are used to demonstrate learning, teacher effectiveness, reading ability, or some other variable beyond the very narrow scope of the standardized measure.

QUALITATIVE RESEARCH

Qualitative research generally focuses on understanding naturally occurring phenomena in real-life settings. It uses systematic observations to study and understand people, places, events, situations, and experiences with all their many variables in all their complexity (Johnson, 2012). Below are seven elements that should be considered when evaluating qualitative research (Leedy & Ormrod, 2010).

Let the Data Speak

You should get the sense that the researcher is willing to let the data speak. That is, the researcher does not start with the answer. Instead, the researcher allows the data collected to inform or change his or her views.

Rigor

The plan for collecting and analyzing data should be systematic and described in a way that invites duplication. Also, the number of observations, their duration, and the quantity of data collected should be sufficient to understand what is being studied. In addition, the duration of the study should be sufficient to collect enough data to answer the research question.

Data Depth and Breadth

The type of data collected should be sufficient to adequately answer the research question or contribute to the purpose of the study. Also, multiple types of data should be collected over time.

Accuracy and Completeness

The description should provide an accurate and complete picture of the person, place, event, situation, or experience being studied. All relevant aspects of the environments studied should be described in a way that enables a thorough understanding of the phenomena being studied.

Coherence

You should be able to easily read and understand the research report. It should make sense. The literature review, research question, methodology, findings, and discussion or conclusion should all be aligned with each element, building upon the previous element.

Logic and Persuasiveness

The researcher should use sound logic to analyze and interpret the data. As well, the findings, conclusions, or recommendations should be a logical extension or application of the data.

Usefulness

You should be able to use the findings to enhance your understanding of similar people, places, events, situations, or experiences.

FINAL WORD

As professional educators and as reading intervention teachers, we must be informed consumers of educational researchers. This chapter provided some basic tips toward this end.

CHAPTER 24

Students with Dyslexia

Dear Dr. Johnson,

I have a K–12 reading license and was considering joining the Orton–Gillingham course that costs over $2,000 and is full for the summer at the Reading Center in [deleted]. Is it beneficial? Please let me know. I applied for the admission and scholarship and I am on the waiting list.

READING INSTRUCTION FOR STUDENTS WITH DYSLEXIA

In Minnesota, where I live, and in many other states, representatives from the International Dyslexia Association (IDA) have lobbied state legislatures to mandate a certain type of reading instruction for students with dyslexia. These mandates prohibit teachers from using their research-based knowledge, expertise, and understanding of the individual readers with whom they work. Instead, they are forced to implement a certain type of instruction for students who are severely struggling readers. Could you imagine if similar mandates were imposed on doctors, therapists, lawyers, dentists, and other professional practitioners? If you had gallbladder problems, for example, would you feel comfortable if your doctor was forced to use a certain type of treatment because the International Gallbladder Association had lobbied your state legislature?

Orton–Gillingham

According to the IDA, the answer for all reading problems seems to be Orton–Gillingham, or something similar. Orton–Gillingham is an approach to teaching reading that uses instruction that is "multisensory, sequential, incremental, cumulative, individualized, phonics-based, and explicit" (Rippel, 2020). The

To enhance the readability of this chapter, many of the original reference citations were removed. A fully cited version of the chapter can be found at *www.OPDT-Johnson.com.*

Orton–Gillingham website says that the approach is "direct, explicit, multi-sensory, structured, sequential, diagnostic, and prescriptive" (see Figure 24.1). If effectiveness were determined by the number of adjectives used to describe it, then Orton–Gillingham would indeed be one of the most effective programs you could buy.

Buy is the operative word here. An individual Orton–Gillingham course costs over $2,000, and associate-level training costs $4,000 plus $250 for materials. Various levels of training and certification can be purchased. What you get for your money is an expensive, Humpty-Dumptian approach to reading instruction where children are taught a specified list of reading subskills in a predetermined order and in a specified way. In other words, the complex act of reading is broken into little bitty pieces so that a highly trained Orton–Gillingham specialist can help children put the little bitty pieces back together again one little bitty piece at a time. The Orton–Gillingham magic ingredient is "multisensory" instruction. This means it uses visual, auditory, and kinesthetic modalities when teaching. In other words, as children are learning, they see things, hear things, and do things.

This is called *multimodal instruction*. Elementary teachers have been using it for years. But an effective meaning-based approach to reading instruction is even more multimodal in its multimodality. I call it *meta-multimodal instruction*. It includes imagination, emotion, and social interaction as well as visual, auditory, and kinesthetic modalities. So effective meaning-based reading instruction would have children see things, hear things, do things, imagine things, emote things, and say things. There you go: meta-multimodal instruction. And I did not charge you $4,000 plus $250 for materials.

What about the research that "proves" the effectiveness of Orton–Gillingham? Besides some of the methodological problems described in Chapter 22, the research used to support the use of Orton–Gillingham often measures students' progress using pseudo-reading or nonreading tasks (Lim & Oei, 2015), uses measures of questionable validity (Hill, 2005), does not use a comparison group (Bas, 2008), is derived from unpublished master's or doctoral theses (Blockinger, 2004), is a study as opposed to peer-reviewed research put out by groups or organizations that have a vested interest in a certain outcome (Arndt, 2006), or makes claims of superiority without controlling for covariates such as gender, socioeconomic status, ethnicity,

> The **Orton–Gillingham approach** is a direct, explicit, multisensory, structured, sequential, diagnostic, and prescriptive way to teach literacy when reading, writing, and spelling do not come easily to individuals, such as those with dyslexia. It is most properly understood and practiced as an approach, and not as a method, program, or system. In the hands of a well-trained and experienced instructor, it is a powerful tool of exceptional breadth, depth, and flexibility.

FIGURE 24.1. Orton–Gillingham as described by Orton–Gillingham. Retrieved from *www.ortonacademy.org/resources/what-is-the-orton-gillingham-approach*.

verbal IQ, or initial skills (Ritchey & Goeke, 2006). Despite the claims that it is heavily research-based, it simply is not (ILA, 2016a; Ritchey & Goeke, 2006).

The ILA and NCTE

The International Literacy Association (ILA) and the National Council of Teachers of English (NCTE) are two professional organizations that I generally turn to when seeking a research-based perspective on literacy learning and instruction. These nonprofit organizations have been around for over 60 and 100 years, respectively, and include thousands of researchers, scholars, teachers, and other educators with a variety of theoretical perspectives but with the single goal of enhancing literacy instruction through research and professional development (as opposed to generating profit). You can trust that position statements issued by these organizations have been vetted and are based on solid, peer-reviewed research. Also, books, journals, and other publications have been reviewed by reviewers with solid literacy-based credentials. Just as the American Medical Association and the National Academy of Medicine and their related professional journals are the guideposts in the medical field, the ILA and NCTE are the two professional organizations that are best positioned to provide an objective, research-based perspective on literacy learning and instruction based on a wide variety of research from a wide variety of fields.

This is what the ILA (2016a) had to say about using Orton–Gillingham approaches with students with dyslexia:

> As yet, there is no certifiably best method for teaching children who experience reading difficulty (Mathes et al., 2005). For instance, research does not support the common belief that Orton–Gillingham-based approaches are necessary for students classified as dyslexic (Ritchey & Goeke, 2006; Turner, 2008; Vaughn & Linan-Thompson, 2003). Reviews of research focusing solely on decoding interventions have shown either small to moderate or variable effects that rarely persist over time, and little to no effects on more global reading skills. Rather, students classified as dyslexic have varying strengths and challenges, and teaching them is too complex a task for a scripted, one-size-fits-all program (Coyne et al., 2013; Phillips & Smith, 1997; Simmons, 2015). Optimal instruction calls for teachers' professional expertise and responsiveness, and for the freedom to act on the basis of that professionalism. (p. 3)

Algorithmic Solutions

To be fair, certain aspects of Orton–Gillingham work for some students for certain aspects of their reading instruction. One teacher with whom I work has been very successful in individual tutoring sessions using parts of Orton–Gillingham; however, she selectively adopts and adapts specific parts as needed for individual students, and she incorporates many of the meaning-based strategies described in this book.

The problem with Orton–Gillingham and similar for-profit programs (Lindamood, Wilson Language Training, Barton System, etc.) is that they try to reduce teaching to an algorithm. An algorithm is a formula for solving problems in which you follow a step-by-step set of procedures in order to achieve a specific outcome. In other words, by correctly following a prescribed set of steps in the specified order, you will be led to a predefined solution. Algorithms are useful in mathematics and computer science for calculation, data processing, and automatic reasoning. For teaching struggling readers? Not so much.

However, Orton–Gillingham and the State of Minnesota would have you believe that if the teaching algorithm is followed explicitly, the teacher can be assured that students will learn to read. And if the algorithm does not work, you run them through the algorithm again . . . and again . . . and again. What these algorithmic programs offer is a false sense of certainty. Despite all the certainty thrown about, research to support the long-term effectiveness of these "direct, explicit, multi-sensory, structured, sequential, diagnostic, and prescriptive" interventions in improving struggling readers' ability to create meaning with print is simply not evident (Compton, Miller, Elleman, & Steacy, 2014).

DEFINING DYSLEXIA

Let us now try to understand what dyslexia is or might be. There is not a single, universal definition or conception of this term. This section looks at two perspectives: (1) a sound-out-words perspective and (2) a meaning-making perspective.

A Sound-Out-Words Perspective

If reading was simply sounding out words, then these first definitions below would be wholly adequate. The IDA (2018) definition below has been replicated by Minnesota and other states:

> Dyslexia is a specific learning disability that is neurological in origin. It is characterized by difficulties with accurate or fluent recognition of words and by poor spelling and decoding abilities. These difficulties typically result from a deficit in the phonological component of language that is often unexpected in relation to other cognitive abilities and the provision of effective classroom instruction.
>
> Secondary consequences may include problems in reading comprehension and reduced reading experience that can impede the growth of vocabulary and background knowledge.

The Mayo Clinic, being a medical institution, uses a medical model to understand dyslexia. It is a "disorder" that must be diagnosed and cured. However, the Mayo Clinic also states, "There's no cure for dyslexia":

> Dyslexia is a learning disorder characterized by difficulty reading. Also called specific reading disability, dyslexia is a common learning disability in children. Dyslexia occurs in children with normal vision and intelligence. Sometimes, dyslexia goes undiagnosed for years and isn't recognized until adulthood.
>
> There's no cure for dyslexia. It's a lifelong condition caused by inherited traits that affect how your brain works. However, most children with dyslexia can succeed in school with tutoring or a specialized education program. Emotional support also plays an important role (in IDA, 2018).

The National Center for Learning Disabilities (2014) defines dyslexia as a type of learning disability related to reading with specific symptoms:

> Dyslexia is the term associated with specific learning disabilities in reading. Although features of LD in reading vary from person to person, common characteristics include:
>
> - difficulty with phonemic awareness (the ability to notice, think about and work with individual sounds in words)
> - phonological processing (detecting and discriminating differences in phonemes or speech sounds)
> - difficulties with word decoding, fluency, rate of reading, rhyming, spelling, vocabulary, comprehension and written expression
>
> Dyslexia is the most prevalent and well recognized of the subtypes of specific learning disabilities. (p. 3)

The Learning Disabilities Association of America (2013) definition of dyslexia includes impaired orthographic processing (the visual system used to form, store, and recall words). Word recognition skills seem to be both a cause and an effect of dyslexia:

> Dyslexia is characterized by deficits in accurate and fluent word recognition. Individuals with dyslexia struggle with word recognition, decoding, and spelling. Reading comprehension is sometimes impaired due to very poor word reading skills. Individuals with dyslexia often have deficits in phonemic and phonological awareness, which refer to the ability to hear, identify and manipulate the sound structure of a spoken word, including its phonemes, syllables, onsets and rimes. Individuals with dyslexia may also have impaired orthographic processing, which interferes with connecting letters and letter combinations with sounds accurately and fluently.

The National Institute of Neurological Disorders and Stroke (n.d.) defines dyslexia as a "brain-based" condition, characterized by difficulties with phonological processing, spelling, and/or rapid visual–verbal responding. Rapid visual–verbal responding means that readers have slower than normal rates of naming letters and individual words that appear in print.

> Dyslexia is a brain-based type of learning disability that specifically impairs a person's ability to read. These individuals typically read at levels significantly lower than expected despite having normal intelligence. Although the disorder varies from person to person, common characteristics among people with dyslexia are difficulty with phonological processing (the manipulation of sounds), spelling, and/or rapid visual–verbal responding.

A Meaning-Making Perspective

But reading is not merely sounding out words; it is creating meaning with print. During this meaning-making process, the brain uses three cueing systems to recognize words, not just one. Also, it is an interactive process between what is in the head and what is on the page. And during the process of reading almost10 times more information flows from the cortex down than from the page up. Based on this fact, all the definitions above are highly inadequate.

The ILA does not provide an official definition of dyslexia, but it does offer two ideas that inform our understanding:

> However, it would be more accurate to say that some children experience difficulty acquiring literacy, which is often related to inadequate phonological analysis skills along with instruction that does not address comprehension, text fluency, phonemic awareness, phonics, automatic word recognition, vocabulary, and writing in ways that motivate children to read and write widely. There is no evidence for the value of inserting the construct dyslexia into this claim. (2016b, p. 8)

> Many researchers accept the idea that dyslexia/severe reading difficulties results from difficulties in analyzing and manipulating sounds in words (Vellutino, Fletcher, Snowling, & Scanlon, 2004). These difficulties, however, do not of themselves allow us to distinguish readers with dyslexia from other readers encountering difficulties, or from younger readers with the same level of reading proficiency. Errors in reading and spelling made by children classified as dyslexic are not reliably different from those of younger children who are not classified as dyslexic. Rather, evidence suggests that readers with similar levels of competence make similar kinds of errors. This does not suggest a greater incidence of dyslexia, but instead that some difficulties in learning to work with sounds are normal. (2016a, pp. 2–3)

Dyslexia can be understood as simply a designation for those on the lower end of the reading continuum (Protopapas & Parrila, 2018; Stanovich, 1994). These would be students who usually score two or more standard deviations below the mean on standardized reading achievement tests. However, Constance Weaver (1998) provides what I have found to be the most apt definition of dyslexia:

> Most educators steeped in miscue analysis would prefer not to think of readers themselves as dyslexic at all. Rather, we might define dyslexia as the ineffective use or coordination of strategies to construct meaning from conceptually appropriate and aurally comprehensible texts. Locating dyslexia within the strategies and their coordinated use, not within the reader, this reconceptualization emphasized the possibility that the ineffectiveness of the strategies may result partly or mostly from teachers' or parents' conceptualizing reading as first and foremost a matter of identifying words, and providing instruction that reflects this view. (p. 300)

SEVEN THINGS WE KNOW ABOUT DYSLEXIA

Depending on studies and definitions, anywhere from 3 to 5% of students are severely struggling readers or students with dyslexia. This is what we know about dyslexia:

1. **Dyslexia is not related to visual problems** (ILA, 2016a; Strauss, 2011a). Students with dyslexia do not perceive letters backwards or jumble up words to any greater degree than beginning readers or readers of similar ability.

2. **Dyslexia is not a brain disorder** (Strauss et al., 2009). There is no reliable evidence to show that the brains of students with dyslexia are qualitatively different from the brains of other students (Moreau, Stonyer, McKay, & Walkie, 2018). The brain-imaging research that purports to demonstrate "dysfunction" or "abnormalities" is fraught with methodological concerns (Bishop, 2013). These concerns are usually related to small sample size, type of subjects used in studies, use of single-word reading tasks, use of the phonological model to define and understand reading, types of data collected, overinterpretation of the data, and kinds of generalizations made based on the data.

This is not to say that there are no differences between the brain images of students with dyslexia and students without. However, many of the differences can be explained by differences in instruction and experience (Vandermosten, Hoeft, & Norton, 2016). These differences largely disappear with the right kinds of instruction and experience (Coles, 2004).

3. **Students with dyslexia often have difficulties analyzing and manipulating sounds in words** (Strauss, 2011a; Ziegler & Goswami, 2005). These students often struggle processing phonological data; but this is not always the case (Hadzibeganovic et al., 2010). As well, the types of word reading errors made by

readers identified with dyslexia are not remarkably different from those made by other struggling readers or from beginning readers at the same level (ILA, 2016b; Weaver, 1994).

4. **Students with dyslexia often have difficulties with spelling** (Snowling, 2008). Spelling proficiency is related to visual memory capacity (Gentry & Gilbert, 2006). Good spellers are better able to store and retrieve letter patterns from their long-term memory than are less able spellers. Since students with dyslexia often have trouble processing phonological data, it follows that this would result in spelling difficulties. This said, spelling has little to do with one's ability to create meaning with print. And drill and practice on weekly spelling lists does little or nothing to help students become better spellers or to enhance their ability to create meaning with print (Krashen, 1989).

5. **More phonics is not the answer.** What students with dyslexia often receive in intervention programs is a steady diet of phonics and low-level reading skills (Allington, 2012). As has been described in other places in the book, phonics-based instruction can lead to increased scores on phonics-based measures in the short term (Hill, 2016); however, there is little transfer of these skills to authentic reading conditions (Pearson & Hiebert, 2013). In addition, there is little evidence to demonstrate that this kind of instruction has any long-term effect on students' ability to create meaning with print (Krashen, 2009; Strauss, 2011a).

This is not to say that phonics instruction is not necessary. Phonics instruction in some form is one important part of an intervention for most students with dyslexia; however, it should occur within a meaningful context to the greatest extent possible (Fawcett & Nicolson, 2007). Phonics instruction should also be part of a balanced literacy program that includes practice reading real books. Children who are given daily opportunities to read make as good or better gains in skills instruction in the long term and typically score higher on tests of reading comprehension (Eldridge, 1991; Krashen, 2016).

6. **There are no standardized prepackaged programs that are effective in helping students with dyslexia create meaning with print** (Gabriel, 2018; ILA, 2016a). Despite the "research-based" claims made by commercial programs such as Orton–Gillingham, Lindamood-Bell LIPs, Simultaneously Multisensory Teaching, Phonics First, Open Court, Fast Forward, or Barton, there are no one-size-fits-all programs that will "cure" dyslexia. The research-based claims made by these for-profit entities should be suspect as they have a financial interest in particular outcomes. Also, you will find no valid research to support the superiority of these skills-based programs in helping struggling readers create meaning with print when compared to a balanced approach to literacy instruction or meaning-based interventions that include extensive reading practice.

Skills-based programs may result in a short-term bump in skills-based measures but do not produce long-term gains in comprehension (Krashen, 2009). Again, some decoding instruction is important; however, children who immerse themselves in good books with daily opportunities to read make as good or better gains in skills instruction in the long term and typically score higher on tests of reading comprehension (Eldridge, 1991; Krashen, 2016).

7. **Students with dyslexia do not need dramatically different kinds of instruction** (Wharton-McDonald, 2011). Students with dyslexia, like all struggling readers, need interventions that provide more intense versions of the kinds of research-based instruction they are currently receiving in a general education setting. As stated in Chapter 1, when an intervention is substantially different from classroom instruction, it creates a splintered curriculum. Here struggling readers are presented with different types of instruction and learn different sorts of skills in different places throughout the day. This makes it harder to develop their reading skills; not easier. As stated earlier in this book, struggling readers need consistency in order to reinforce developing skills. This is not to say that there are not differences in instruction between students with and without dyslexia, but the differences are in emphasis and intensity, not in kind.

As stated in a previous chapter, intensity here refers to (1) more time, (2) more time-on-task, (3) more time engaged in authentic literacy activities [reading and writing], and (4) smaller instructional groups (three to seven students). Intense, supplemental instruction (or an intervention) can occur within or outside of a general education classroom setting. When students leave the general education classroom for this supplemental instruction, the big question is always, what will you have them miss?

INTERVENTIONS FOR STUDENTS WITH DYSLEXIA

Intervention sessions for students with dyslexia should occur no less than 4 days a week and should include variations of the same seven elements described in Chapter 5 and listed again in Figure 24.2. This would be part of a Tier 3 intervention in an RTI context.

Classroom Supports for Students with Dyslexia

The resources and supports discussed below should be available in the classroom for students who show characteristics of dyslexia. Many of these supports are appropriate for all learners in a classroom.

1. **Word work.** Direct, explicit, and systematic instruction and practice related to letters and letter patterns. This includes synthetic phonics, analytic phonics, and large unit phonics.
2. **Word identification.** Direct, explicit, and systematic instruction and practice related to the four word identification strategies: (a) analogy, (b) morphemic analysis, (c) context clues, and (d) phonics.
3. **Maze and cloze work.** Students practice identifying words within sentences based on context clues. These can also be used as pre- or postreading activities or as reinforcement of word work (see Chapter 10).
4. **Comprehension.** Direct, explicit, and systematic instruction and practice related to the cognitive processes used in comprehension as well as study skills strategies.
5. **Reading practice.** Students are able to read and respond to authentic texts that they have chosen. This could also include teacher read-alouds (Braunger & Lewis, 2006) and scaffolded oral reading (Johnson, 2016b).
6. **Fluency work.** Repeated reading and other activities used to develop fluency.
7. **Writing.** LEA, simple one- or two-sentence writing activities, as well as the types of process writing instruction and activities used in writing workshops.

FIGURE 24.2. Elements to include in a reading intervention.

Emotional Support

Reading things takes up much of daily instruction in most classrooms. Reducing the stigma of reading problems will enhance learning. The first thing I say when working with struggling readers of any age is, "Lots of people have reading problems. It's no big deal. We can help." Also, check-ins are helpful, such as "How's it going? What can I do to help?" Of course, emotional supports and check-ins are appropriate for all students.

Audio Books

Students with dyslexia need to be exposed to the same vocabulary, concepts, systems of thinking, and language structures as their peers so that they do not to fall behind. Audio versions of any textbook used in a K–12 public school setting should be made available. Also, during free voluntary reading (reading practice) audio-recorded narrative texts should be made available to students.

Speech-to-Text Programs

Most computers come with speech-to-text programs that enable students to have their oral text converted directly into written text. Encourage students to use these programs for classroom assignments, including writing assignments. These programs also read written text back to students. Both should be used interchangeably.

Smaller Parts

Students with dyslexia can become overwhelmed with too much reading instruction (or other instruction). Instruction should be broken into smaller, manageable parts. This does not mean that you need to reduce the overall time, instead instruction should be brief and briskly paced, followed by strategies that get students actively involved. The strategy could be as simple as "Turn to a neighbor and share an important idea." The point is, the brain learns best when instruction is provided in small bits, followed by a chance to do something meaningful with the new instructional input. The human brain does not learn well when presented with large blobs of instruction followed by meaningless practice.

Pause-and-Process Time

Insert pause-and-process (P&P) time into instruction (Johnson, 2016b). Instead of extended exposure to a single instructional element, use brief bits of instruction or instructional activities with small bits of P&P time. This enables students to think about and fully process the instructional input. Inserting these small breaks into the learning sessions enables students to engage all parts of the brain and to integrate new information with knowledge already stored in long-term memory. This is why, in a meaning-based intervention, it is recommended that each individual activity be between 2 and 8 minutes in duration with 15- to 60-second breaks between each. The P&P break could be something as simple as "How do you think you did on that one?" or "Did you notice how you stopped to see if that sentence made sense?" or "All right, what do you think we'll do next?" Anything to pause, create a break, and make a personal interaction with the individual student or students will work here.

Simplified Homework Assignments

Students with dyslexia often learn more if their homework assignments are lightened. Keep in mind the purpose of homework: When used effectively, homework reinforces learning and provides opportunities to extend and practice what is learned in class. As such, students should be able to complete homework assignments with high rates of success (Alleman et al., 2010). While some homework is helpful, too much homework can reduce learning. In other words, a little homework is good, but that does not mean that more homework is better. And homework should not be used, as is commonly the case, as a measuring and sorting device.

Also, the developmental level of children should be considered when assigning homework. Children need to be children, and they need to be outside playing with friends. Any homework assigned before middle school should be minimal. In the same way, adolescents need to socialize with friends and discover who they are and want to be. Thus, when assigning homework at these levels, time should be allotted in every class period to complete some or all of it (Johnson, 2019). This enables the teacher to provide feedback and guidance. The academic development of students should not take place at the expense of their emotional, personal, and social development.

Guided Notes or Outlines for Lectures and Reading Assignments

Guided notes is a strategy in which the teacher gives students a content outline before a class lecture or textbook reading assignment. The notes include the basic structure of the information to be learned, with some or most of the information filled in. This acts as a scaffold. Students must then fill in the blanks as they listen or read.

Assistive Technology

Assistive technology can be something as simple as audio recorders for class lectures and spell-check devices for writing. There are also reading pens: you move the pen over the words on the page, and the text appears on the computer screen. This is good as a note-taking device, and in addition, the text can be read back by the computer. There are also reading pens that can read the text aloud. These currently are fairly expensive, however.

Peer-Mediated Learning Activities

Peer-mediated activities include shared reading (Johnson, 2016b), cooperative learning activities, T-talks (Johnson, 2019), or any other strategy that creates social interaction around books and the content to be learned.

The Importance of Voluntary Reading for Students with Dyslexia

Chapter 14 mentioned research conducted by Roseline Fink (1996, 1998). To review, she interviewed successful men and women with dyslexia to see why they were able to be so successful despite their profound "disability." She discovered that all these successful adults were allowed to immerse themselves in books and read in areas of interest as children. They developed expertise, built conceptual and vocabulary knowledge, and became familiar with the schemes and structures of the types of texts found in their field. This background knowledge was more important for facilitating reading accuracy and comprehension than letter clues. That is, marginal decoders used context to create meaning with print. Low-level skill mastery was not a prerequisite for higher-level thinking and skill construction.

The instructional implications are clear. First, teachers must help all students, but especially students with dyslexia to discover areas of interest. This is done by presenting a wide variety of topics in classes and class discussions, using book talks in which students talk about books and topics of interest, and by having a wide variety of books and other reading material on a wide variety of topics available to students. Second, teachers must allow for daily opportunities to select and read books and other reading materials of interest to students as part of reading instruction.

FINAL WORD

I have presented my views on dyslexia and Orton–Gillingham in this chapter. They are well referenced, based on solid, peer-reviewed research, and built upon the research-based theoretical perspective elucidated throughout this book. I have presented similar views to different people and groups, both in person and online. Sometimes through the haze of emotion that this topic seems to generate, the seven important points that follow do not seem to be clearly heard.

1. **Early interventions.** I want to be absolutely clear on this point: Everybody believes that early interventions are incredibly important for all students who are struggling readers. This includes students with dyslexia. The question has always revolved around what types of interventions are most effective for struggling readers (including students with dyslexia). As described in this chapter and many places in this book, there is no single approach; there is no one-size-fits-all program.

2. **Short-term bumps.** Skills-based programs such as Orton–Gillingham often lead to short-term bumps in skills-based measures. This result has never been in question. If you teach something, you are going to get higher scores on posttest measures of that same something. The questions have always been, do these short-term bumps transfer to authentic reading contexts, and do they result in long-term gains in valid measures of comprehension?

3. **Exposure to print.** Any exposure to print will be helpful. Additional exposure to print, even nonsensical print such as that included in skills-based programs will be of some benefit to students, especially when compared to students who have had no additional exposure to print. The following question has always arisen: Are these frequent exposures to nonsensical print of more benefit to struggling readers than frequent exposures to high-quality text accompanied by direct instruction related to letters and letter patterns. In other words, is a scripted approach

like Orton–Gillingham more effective than a meaning-based approach in which an expert reading teacher is empowered to make the choices best for individual students?

4. **Direct instruction.** Everybody believes that direct instruction used as a pedagogical strategy is a necessary part of any reading intervention. However, when it is used as an approach to reading instruction, does direct instruction result in the acquisition of the higher cognitive processes necessary for advanced reading and thinking? And will direct instruction of low-level reading subskills provide struggling readers with the tools they need to create meaning with print?

5. **Expert teacher.** Students with dyslexia need expert reading teachers. Everyone agrees with this statement. The teacher is the most significant variable in determining the quality instruction students receive and the amount of learning that takes place. The question is, will we allow expert reading teachers to use their expertise and experience to meet the needs of the students with whom they work? Or will they be mandated to implement scripted programs with fidelity? Also, is an expert reading teacher one who knows how to implement a particular program or system? Or is an expert reading teacher one who understands how the brain creates meaning with print, who has read a wide range of research related to literacy learning, and who knows and is able to implement a wide range of pedagogical strategies based on the needs of the students with whom that teacher works?

6. **Systematic phonics instruction.** Everybody believes that some form of systematic phonics instruction is necessary, but what system and what form? Who gets to decide what skills will be included in the system? Who gets to decide what system and form will be used to teach these skills? And who gets to decide what system will be used for demonstrating and documenting those skills? Will it be expert reading teachers with daily interaction with their students? Or will it be some entity outside the classroom who knows nothing of the students, teachers, or teaching situations?

7. **Research-based reading instruction.** Everybody believes that a wide body of peer-reviewed research should be used to make decisions about reading instruction and interventions. Everyone also believes that reading teachers should only use those pedagogical strategies that are evidence-based. But who gets to decide what counts as evidence? Who gets to make these important epistemological assumptions for all of us? Will the same simplistic view of research that is used to understand organisms in a petri dish be used to mandate what research methodologies can be used to understand human beings interacting in the real world? Or will a more complex understanding of research be used to navigate the multitude of variables associated with human learning?

PART VI
ISSUES IN SPECIAL EDUCATION

CHAPTER 25

Problems in the Special Education World

THE SYSTEM IS BROKEN

I have encountered many incredible teachers in the field of special education. However, they are often stuck in a system that is broken that often does not allow them to be incredible. In this broken system, learning is measured only by standardized test scores. If it cannot be quantified, it cannot be learned. If it was not quantified, it was not learned. Students whose test scores fall below a certain percentile ranking are thought to have a learning disability. These students are sent off to "Special Ed World." In this purgatorial "special" place located apart from the general education classroom, students are given a prescribed special treatment that special education teachers must implement with fidelity. However, one of the many problems with Special Ed World as currently configured is that once students become entangled in the special education machinery, they are lost forever. They rarely return.

Theoretical Constructs

Examine the prominent journals within the field of special education and look at the types of standards assigned to teacher preparation programs in special education and you will see one of the causes of the broken system. Despite a wealth of varying types of research data from a wide range of sources supporting a neurocognitive model of reading, the predominant theoretical construct used to understand reading and guide reading research within the field of special education is still the phonological processing model. Reading is understood to be merely sounding out words.

This unquestioning fealty to the phonological processing model has rendered a wealth of research data collected from a variety of fields irrelevant or nonexistent. This would not be problematic if the field was largely successful in helping struggling readers. But this is not the case. In special education programs for learning disabilities, students rarely experience accelerated reading once they begin special education services. Since 70–80% of all students receiving special education services have problems related to literacy, this is highly problematic.

Research Paradigms

The theoretical construct above is directly related to what might be called paradigmatic parochialism. The field of special education places an overreliance on a single type of research method to the exclusion of all other types of research. This research paradigm reflects an outdated Newtonian mechanistic paradigm used to understand and come to know reality. Here, things exist only to the extent to which they can be quantified. Controlled experimental research is the exclusive and epistemologically privileged way of determining causality and making claims as to what constitutes knowledge. Measuring is equated with knowing, by which the illusion of certainty is constructed.

This paradigmatic parochialism is further confirmed by the Standards for Evidence-Based Practices in Special Education, released by the Council for Exceptional Children (CEC). The CEC is the major professional organization in the field of special education. This organization has declared that only quantitative data gleaned from highly controlled experimental designs are worthy of determining which pedagogical practices are "evidence-based." The exclusive use of these methods to the exclusion of all other ways of seeing and knowing is detrimental to the field of special education. As described in earlier chapters, the same research methods used to study the physical world in the artificial confines of a controlled laboratory setting are the only methods that are used to study and make causal assertions about human beings in real-world educational settings. This methodological incarceration creates a narrow and distorted view of the very educational reality it seeks to examine. The result is a paradigmatic peephole through which a complex world is observed.

This is in contrast with a holistic, postmodern paradigm that includes systems theory and an interconnected view of an unfolding universe based on quantum physics. Here, it is recognized that any single part (variable) can only be understood within the context of the whole. Reality is not composed of fragmented parts but of self-organizing systems that are both interactive and interdependent. All entities within this holistic reality are understood in terms of patterns, connections, interconnections and relationships, all of which influence each other. The research paradigm that emerges here includes a variety of methods that fully examine reality.

This examination includes attention to processes as well as products in fully understanding phenomena. In this context, certainty is never achieved; instead, uncertainty is reduced.

Instructional Practice

The interconnections between research paradigms and instructional practices within the field of special education are exemplified in the 22 "high-leverage practices" for special education identified by the CEC. The term *high leverage* reflects the mechanistic research paradigm in which cause–effect relationships are converted into stimulus–response instructional techniques. In much the same way that a mouse is "leveraged" into pressing a bar in a Skinner box, students are to be "leveraged" or manipulated into producing predetermined behaviors that represent measurable learning objectives. Learning is said to have occurred when students display the appropriate behavioral response to an instructional stimulus.

In Special Ed World, direct instruction is the predominant tool used to leverage students toward measurable objectives. As stated in previous chapters, direct instruction is effective for learning low-level skills. It is extremely ineffective for developing high-level thinking, understanding complex concepts, and acquiring sophisticated skills. The subsequent problem is that students in Special Ed World are force-fed an interminable array of mind-numbing lessons that use direct instruction to teach low-level concepts and skills. As a result, they have few opportunities to participate in activities that would enable them to develop complex thinking and deeper understandings of the world. You do not have to control any variables to understand that if only low-level skills are taught, only low-level learning occurs. Thus, in Special Ed World, the myth of the learning disability is perpetuated by the very system designed to make it go away.

The predominant use of direct instruction leveraging practices used in Special Ed World stands in contrast to the wide array of pedagogical practices based on the more complex understanding of human learning that has emerged from fields outside of special education. Here it is recognized that learning is a natural and innate human condition. As such, learning disabilities do not exist. In fact, much of what has been labeled a learning disability is actually a learning-certain-things disability, a learning-in-certain-ways disability, or an educational systems disability.

THE ANSWER

There is a malfunction in the special education machinery as it is now configured. The malfunction will not be fixed by installing yet another research-based pedagogical part or by tinkering with the existing machinery. These are simplistic solutions to a deeper, more complex problem. Change will occur only if, and how much, the field of special education is able to move away from the restrictive theoretical constructs and parochial paradigms that have stymied its ability to evolve in recent years. Toward this end, we need to divest ourselves of simplistic understandings of reading, learning, and research, and instead reimagine and embrace a more expansive view of humans creating meaning with print, human learning, and human research.

Epilogue

As I said in the Preface of this book, I wish I had the knowledge and skills back in 1983 to help my student Erik. What we do and do not know about literacy instruction has a real-world impact on students' lives, now and in the future. This is illustrated by three recent messages from students in my graduate literacy methods course.

> Dr. Johnson,
>
> I have a student who came to me this last Fall. His eighth-grade teacher sent carryover assignments with phonics and sight words. This young man absolutely HATED reading or anything close to it. As a result of this course, I changed my approach. I am teaching him during extended school year right now. He is traveling and doing a lot of geocaching. He is reading me pamphlets from state parks, using so much language to tell me about his experiences, and I've learned more about his interests. He's "reading" about animals on the National Geographic Kids site. I tell him about cool and iconic landmarks based on his travel destinations and he reads about them and then tells me all about his experience. (He loves zombies and aliens. He journaled his own imagined story about aliens coming to school after visiting Area 51.) I love the term "driting." That is so relatable with my student population. To this young man, reading meant boring and mundane work. His parents and I fell into this trap of measuring reading ability based on word recognition, fluency and phonics.
>
> As a new teacher, I felt MY own skills were measured by students' abilities to show advancement with standardized testing. Now I allow myself to step outside that perceived expectation, use the language and messages from this class and apply them. Unfortunately, and embarrassingly, direct instruction was

my method until I understood that it was a tool and not a method. I know that measurable outcomes are important. However, what and how I measure are now more practical. What I've taken from this class may not come across on the upcoming exam. My real learning might be instead measured by this student enjoying reading and my own excitement to teach him reading again.

Dear Dr. Johnson,

I've been using what you've taught in your class and in your book for my work with middle school kids who are struggling. "Making meaning with print" is a mantra that is stuck in my head. Of course, I have anecdotal evidence from my own son, who is now in 9th grade and HATES to read. I'm not sure that will ever change, and I'm convinced it's because of all the Orton–Gillingham tutoring.

This year, District _______ (starting in sixth grade) moved to an L.A. curriculum that is a reader's workshop model. There are mini-lessons, a reader's notebook, and students are picking high-quality books that are of interest to them and at their level. Of course, there are kinks to work out, but it is in the right direction. This is exactly what you taught us!!

Dr. Johnson,

I am a mom of two children who struggle with reading because they learn differently. Neurologically, their brains are wired differently. My sons are misunderstood. As a parent, I have 15 years of experience working with special education teachers, reading IEPs, signing consent forms for IEPs, most of which contained the language of special education. As the years went on, I felt our two children got lost in the process of teaching vs. the art of learning. They fell into the chasm of being taught to testing standards vs. learning from reading or the joy that reading can bring.

This is partially what inspired my career change, going from a nurse of 20 years, to a special education teacher. I wanted to bring in my passion for working with kids who learn differently and are misunderstood into the classroom. I envisioned using my parenting perspective to not only change the way kids experience classroom learning. We all learn differently. We all have gifts to bring to this world. We all have our own special needs. Just because some kids learn differently doesn't mean they have a learning disability.

As a special education teacher, I fell into the trap of using the school language that I didn't like. I fell into the trap of measuring student success by looking at their testing outcomes vs. my teaching effectiveness. To be the teacher I envisioned and desired to be, I feel like I need to get out of that trap. (Standardized testing is a valuable tool that has its place, but I agree with you that you should challenge yourself to use other student-centered, measurable outcomes!)

> Then I took your class. It reinforced my passion. It felt safe to step outside the box to *teach differently* so that students who *learn differently* will indeed learn to love reading. I put this "enjoy reading" concept into practice. The PURPOSE of teaching reading is important. HOW we teach them is important. WHY we teach them is THE MOST important. We teach them so that they will LOVE to read. Through reading, students can explore the world, create ideas, and use their imagination. What better lesson to teach children than to teach them to enjoy reading?

There are no magical one-size-fits-all programs that work best for all students. There are no super-secret special education strategies that only specially trained special education teachers can implement. Instead, there are magical teachers who have a variety of research-based tools in their teaching toolbox. These tools are adopted and adapted to meet the unique needs of each of their students.

References

Adams, M. J. (1990). *Beginning to read: Thinking and learning about print*. Cambridge, MA: MIT Press.

Alitto, H., & Usrey, W. (2003). Corticothalamic feedback and sensory processing. *Current Opinion in Neurobiology, 13,* 440–445.

Alleman, J., Brophy, J., Knighton, B., Ley, B., Botwinski, B., & Middlestead, S. (2010). *Homework done right: Powerful learning in real-life situations.* Thousand Oaks, CA: Corwin.

Allington, R. L. (1994). The schools we have: The schools we need. *The Reading Teacher, 48*(1), 14–29.

Allington, R. L. (2002). Research on reading/learning interventions. In A. Farstrup & S. J. Samuels (Eds.), *What research has to say about reading instruction* (3rd ed., pp. 261–290). Newark, DE: International Reading Association.

Allington, R. L. (2011). Research on reading/learning disability interventions. In S. J. Samuels & A. E. Farstrup (Eds.), *What research has to say about reading instruction* (4th ed., pp. 236–264). Newark, DE: International Reading Association.

Allington, R. L. (2012). *What really matters for struggling readers: Designing research-based programs*. Boston: Pearson.

Allington, R., & McGill-Franzen, A. (2017). Comprehension difficulties and struggling readers. In S. Israel (Ed.), *Handbook of research on reading comprehension* (2nd ed., pp. 271–292). New York: Guilford Press.

Almasi, J. F., Palmer, B. M., Madden, A., & Hart, S. (2011). Interventions to enhance narrative comprehension. In A. McGill-Franzen & R. Allington (Eds.), *Handbook of reading disability research* (pp. 329–344). New York: Routledge.

Altwerger, B. (2005). *Reading for profit: How the bottom line leaves kids behind.* Portsmouth, NH: Heinemann.

Anderson, R. (2013). Role of the reader's schema in comprehension, learning, and memory. In A. Alvermann, N. Unrau, & R. Ruddell (Eds.), *Theoretical models and process of reading* (6th ed., pp. 476–488). Newark, DE: International Reading Association.

Arndt, E. J. (2006). *Orton–Gillingham approach.* Tallahassee: Florida Center for Reading Research.

Atwell, N. (1998). *In the middle: New understandings about writing, reading, and learning* (2nd ed.). Portsmouth, NH: Boynton/Cook.

Averill, O. H., Baker, D., & Rinaldi, C. (2014). A blueprint for effectively using RTI intervention block time. *Intervention in School and Clinic, 50*(1)¸ 29–38.

Bas, O. (2008). Teaching literacy with multisensory approach to a dyslexic child who has hearing difficulty and attention deficit disorder (ADD): A case study. *Cagdas Egitim Dergisi, 351,* 21–27.

Bentum, K. E., & Aaron, P. G. (2003). Does reading instruction in learning disabilities resources rooms really work?: A longitudinal study. *Reading Psychology, 24,* 361–382.

Berends, I. E., & Reitsma, P. (2004). Addressing semantics promotes the development of reading fluency. *Applied Psycholinguistics, 27,* 247–265.

Binder, K. S., Duffy, S. A., & Rayner, K. (2001). The effects of thematic fit and discourse context on syntactic ambiguity resolution. *Journal of Memory and Language, 44,* 297–324.

Bishop, D. (2013). Research review: Emanuel Miller Memorial Lecture 2012—Neuroscientific studies of intervention for language impairment in children: Interpretive and methodological problems. *Journal of Child Psychology and Psychiatry, 54*(3), 247–259.

Block, C. C., & Lacina, J. (2009). Comprehension instruction in kindergarten through grade three. In S. Israel & G. Duffy (Eds.), *Handbook of research on reading comprehension.* (pp. 494–509). New York: Routledge.

Blockinger, K. L. (2004). *The impact of daily Orton–Gillingham drill on reading skills.* Unpublished master's thesis, Gratz College, Melrose Park, PA.

Borzabadi, A. B. (2011). The effect of regular practice with cloze passages on EFL students' reading ability. *Theory and Practice in Language Students, 1,* 941–946.

Bracey, G. (2006). *Reading educational research: How to avoid getting statistically snookered.* Portsmouth, NH: Heinemann.

Bradley, B., & Reinking, D. (2011). Revisiting the connection between research and practice using formative design experiments. In N. Duke & M. Mallette (Eds.), *Literacy research methodologies* (2nd ed., pp. 188–212). New York: Guilford Press.

Braunger, J., & Lewis, J. P. (2006). *Building a knowledge based in reading* (2nd ed.). Urbana, IL: National Council of Teachers of English.

Brown, A. L., Palinscar, A. S., & Armbruster, B. B. (2013). Instructing comprehension-fostering activities in interactive learning situations. In D. Alvermann, N. Unrau, & R. Ruddell (Eds.), *Theoretical models and processes of reading* (pp. 657–689). Newark, DE: International Reading Association.

Bruner, J. (1977). *The process of education.* Cambridge, MA: Harvard University Press.

Cartwright, K. (2015). *Executive skills and reading comprehension.* New York: Guilford Press.

Chall, J. S. (1989). Learning to read: The great debate 20 years later. *Phi Delta Kappan, 70,* 521–538.

Christenbury, L., Bomer, R., & Smagorinsky, P. (2009). Introduction. In L. Christenbury, R. Bomer, & P. Smagorinsky (Eds.), *Handbook of adolescent literacy research* (pp. 3–13). New York: Guilford Press.

Code, L. (1993). Taking subjectivity into account. In L. Alcoff & E. Potter (Eds.), *Feminist epistemologies* (pp. 15–48). New York: Routledge.

Coles, G. (2004). Danger in the classroom: "Brain glitch" research and learning to read. *Phi Delta Kappan, 85*(5), 344–351.

Compton, D., Miller, A., Elleman, A., & Steacy, L. (2014). Have we forsaken reading theory in the name of "quickfix" interventions for children with reading disability? *Scientific Studies of Reading, 18,* 55–73.

Couter, R., Flynt, E., & Cooter, K. (2013). *The Flynt/Cooter comprehensive reading inventory* (2nd ed.). Boston, MA: Pearson.

Coyne, M. D., Simmons, D. C., Hagan-Burke, S., Simmons, L. E., Hagan-Burk, S., Simmons, L., . . . Rawlinson, D. (2013). Adjusting beginning reading intervention based on student performance: An experimental evaluation. *Exceptional Children, 80*(1), 25–44.

Cunningham, P., & Allington, R. (2007). *Classrooms that work: They can all read and write* (3rd ed.). Boston: Allyn & Bacon.

Cunningham, P. M., & Cunningham, J. W. (2002). What we know about how to teach phonics. In A. Farstrup & S. J. Samuels (Eds.), *What research has to say about reading instruction* (3rd ed., pp. 87–109). Newark, DE: International Reading Association.

Darling-Hammond, L. (1999). *Teacher quality and study achievement: A review of state policy evidence.* Seattle: Center for the Study of Teaching and Policy, University of Washington.

Darling-Hammond, L., Holtzman, D. J., Gatlin, S. J., & Heilig, J. V. (2005). *Does teacher certification matter?: Evidence about teacher certification, Teach for America, and teacher effectiveness.* Chapel Hill, NC: Southeast Center for Teaching Quality.

Darling-Hammond, L., & Youngs, P. (2002). Defining "highly qualified teachers": What does "scientifically-based research" actually tell us? *Educational Researcher, 31*(9), 13–25.

Deno, S. L., & Marston, D. (2006). Curriculum-based measurement of oral reading: An indicator of growth in fluency. In S. J. Samuels & A. E. Farstrup (Eds.), *What research has to say about fluency instruction* (pp. 179–203). Newark, DE: International Reading Association.

Denton, C. A., Vaugh, S., & Fletcher, J. M. (2003). Bringing research-based practice in reading intervention to scale. *Learning Disabilities Research and Practice, 18*(3), 201–211.

Dolch, E. W. (1936). A basic sight vocabulary. *The Elementary School Journal, 36,* 456–460.

Dole, J. A., Nokes, J. D., & Drits, D. (2009). Cognitive strategy instruction. In S. Israel & G. Duffy (Eds.), *Handbook of research on reading comprehension* (pp. 347–373). New York: Routledge.

Donnelly, N., & Davidoff, J. (1999). The mental representations of faces and houses: Issues concerning parts and wholes. *Visual Cognition, 6,* 319–343.

Dudley-Marling, C. (2011). Research in in classrooms: Getting beyond "what works." *Learning Disability Quarterly, 34,* 141–149.

Duke, N., & Mallette, M. (Eds.). (2011). *Literacy research methodologies* (2nd ed.). New York: Guilford Press.

Duke, N. K., Pearson, P. D., Strachan, S. L., & Billman, A. K. (2011). Essential elements of fostering and teaching reading comprehension. In S. J Samuels & A. E. Farstrup (Eds.), *What research has to say about reading instruction* (4th ed., pp. 51–93). Newark, DE: International Reading Association.

Ehri, L. C. (2005). Learning to read words: Theory, findings, and issues. *Scientific Studies of Reading, 9,* 167–188.

Eldridge, L. (1991). An experiment with a modification whole language approach in first-grade classrooms. *Reading Research and Instruction, 30,* 21–38.

Elliott, J. G., & Grigorenka, E. L. (2014). *The dyslexia debate.* New York: Cambridge University Press.

Engel, A. K., Fries, P., & Singer, W. (2001). Dynamic predictions: Oscillations and synchrony in top-down processing. *Nature Reviews Neuroscience, 2,* 704–716.

Eppley, K., & Dudley-Marling, C. (2018). Does direction instruction work?: A critical assessment of direct instruction research and its theoretical perspective. *Journal of Curriculum and Pedagogy, 14,* 1–20.

Erickson, K. A., & Koppenhaver, D. A. (1995). Developing a literacy program for children with severe disabilities. *The Reading Teacher, 48*(8), 676–684.

Fautsch-Patridge, T., McMaster, K. L., & Hupp, S. C. (2011). Are current reading findings applicable to students with intellectual disabilities? In S. J. Samuels & A. Farstrup (Eds.), *What research has to say about reading instruction* (4th ed., pp. 215–235). Newark, DE: International Reading Association.

Fawcett, A. J., & Nicolson, R. I. (2007). Dyslexia, learning, and pedagogical neuroscience. *Developmental Medicine and Child Neurology, 49*(4), 306–311.

Fink, R. (1996). Successful dyslexics: A constructivist study of passionate interest reading. *Journal of Adolescent and Adult Literacy, 39*(4), 268–280.

Fink, R. (1998). Literacy development in successful men and women with dyslexia. *Annals of Dyslexia, 48,* 331–346.

Fink, R. (2006). *Why Janie and Johnny couldn't read—and how they learned.* Newark, DE: International Reading Association.

Flood, J., Lapp, D., & Fisher, D. (2005). Neurological impress method plus. *Reading Psychology an International Quarterly, 26*(2), 147–160.

Fry, E. (1998). The most common phonograms. *The Reading Teacher, 51,* 620–622.

Gabriel, R. (2018). Preparing literacy professionals: The case of dyslexia. *Journal of Literacy Research, 50*(2), 262–270.

Gaskins, I. W. (2011). Interventions to develop decoding proficiencies. In A. McGill-Franzen & R. L. Allington (Eds.), *Handbook of reading disability research* (pp. 289–306). New York: Routledge.

Gazzaniga, M., Ivry, R., & Mangun, G. (2000). *Cognitive neuroscience: The biology of the mind* (2nd ed.). New York: Norton.

Gee, J. (2012). *Social linguistics and literacies: Ideology in discourses* (4th ed.). New York: Routledge.

Gee, J. (2019). Reading as situation language: A sociocultural perspective. In D. Alvermann, N. Unrau, M. Sailors, & R. Ruddel (Eds.), *Theoretical models and process of literacy* (7th ed., pp. 105–117). New York: Routledge.

Gentry, R. L., & Gilbert, J. W. (2006). *Breaking the code: The new science of beginning reading and writing.* Portsmouth, NH: Heinemann.

Goodman, K. S., Fries, P. H., & Strauss, S. L. (2016). *Reading the grand illusion: How and why people make sense of print.* New York: Routledge.

Goodman, K. S., & Goodman, Y. M. (2009). Helping readers make sense of print: Research that supports a whole language pedagogy. In S. E. Israel & G. Duffy (Eds.), *Handbook of research on reading comprehension* (pp. 91–114). New York: Routledge.

Goodman, K., Goodman, Y., & Allen, K. (2017). Reading on helping readers make sense of print. In S. Israel (Ed.), *Handbook of research on reading comprehension* (2nd ed., pp. 84–107). New York: Guilford Press.

Goodman, Y., Martens, P., & Flurkey, A. (2016). Revaluing readers: Learning from Zachary. *Language Arts, 93,* 213–223.

Graney, S. B., Martinez, R. S., Missall, K. N., & Arick, O. T. (2010). Universal screening of reading in late elementary school: R-CBM versus CBM maze. *Remedial and Special Education, 31,* 368–377.

Gunning, T. (2014). *Assessing and correcting reading and writing difficulties: A student-centered approach* (5th ed.). Boston: Pearson.

Guthrie, J. T., Wigfield, A., Metsala, J. L., & Cox, K. E. (2004). Motivational and cognitive predictors of text comprehension and reading amount. In B. Ruddel & N. Unrau (Eds.), *Theoretical models and processes of reading* (5th ed., pp. 929–953). Newark, DE: International Reading Association.

Hadzibeganovic, T., van den Noort, M., Bosch, P., Perc, M., van Kralingen, R., Mondt, K., & Coltheart, M. (2010). Cross-linguistic neuroimaging and dyslexia: A critical view. *Cortex, 46,* 1312–1316.

Harman, W. (1994). A re-examination of the metaphysical foundations of modern science: Why is it necessary. In W. Harman & J. Clark (Eds.), *New metaphysical foundations of modern science* (pp. 1–14). Sausalito, CA: Institute of Noetic Sciences.

Hattie, J., & Yates, G. (2014). *Visible learning and the science of how we learn.* New York: Routledge.

Hawkins, J. (2004). *On intelligence.* New York: Holt.

Helmut, L. (2005). When context hinders!: Learn–test compatibility in face recognition. *Quarterly Journal of Experimental Psychology, 58,* 235–250.

Hill, D. R. (2016). Phonics based reading interventions for students with intellectual disability: A systematic literature review. *Journal of Education and Training Studies* 4(5), 205–214.

Hill, V. (2005). Through the past darkly: A review of the British Ability Scales Second Edition. *Child and Adolescent Mental Health, 10,* 87–98.

Hoffman, J. (2017). Comprehension is not simple: Considering the persistent dangers in the simple view of reading comprehension. In S. Israel (Ed.), *Handbook of research on reading comprehension* (2nd ed., pp. 57–69). New York: Guilford Press.

Hruby, G. G. (2011). Minding the brain. *Journal of Adolescent and Adult Literacy, 55,* 316–321.

Hruby, G. G., & Goswami, U. (2013). Educational neuroscience for reading researchers. In N. J. Unrau & R. B. Ruddell (Eds.), *Theoretical models and process of reading* (pp. 558–588). Newark, DE: International Reading Association.

Hushusius, L. (1994). Freeing ourselves from objectivity: Managing subjectivity or turning toward a participatory mode of consciousness? *Educational Researchers, 23,* 15–22.

Iano, R. (1987). Rebuttal: Neither the absolute certainty of prescriptive law nor a surrender to mysticism. *Remedial and Special Education,* 8, 52–61.

International Dyslexia Association. (2018). Definition of dyslexia. Retrieved from *www.dyslexia-reading-well.com/dyslexia-definition.html.*

International Literacy Association. (2016a). *Dyslexia* [Research advisory]. Newark, DE: Author.

International Literacy Association. (2016b). *Dyslexia: A response to the International Dyslexia Association* [Research advisory addendum]. Newark, DE: Author.

International Literacy Association. (2017a). *Literacy assessment: What everyone needs to know.* Newark, DE: Author.

International Literacy Association. (2017b). *The roles of standardized reading tests in schools.* Newark, DE: Author.

International Literacy Association. (2018a). *Beyond the numbers: Using data for instructional decision making.* Newark, DE: Author.

International Literacy Association. (2018b). *Democratizing professional growth with teachers: From development to learning.* Newark, DE: Author.

International Literacy Association. (2018c). *The power and the promise of read-alouds and independent reading* [Literacy leadership brief]. Newark, DE: Author.

International Literacy Association. (2019). *Creating passionate readers through independent reading* [Literacy leadership brief]. Newark, DE: Author.

International Reading Association. (2010). Response to intervention: Guiding principles for educators from the international reading association. Retrieved from *www.literacyworldwide.org/docs/default-source/where-we-stand/rti-brochure.pdf?sfvrsn=6.*

Jennings, J., Caldwell, J., & Lerner, J. (2010). *Reading problems: Assessment and teaching strategies* (6th ed.). Boston: Pearson.

Jensen, E. (2005). *Teaching with the brain in mind* (2nd ed.). Alexandria, VA: ASCD.

Jensen, E. (2009). *Teaching with poverty in mind: What being poor does to kids' brains and what schools can do about it.* Alexandria, VA: ASCD.

Johns, J., Elish-Piper, L., & Johnson, B. (2016). *Basic reading inventory: Kindergarten through grade twelve and early literacy assessments* (12th ed.). Dubuque, IA: Kendall Hunt.

Johnson, A. (1995). I was a less able reader: What concert choir taught me about reading instruction. *Reading Horizons, 35,* 430–441.

Johnson, A. (2000). *Up and out: Using thinking skills to enhance learning.* Needham Heights, MA: Allyn & Bacon.

Johnson, A. (2012). *A short guide to action research* (4th ed.). Boston: Pearson.

Johnson, A. (2016a). *Academic writing: Process and product.* Lanham, MD: Rowman & Littlefield.

Johnson, A. (2016b). *10 essential instructional elements for students with reading difficulties: A brain-friendly approach.* Thousand Oaks, CA: Corwin.

Johnson, A. (2017). *Teaching strategies for all teachers.* Lanham, MD: Rowman & Littlefield.

Johnson, A. (2019). *Essential learning theories and their applications.* Lanham, MD: Rowman & Littlefield.

Julia, E. (2006). Researching children's experience hermeneutically and holistically. *Alberta Journal of Educational Research, 52,* 111–126.

Kershner, J. R. (2016). Network dynamics in dyslexia: Review and implications for remediation. *Research in Developmental Disabilities, 59,* 24–34.

Klinger, J., & Boardman, A. (2011). Addressing the "research gap" in special education through mixed methods. *Learning Disability Quarterly, 34,* 208–218.

Koch, C. (2004). *The quest for consciousness: A neurobiological approach.* Englewood, CO: Roberts & Company.

Krashen, S. D. (1989). We acquire vocabulary and spelling by reading: Additional evidence for the input hypothesis. *Modern Language Journal, 73,* 440–464.

Krashen, S. D. (2004). *The power of reading: Insights from research* (2nd ed.). Portsmouth, NH: Heinemann.

Krashen, S. (2009). Does intensive decoding instruction contribute to reading comprehension? *Knowledge Quest, 37,* 72–74.

Krashen, S. (2016). The researcher's perspective: The purpose of education, free voluntary reading, and dealing with the impact of poverty. *School Libraries Worldwide, 22,* 1–7.

Kucer, S. (2013). Processing factors, academic discourses, and local and global comprehension. *Language and Literacy, 15,* 56–76.

Kucer, S. B. (2014). *Dimensions of literacy: A conceptual base for teaching reading and writing in school settings* (4th ed.). New York: Routledge.

Kucer, S. (2016). Accuracy, miscues, and the comprehension of complex literacy and scientific texts. *Reading Psychology, 37,* 1076–1095.

Kucer, S. (2017). The monitoring and responding behaviours of proficient fourth grade readers to miscues on a complex scientific text. *Literacy, 51,* 154–161.

Kuder, S. J., & Hasit, C. (2002). *Enhancing literacy for all students.* Upper Saddle River, NJ: Merrill Prentice Hall.

Kuhn, M. R., & Stahl, S. A. (2013). Fluency: Developmental and remedial practices—revisited (pp. 385–411). In D. Alvermann, N. J. Unrau, & R. B. Ruddell (Eds.), *Theoretical models and process of reading* (6th ed.). Newark, DE: International Reading Association.

Kuhn, T. (1996). *The structure of scientific revolutions* (3rd ed.). Chicago: University of Chicago Press.

Learned, J. E., Stockdill, D., & Moje, E. B. (2013). Integrating reading strategies and knowledge building in adolescent literacy instruction. In S. J. Samuels & A. E. Farstrup (Eds.), *What research has to say about reading instruction* (4th ed., pp. 159–185). Newark, DE: International Reading Association.

Learning Disabilities Association of America. (2013). Dyslexia. Retrieved from *https://ldaamerica.org/disabilities/dyslexia.*

Leedy, P. D., & Ormrod, J. E. (2010). *Practical research: Planning and design* (9th ed.). Boston: Pearson

Lefrancois, G. R. (2011). *Theories of human learning: What the professor said* (6th ed.). Belmont, CA: Thomson Wadsworth.

Leslie, L., & Caldwell, J. (2017). *Qualitative reading inventory* (7th ed.). Boston, MA: Pearson.

Lim, J., Reiser, R., & Olina, Z. (2009) The effects of part-task and whole-task instructional approaches on acquisition and transfer of a complex cognitive skill. *Educational Technology Research and Development, 57,* 61–77.

Lim, L., & Oei, A. C. (2015). Reading and spelling gains following one year of Orton–Gillingham intervention in Singaporean students with dyslexia. *British Journal of Special Education, 42,* 374–389.

Lipson, M. Y., & Wixson, K. K. (2009). *Assessment and instruction of reading and writing difficulties: An interactive approach.* Boston: Pearson.

Lyons, M. N., Green, R., Raiford, S., Tsemunhu, R., Pate, J., & Baldy, T. (2013). The relationship between teacher empowerment and school performance. *National Teacher Education Journal,* 6(2), 11–20.

Martin, N. M., & Duke, N. K. (2011). Interventions to enhance informational text comprehension. In A. McGill-Franzen & R. Allington (Eds.), *Handbook of reading disability research* (pp. 345–361). New York: Routledge.

Marzano, R. J., Pickering, D. J., & Pollock, J. E. (2001). *Classroom instruction that works: Research-based strategies for increasing student achievement.* Alexandria, VA: ASCD.

Mathes, P. G., Denton, C. A., Fletcher, J. M., Anthony, J. L., Francis, D. J., & Schatschneider, C. (2005). The effects of theoretically different instruction and student characteristics on the skills of struggling readers. *Reading Research Quarterly, 40*(2), 148–182.

McCoy, A. R., & Reynolds, A. J. (1999). Grade retention and school performance: An extended investigation. *Journal of School Psychology, 37*(3), 273–298.

Minnesota Department of Education. (2013). Developing standards-based IEP goals and objectives. Retrieved from *www.lcsc.org/cms/lib6/MN01001004/Centricity/Domain/21/MDE%20Discussion%20guide.April2013.pdf.*

Moreau, D., Stonyer, J. E., McKay, N. S., & Walkie, K. E. (2018). No evidence for systematic white matter correlates of dyslexia: An activation likelihood estimation meta-analysis. *Brain Research, 1683,* 36–47.

Moustafa, M. (1997). *Beyond traditional phonics.* Portsmouth, NH: Heinemann.

Moustafa, M. (1998). Reconceptualizing phonics instruction. In C. Weaver (Ed.), *Reconsidering a balanced approach to reading* (pp. 135–158). Urbana, IL: National Council of Teachers of English.

National Center for Learning Disabilities. (2014). *The state of learning disabilities* (3rd ed.). New York: Author. Retrieved from *www.ncld.org/wp-content/uploads/2014/11/2014-State-of-LD.pdf.*

National Governors Association Center for Best Practices & Council of Chief State School Officers. (2010). *Common Core State Standards for English language arts and literacy in history/social studies, science, and technical subjects.* Washington, DC: Authors. Retrieved from *www.corestandards.org/ELA-Literacy/RF/5.*

National Institute of Neurological Disorders and Stroke. (n.d.). Dyslexia information page. Retrieved from *www.ninds.nih.gov/Disorders/All-Disorders/Dyslexia-Information-Page.*

National Reading Panel. (2000). Teaching children to read: An evidence-based assessment of the scientific research literature on reading and its implication for reading instruction. Retrieved from *www.nationalreadingpanel.org.*

Oladele, A. O. (2013). The efficacy of neurological impress method and repeated reading on reading fluency of children with learning disabilities in Oyo State, Nigeria. *International Scholarly and Scientific Research and Innovation 7*(1), 187–190.

Parodi, G. (2013). Reading–writing connections: Discourse-oriented research. In D. Alvermann, N. J. Unrau, & R. B. Ruddell (Eds.), *Theoretical models and process of reading* (pp. 957–977). Newark, DE: International Reading Association.

Paulson, E. J. (2005). Viewing eye movements during reading through the lens of chaos theory: How reading is like the weather. *Reading Research Quarterly, 40*(3), 338–358.

Paulson, E. J., & Freeman, A. E. (2003). *Insight from the eyes: The science of effective reading instruction.* Portsmouth, NH: Heinemann.

Paulson, E. J., & Goodman, K. S. (2008). Re-reading eye-movement research: Support for transactional models of reading. In A. Flurky, E. Paulson, & K. Goodman (Eds.), *Scientific realism in studies of reading* (pp. 25–50). New York: Erlbaum.

Pearson, P. D., & Cervetti, G. (2017). The roots of reading comprehension instruction. In S. Israel (Ed.), *Handbook of research on reading comprehension* (2nd ed., pp. 12–56). New York: Guilford Press.

Pearson, P. D., & Hiebert, E. H. (2013). National reports in literacy: Building a scientific base for practice and policy. In D. Alvermann, N. J. Unrau, & R. B Ruddell (Eds.), *Theoretical models and processes of reading* (6th ed., pp. 1133–1149). Newark, DE: International Reading Association.

Peterson, M., & Hittie, M. (2010). *Inclusive teaching: The journey toward effective schools for all.* Columbus, OH: Merrill.

Phillips, G., & Smith, P. (1997). *A third chance to learn: The development and evaluation of specialized interventions for young children experiencing the greatest difficulty in learning to read.* Wellington: New Zealand Council for Educational Research.

Poplin, M. (1988). The reductionistic fallacy in learning disabilities: Replicating the past by reducing the present. *Journal of Learning Disabilities, 21,* 389–400.

Poplin, M. (2011). Valuing a plurality of research methodologies and instructional ideologies in classroom research. *Learning Disabilities Quarterly, 34,* 150–152.

Portes, P., & Salas, S. (2009). Poverty and its relation to development and literacy, In L. Morrow, R. Rueda, & D. Lapp (Eds.) *Handbook of research on literacy and diversity* (pp. 98–113). New York: Guilford Press.

Pressley, M., Wharton-McDonald, R., & Mistretta, J. (1998). Effective beginning literacy instruction: Dialectical, scaffolded and contextualized. In J. Metsala & L. Ehri (Eds.), *Word recognition in beginning literacy* (pp. 357–373). Mahwah, NJ: Erlbaum.

Protopapas, A., & Parrila, R. (2018). Is dyslexia a brain disorder? *Brain Sciences, 8*(4), 61.

Rasinski, T. V., Padak, N. D., & Fawcett, G. (2010). *Teach children who find reading difficult* (4th ed.). Boston: Allyn & Bacon.

Rasinski, T. V., & Samuels, S. J. (2011). Reading fluency: What it is and what it is not. In S. J. Samuels & A. E. Farstrup (Eds.), *What research has to say about reading instruction* (4th ed., pp. 94–114). Newark, DE: International Reading Association.

Rayner, K., Liversedge, S. P., White, S. J., & Vergilino-Perez, D. (2003). Reading disappearing text: Cognitive control of eye movements. *Psychological Science, 14,* 385–388.

Rayner, K., & Well, A. D. (1996). Effects of contextual constraint on eye movements in reading: A further examination. *Psychonomic Bulletin and Review, 3,* 504–509.

Revlin, R. (2013). *Cognition: Theory and practice.* New York: Worth.

Ricketts, J., Davies, R., Masterson, J., Morag, S., & Duff, F. (2016). Evidence for semantic involvement in regular and exception word reading in emergent readers of English. *Journal of Experimental Child Psychology, 150,* 330–345.

Rippel, M. (2020). *The Orton–Gillingham approach to reading and spelling.* Eagle River, WI: All About® Learning Press.

Ritchey, K. D., & Goeke, J. L. (2006). Orton–Gillingham and Orton–Gillingham-based reading instruction: A review of the literature. *Journal of Special Education, 40,* 171–183.

Roberts, G., Torgesen, J. K., Boardman, A., & Scammacca, N. (2008). Evidence-based strategies for reading instruction of older students with learning disabilities. *Learning Disabilities Research and Practice, 23,* 63–69.

Roes, B., & Burns, P. (2011). *Informal reading inventory: Preprimer to twelfth grade* (8th ed.). Boston, MA: Cengage Learning.

Ruddell, R., & Unrau, N. (2013). Reading as a motivated meaning-constrion process: The reader, the text, and the teacher. In D. Alvermann, N. Unrau, & R. Ruddell (Eds.), *Theoretical models and process of reading* (6th ed., pp. 1015–1068). Newark, DE: International Reading Association.

Samuels, S. J. (2013). Toward a theory of automatic information processing reading, revisited. In D. Alvermann, N. J. Unrau, & R. B. Ruddell (Eds.), *Theoretical models and process of reading* (6th ed., pp. 698–718). Newark, DE: International Reading Association.

Scanlon, D. M. (2011). Response to intervention as an assessment approach. In A. McGill-Franzen & R. L. Allington (Eds.), *Handbook of reading disability research* (pp. 139–148). New York: Routledge.

Schunk, D. H., & Zimmerman, B. J. (2006). Competence and control beliefs: distinguishing the means and ends. In P. A. Alexander & P. H. Winne (Eds.), *Handbook of educational psychology* (pp. 349–367). Mahwah, NJ: Erlbaum.

Seriven, M. (1994). The psycho-logical foundations of modern science. In W. Harman & J. Clark (Eds.), *New metaphysical foundations of modern science* (pp. 47–80). Sausalito, CA: Institute of Noetic Sciences.

Shanker, J., & Cockrum, W. (2019). *Ekwall/Shanker reading inventory* (7th ed.). Boston, MA: Pearson

Shaywitz, S. E., Morris, R., & Shaywitz, B. A. (2008). The education of dyslexic children from childhood to young adulthood. *Annual Review of Psychology, 59,* 451–475.

Shaywitz, S. E., & Shaywitz, B. A. (2008). Paying attention to reading: The neurobiology of reading and dyslexia. *Development and Psychopathology, 20,* 1329–1349.

Sherman, S., & Guillery, R. (2002). The role of the thalamus in the flow of information to the cortex. *Philosophical Transactions of the Royal Society of London, 357,* 1695–1708.

Siegel, D. J. (2007). *The mindful brain.* New York: Norton.

Silliman, E. R., & Wilkinson, L. C. (1994). Discourse scaffold for classroom intervention. In G. P. Wallach & K. G. Butler (Eds.), *Language learning disabilities in school-age children and adolescents* (pp. 27–52). New York: Merrill/Macmillan.

Sillito, A., & Jones, H. (2002). Corticothalamic interactions in the transfer of visual information. *Philosophical Transactions of the Royal Society of London, 357,* 1739–1752.

Simmons, D. (2015). Instructional engineering principles to frame the future of reading intervention research and practice. *Remedial and Special Education, 36*(1), 45–51.

Snow, C. E., Burns, M. S., & Griffin, P. (Eds.). (1998). *Preventing reading difficulties in young children*. Washington, DC: National Academy Press.

Snowling, M. J. (2008). Specific disorders and broader phenotypes: The case of dyslexia. *Quarterly Journal of Experimental Psychology, 61*(1), 142–156.

Spear-Swerling, L. (2013). A road map for understanding reading disabilities and other reading problems, redux. In D. Alvermann, N. Unrau,& R. Ruddell (Eds.), *Theoretical models and processes of reading* (6th ed., pp. 412–436). Newark, DE: International Reading Association.

Springer, S. E., Dole, J. A., & Hacker, D. J. (2017). The role of interest in reading comprehension. In S. Israel (Ed.), *Handbook of research on reading comprehension* (2nd ed., pp. 57–69). New York: Guilford Press.

Stanovich, K. E. (1994). Annotation: Does dyslexia exist? *Journal of Child Psychology and Psychiatry, 35*(4), 579–595.

Strauss, S. (2005). *The linguistics, neurology, and politics of phonics: Silent "E" speaks out*. New York: Routledge.

Strauss, S. L. (2011a). Neuroscience and dyslexia. In A. McGill-Franzen & R. L. Allington (Eds.), *Handbook of reading disability research* (pp. 79–90). New York: Routledge.

Strauss, S. L. (2011b). Reading theory, constructivist psychology, and emerging concepts in neuroscience: Implications for a model of human consciousness. *Functional Neurology, Rehabilitation, and Ergonomics, 1,* 147–161.

Strauss, S. L. (2014). The political economy of dyslexia. *Monthly Review,* 66(4), 35–47.

Strauss, S. L., Goodman, K. S., & Paulson, E. J. (2009). Brain research and reading: How emerging concepts in neuroscience support a meaning construction view of the reading process. *Education Research and Review,* 4(2), 21–33.

Strickland, D. S. (2002). The importance of effective early intervention. In A. Farstrup & S. J. Samuels (Eds.), *What research has to say about reading instruction* (3rd ed., pp. 69–86). Newark, DE: International Reading Association.

Swanson, E., & Vaughn, S. (2011). Implementing a response to intervention model to improve reading outcomes for all students. In S. J. Samuels & A. E. Farstrup (Eds.), *Reading instruction: What research has to say*. Newark, DE: International Reading Association.

Sweet, R. W. (2016). A century of miseducation of America's teachers, from the National Right to Read Foundation. Retrieved from *www.nrrf.org/century-miseducation-americas-teachers*.

Tompkins, C. (2011). *Literacy in the early grades: A successful start for preK–4 readers and writers* (3rd ed.). Boston: Pearson.

Torgesen, J. K. (2009). The Response to Intervention Instructional Model: Some outcomes from a large-scale implementation in reading first schools. *Child Development Perspectives, 3,* 38–40.

Torgesen, J., Alexander, A., Wagner, R., Rashotte, C., Voeller, K., & Conway, T. (2001). Intensive remedial instruction for children with severe reading disabilities: Immediate and long-term outcomes from two instructional approaches. *Journal of Learning Disabilities, 34,* 33–58.

Torgesen, J. K., Wagner, R. K., & Rashotte, C. A. (2012). Test of Word Reading Efficiency–Second Edition. *Canadian Journal of School Psychology, 30,* 320–326.

Torgesen, J., Wagner, R., Rashotte, C., Herron, J., & Lindamood, P. (2009). Computer-assisted instruction to prevent early reading difficulties in students at risk for dyslexia: Outcomes from two instruction approaches. *Annals of Dyslexia, 60,* 40–56.

Torgesen, J., Wagner, R., Rashotte, C., Rose, E., Lindamood, P., Lindamood, P., . . . Garvin, C. (1999). Preventing reading failure in young children with phonological processing disabilities: Group and individual response to instruction. *Journal of Educational Psychology, 91,* 579–593.

Tunmer, W., & Nicholson, T. (2011). The development and teaching of word recognition skills. In M. Kamil, P. Pearson, E. Moje, & P. Afflerbach (Eds.), *Handbook for reading research: Volume IV* (pp. 403–431). New York: Routledge.

Turner, H. M. (2008). This systematic review empirically documents that the effectiveness of Orton–Gillingham and Orton–Gillingham-based reading instruction remains to be determined. *Evidence-Based Communication Assessment and Intervention, 2*(2), 67–69.

Unrau, N., Alvermann, D., & Sailors, M. (2019). Literacies and their investigation through theories and models. In D. Alvermann, N. Unrau, M. Sailors, & R. Ruddell (Eds.), *Theoretical models and processes of literacy* (7th ed., pp. 3–34). New York: Routledge.

U.S. Department of Education. (2006, August 14). Rules and regulations: Assistance to states for the education of children with disabilities and preschool grants for children with disabilities. *Federal Register, 71*(156), 46546–46845.

U.S. Deparment of Education. (2007). Final regulations on modified academic achievement standards. Retrieved from *https://www2.ed.gov/policy/speced/guid/modachieve-summary.html.*

Valencia, S. W., & Buly, M. R. (2004). Behind test scores: What struggling readers really need. *The Reading Teacher, 57,* 520–531.

Vandermosten, M., Hoeft, F., & Norton, E. S. (2016). Integrating MRI brain imaging studies of pre-reading children with current theories of developmental dyslexia: A review and quantitative meta-analysis. *Current Opinion in Behavioral Sciences, 10,* 155–161.

Vaughn, S., & Fletcher, J. (2012). Response to intervention with secondary school students with reading difficulties. *Journal of Learning Disabilities, 45,* 244–256.

Vaughn, S., & Linan-Thompson, S. (2003). What is special about special education for students with learning disabilities? *Journal of Special Education, 37*(3), 140–147.

Vellutino, F., Fletcher, J., Snowling, M., & Scanlon, D. (2004). Special reading disability (dyslexia): What have we learned in the past four decades? *Journal of Child Psychology and Psychiatry, 45*(1), 2–40.

Wagner, R., Torgesen, J., Rashotte, C., & Pearson N. (1999). *The Comprehensive Test of Phonological Processing.* Torrance, CA: WPS.

Weaver, C. (1994). Reconceptualizing reading and dyslexia. *Journal of Childhood Communication Disorders, 16*(1), 23–35.

Weaver, C. (1998). Reconceptualizing dyslexia. In C. Weaver (Ed.), *Practicing what we know: Informed reading instruction.* Urbana, IL: National Council of Teachers of English.

Weaver, C. (2002). *Reading process and practice* (3rd ed.). Portsmouth, NH: Heinemann.

Weaver, C. (2009). *Reading process*. Portsmouth, NH: Heinemann.

Wharton-McDonald, R. (2011). Expert classroom instruction for students with reading disabilities: Explicit, intense, targeted . . . and flexible. In A. McGill-Franzen & R. S. Allington (Eds.), *Handbook of reading disability research* (pp. 265–272). New York: Routledge.

Wheelock, W., Campbell, C., & Silvaroli, N. (2011). *Classroom reading inventory* (12th ed.). New York: McGraw-Hill.

White, T. G., Sowell, J., & Yanagihara, A. (1989). Teaching elementary students to use word-part clues. *The Reading Teacher, 42,* 302–308.

Wiederholt, J. L., & Bryant, B. R. (1992). *Gray Oral Reading Test: Examiner's manual* (3rd ed.). Austin, TX: PRO-ED.

Wixson, K. K., Lipson, M. Y., & Valencia, S. W. (2014). Response to intervention for teaching and learning in language and literacy. In A. Stone, E. Silliman, B. Ehren, & G. Wallach (Eds.), *Handbook of language and literacy: Development and disorders* (2nd ed., pp. 637–653). New York: Guilford Press.

Wixson, K. K., & Valencia, S. W. (2011). Assessment in RTI: What teachers and specialists need to know. *The Reading Teacher, 64,* 466–469.

Woodcock, R. (2011). *Woodcock Reading Mastery Tests* (3rd ed.). Boston: Pearson.

Woods, M. L., & Moe, A. (2015). *Analytical reading inventory: Comprehensive standards-based assessment for all students including gifted and remedial* (10th ed.). Boston, MA: Pearson.

Zeno, S. M., Ivens, S. H., Millard, R. T., & Duvvuri, R. (1995). *The educator's word frequency guide.* New York: Touchstone Applied Science Associates.

Ziegler, J. C., & Goswami, U. (2005). Reading acquisition, developmental dyslexia, and skilled reading across languages: A psycholinguistic grain size theory. *Psychological Bulletin, 131*(1), 3–29.

Zirkel, P. A., & Rose, T. (2009). Scientifically based research and peer-reviewed research under the IDEA: The legal definitions, applications, and implications. *Journal of Special Education Leadership, 22*(1), 36–50.

Index

Note. *f* following a page number indicates a figure.

B

C

D

E

F

L

M

N

O

P

Q

R

S

T

V

W

Z